THE HEALING

THE HEALING

GAYL JONES

BEACON PRESS
BOSTON

BEACON PRESS

25 Beacon Street

Boston, Massachusetts 02108-2892

http://www.beacon.org

BEACON PRESS BOOKS

are published under the auspices of

the Unitarian Universalist Association of Congregations.

03 02 01 00 99 98   8 7 6 5 4 3 2 1

Text design by Anne Chalmers

Composition by Wilsted & Taylor Publishing Services

Library of Congress Cataloging-in-Publication Data

Jones, Gayl.

The healing / Gayl Jones.

p. cm.

ISBN 0-8070-6314-2

I. Title.

PS3560.0483H34 1998

813'.54—dc21   97-33325

BOOK

ONE

CHAPTER ONE

I open a tin of Spirit of Scandinavia sardines, floating in mustard sauce.
The woman on the bus beside me grunts and leans toward the aisle.
She's a smallish, youngish, short-haired woman, small Gypsy earrings
in her ears, looks kinda familiar. I offer her some of them sardines, but
she grunts and leans farther toward the aisle. I nibble the sardines with
one of those small plastic forks and stare out the window. The sun hit-
ting the window makes a rainbow across a field of straw pyramids.
There's a few horses and cows grazing in the meadow, a whitewashed
barn and a farmhouse, one of them three-story farmhouses, and there's
one of them little tin-roofed sheds built onto the farmhouse. It looks like
one of them painted scenes, you know the sorta landscape paintings you
can buy at them flea markets. Or the sort of landscapes that you see on
television, where the different artists teach you how to paint pictures.
You can learn how to paint pictures in oil or watercolor, and they teach
you the secrets of painting and make it seem like almost anyone can
be an artist, at least be able to paint pictures in their style of painting.
A Bible's open in my lap. I'm holding it cater-cornered, trying to keep the
sardine oil off the pages, or the mustard sauce. When I finish the tin
of sardines, I drink the mustard sauce. The woman beside me grunts
again. I glance over at her, at them Gypsy earrings. She's got smallish,
almost perfect-shaped ears, and is a little but full-mouthed woman.
Most people likes sardines, or likes the taste of them sardines, but maybe
she thinks it's too countrified to be eating them sardines on the Grey-
hound bus, even Spirit of Scandinavia sardines. Ever since I seen that
movie about the middle passage, though, and they talked about them

Africans coming to the New World being packed in them slave ships like sardines in a can, and even showed a drawing of them Africans, that's supposed to be a famous drawing, so every time I eat sardines I think of that. Of course, I still likes the taste of that, and I don't think she refuse them sardines on account of that metaphor, though, 'cause I'm sure there's plenty of people eats sardines and don't think of that metaphor. I deposit the tin in a plastic bag that's already brimming with paper cups, Coke cans, and crumbled paper napkins, then I open a bag of corn tortillas, you know the ones usedta use the bandito to advertise themselves, till the Mexican-American people protested about that bandito, though I remember hearing a song once about a real bandito, not one of those commercialized banditos, but one of those social bandits that the people themselves sing about, like they're heroes.

You teach Sunday school? the woman asks, her head still tilted toward the aisle.

Naw, I'm a faith healer, I say. I give her one of my brochures. I start to ask her whether them sardines reminds her of the middle passage, but I don't, 'cause everybody, like I said, don't think of that metaphor. So I just give her one of my brochures. That brochure don't have no famous drawings in it, like the middle passage, though. It just got a few clippings talking about the people I've healed, some of them famous, but mostly ordinary-type peoples.

She don't say anything, and don't look at the brochure, though she's probably thinking a brochure commercializes the profession of faith healing, that is, if you can call faith healing a profession. I think she going to put that brochure in that trash bag with that sardine can and them paper cups, Coke cans, and crumbled paper napkins, but she don't, she put it in her pocketbook, one of them Moroccan leather pocketbooks, look like real Moroccan leather, not that imitation Moroccan leather. Course some people say that that real Moroccan leather don't look no different from the imitation Moroccan leather, 'cause the people that makes imitation Moroccan leather is more subtle and sophisticated than in the old days when you could tell imitation leather from real leather. You can buy you imitation purses these days, even Gucci, and think it's real. When she put that brochure in her pocketbook, though, I see one of them paperback books peeking out. I don't see the title of that book, though it seem like it the name of some kinda insect, a mosquito or something like that. Maybe it's a book about them African mosquitoes. I know about them African mosquitoes. And them Caribbean mosquitoes. I got me a friend nicknamed Mosquito, though she ain't named after none of them African or Caribbean mosquitoes. Her real name Nadine. I don't call her Mosquito myself, I call her Nadine. And she also got coupla them magazines, I mean the young woman I give my faith healing brochure. I'm thinking maybe she's reading *Essence* or one of them type magazines, you know, for the African-American woman, but it ain't, it's *Scientific American* and *Popular Culture*. It look kinda like *National Geographic* 'cept it say *Popular Culture*. I like that *National Geographic* myself. But them Americans on the cover of the *Popular Culture* magazine with they tattoos and nose rings and sculptured and painted hairdos kinda look like the kinda folks you usedta just see in the *National Geographic*–type magazines. But now people all over the world look like they could be in them *National Geographic*–type magazines, and not just the so-called primitive peoples.

She ain't say anything about that faith healing, though, that woman with the Gypsy earrings, but I know what she's thinking: that I'm some kinda charlatan and mercenary, or some kinda crazy woman. All that. If I ain't a faker, then I'm a crazy woman that just believes in her own fakery. There's people like that; they's innocent believers, or gullible believers, but it's they own fakery or somebody else's fakery they believe in. And it might not be fakery, it might just be other people believe it to be fakery. You don't always know fakery from fakery. 'Cause I can tell she's one of them skeptical types. One of them skeptics. Gotta be a skeptic to be reading that *Scientific American*, 'cause ain't that the magazine of the skeptical. The gullible reads the *National Enquirer*. Or maybe they ain't gullible, but just likes to be entertained. Fictional science and popular fantasy. And a lot of movie stars. You's got to have a lot of movie stars in a magazine to interest popular culture. Maybe I'm a crazy woman, though, 'cause there's been plenty to say I'm crazy, but in the small tank town I'm going to they'll welcome me. At least those who believe. The others, well, you know, when they witness the healings, then they'll come 'round. Most of them, anyway. In my head, I've already got pictures of my destination, as clear and vivid as if I was already there. And all them little southern and midwestern tank towns, they's all alike. I don't have to describe them little tank towns to you, 'cause they're all alike. I don't know why they call 'em tank towns, though. Them little towns. I think they call 'em tank towns on account of them water tanks, you know them water tanks, where the trains stop to take on water. And that water tank is always higher than all them little buildings in them towns.

I don't know if the modern trains still use water, but them old steam locomotives usedta stop in them little tank towns to take on water. They didn't have depots in a lot of them little towns, 'cause some of them was too small to even have depots, but they'd have them tanks. In some of them little western and southwestern towns where there's always droughts, probably them tanks collects water for the people themselves and not just for them trains. Sometimes the names of the towns themselves are printed on them tanks, you know, or the chief industry in the town sometimes uses them to advertise theyselves. The chief industry might be wine making or cigar making or coal mining or tractor manufacturing or maybe it's a cannery town, then the name of the town's leading employer is on that tank. Maybe that's free advertising for that employer, so's that employer'll stay in that little tank town and not take his business to Mexico or Korea. If it's one of them little tourist towns, though, the chief industry is the town itself. Then the name of the town itself is on that tank. Anyway, I think that's why they call 'em tank towns. If you ain't from a little tank town yourself, you've probably seen 'em on television or at the movies, one of them documentaries on television or one of them movies about ordinary working-class people. I remember there was a controversy when one of them movie stars bought herself a little tank town, bought herself her own little town, though I don't remember if that little town had a tank in it, though. I remember some of them townspeople was glad to have a movie star buy their town, and others were complaining that that movie star ain't done a thing for them but to buy their town. That movie star ain't done a thing for us since she bought our town, said one of the people in one of the newspaper articles where they talked about that movie star and her buying that town. Then the newspaper reporter asked them people whether they'd ever even seen that movie star in their town, and most of them said they'd never even seen her in their town. We seen her in the town when she first bought the town, one of them said. But after she bought the town they ain't seen her in the town. She didn't buy the town like in the movies, though, where this corrupt person is supposed to own the whole town and control the people in that town, and's got his hired gangsters to help him control the town, but her notion were the notion of a virtuous person buying a town so's to make it a better town. I guess they had visions of glory when she bought their town, her being a movie star, and their visions of glory wasn't satisfied, so they started complaining, or that newspaper reporter encouraged them to complain about that movie star so's he could get a story. Course there was others didn't want anybody to buy their town, movie star or not, or whether the movie star a virtuous movie star or a corrupt one. They wanted to own their own town. But whenever they talk about one of them little tank towns, they always show the town's tank that's usually got the name of the town on it or the chief industry. 'Cause them little tank towns don't have anything like the Golden Gate Bridge or the Empire State Building or Lady Liberty or even them Las Vegas casinos to give them distinction, so they show the town's tank. If somebody like Wayne Newton is from one of them little towns, they might put the name of Wayne Newton on that tank. This is Wayne Newton's town, it might say. It don't mean he owns the town, it means it's the town where's he's from, and the town's claim to fame. And it ain't just little southern towns that's tank towns, though, there's little towns up North that's tank towns too. Little towns in Maine and New Jersey and Connecticut and Pennsylvania, and somebody said that all the towns in Rhode Island is tank towns, though I don't remember seeing any tanks in any of them Rhode Island towns. But them that ain't got them water tanks, though, they still call 'em tank towns. So that tank town is just a metaphor for them little towns.

Anyway, in this little tank town, I'm supposed to stay with this woman name Martha Gaines, who right now's making ginger cakes, some of them egg salad sandwiches and probably some of that strawberry pie. This region's supposed to be known for its strawberry pie. And Martha Gaines supposed to make the best strawberry pie. If this region known for its strawberry pie, and Martha Gaines make the best strawberry pie in the region, then she must make the best strawberry pie in the nation and maybe even the best strawberry pie in the world. She ain't thought, though, to commercialize them strawberry pies and refer to them as Martha Gaines' strawberry pies. She could commercialize them strawberry pies, call them Martha Gaines' strawberry pies and sell them all over the world. I think she still work at one of them little factories in the area, though, one of them little doll-making factories. I think they make them Kewpie dolls, them little types of carnival dolls and them little dolls that's sold in gift shops. And she don't even get to put her name on them dolls that she makes; she's got to put the company name on them little dolls. And that's even the Kewpie dolls that is her own original design. I don't think she gets to make Kewpie dolls her own original design, though. I think them manufacturing companies like that have got they standard design. So's anyone who makes they Kewpie dolls makes the same design, though they's got several different designs for them Kewpie dolls. Course this region better known for its tobacco and its thoroughbreds, and there's a place in the area called Wigwam Village near Cave City, I think Cave City is somewhere near here, where you can spend the night sleeping in a wigwam, the motel is made up of these little wigwams or tepees, so that attracts a lot of tourists to the region, them people that's got a romance about them wigwams and tepees. 'Cause there's people that might not know one Native American or want to know 'em, but they romances their wigwams and tepees. I don't believe that it's in the ownership of true Native Americans, that Wigwam Village, though I think once that Wigwam Village or another Wigwam Village, they hired someone with a little Cherokee in 'em that poses as a full breed to tell the tourists Cherokee tales, or whatever the dominant Native American tribe in this area, I think Cherokees, but in the culinary arts, this region known for its strawberry pie. I told my friend Nadine about that Wigwam Village and she say she wouldn't stay in a wigwam or a tepee neither unless it were a real wigwam or tepee and in the ownership of a true Native American. I don't know what's the difference between a wigwam and a tepee myself, but I likes them strawberry pies, though. I asked Nadine, though, whether Native Americans has got they own cuisine, though, like other peoples, because I ain't never seen no Native American restaurants like other peoples' restaurants. She say that most American food has got Native American origins, and especially anything that's got corn in it, except she don't use the word corn for corn, she use another word for corn. I think she say maize. Like when I was in the Southwest I made sure I had me some of that fried cactus and some of them tacos that weren't Taco Bell tacos. Them tacos is made from corn, but you can also have wheat tacos. Any of y'all see that futuristic movie where all the restaurants supposed to be Taco Bell?

Maybe these tank towns is all alike, but in the culinary arts there's still some distinction. Even though McDonald's and Colonel Sanders and Taco Bell and McDonald's and Colonel Sanders and Taco Bell architecture is everywhere, you still find some distinction in certain of the culinary arts. In the evening we'll go to the basement of the Freewill Baptist Church and then I'll show 'em my miracles and wonders. Of course they's always three kinds of people there: them that believes without questioning, those that believe only when it's themselves being healed, and those who could suck a cactus dry—they ain't got cactus in this region, but the region I just come from, little town name Cuba, New Mexico—and'ud still tell you it ain't got no juice in it. I'll tell y'all the truth. If I wasn't the one doing the healing, I'd be among the tough nuts.

That's a big beautiful Bible you got there, the woman says.

Thank you.

It's one of those King James Editions put out by the Spiritual Harvest Bible Company. And Nicholas is on his way there to meet me, catching a plane from Kodiak Island, that's in Alaska, where he bought himself some land. He tell me he always have him them dreams of going to Alaska, though, ever since he were a youngster, during the days when

Alaska first joined the Union, and again when they was working on the pipeline, when there was a lot of mens going up there to Alaska to work on that pipeline, maybe even that Anchorage, and then he heard about that Kodiak Island. Kodiak Island, not Kodak. I think there's bears that inhabit that island. Ain't they got bear that they refers to as Kodiak bears. Then they's got the Eskimo people. I don't know if they inhabits that island, them Inuit and them Inupiaq peoples. I remember when one of them talk shows was doing a segment, though, maybe Sally Jessy Raphael or Geraldo, though probably Sally Jessy Raphael, on the men from Alaska and was trying to match them up with women, and them men from Alaska even had they own magazine advertising theyselves, and wasn't a Inuit or Inupiaq amongst them. I think there were one African American, though, that kinda remind me of one of them men in that singing group, the Village People, who somebody said is all supposed to be American masculine stereotypes or American stereotypes of the masculine hero—the "Indian," the cowboy, the soldier, the construction worker, the cop. Like them men that dances for them women in the nightclubs, you know, usually they costumes theyselves to resemble the masculine stereotypes of men. But Nicholas, even Nicholas kinda resemble them masculine stereotypes of men. Maybe this the last time he'll come along to bear witness to that first healing, that Nicholas, though, 'cause he's been hinting about retiring from the faith healing business, you know, saying that I can tell about my own first healing my own self better than any other witness. I thought about hiring me another "witness" but that would be duplicitous and Nicholas the true one witnessed the first true healing, and that ain't the same as a hired witness. He's thinking of maybe going into the private investigations business or maybe opening himself up a little shop, maybe selling sporting gear for the fishermen-tourists, up there on that island. Seem like he would be good at that private investigations business, for although he might resemble one of them masculine hero types, he still seem like he too much of a thinking man to be content with just selling sporting gear for the fishermen-tourists. Anyway, he's bought hisself some land up there in Alaska. I think he's originally from Denver, Colorado, somewhere out there in Colorado. To tell the truth, I ain't really sure where Nicholas from, though I think it's Colorado. It ain't Boley, though I remember once him telling me about that town of Boley, Colorado, supposed to be a town originally chartered by African Americans, one of they own towns. Least I think it's Nicholas told me about Boley. He ain't from Boley hisself, though.

Course there's probably a lot of fakers that hires theyselves witnesses, y'all know like them evangelist fakers—there's true evangelists and there's evangelist fakers—and some of them probably do better witnessing than the true witnesses. You know, maybe one of them evangelist fakers have a true witness to they healings, but the people don't believe the true witness so's they's got to hire theyselves a fake witness, 'cause the fake witness to the healings is more believable than the true witness. Now I'm wondering whether that would make the healer a faker, if the healings theyselves is real, but the healer got to hire a fake witness, 'cause even the true believers don't believe the true witness. 'Cause maybe the fake witness got more confabulatory imagination than the true witness that just got a knowledge of the healings. Ain't one of them scientists say something like that, about imagination being superior to knowledge in them scientific experiments and scientific theories. But Nicholas he say that I can tell about my own first healing my own self better, though, than any hired witness. Maybe that's the truth. All I know is that Nicholas himself usedta tell the tale with more fanfare, more flourish, more confabulatoriness. And when he tells about that healing, it sounds like a true tale; it don't sound like no confabulatory tale. Least the way he usedta tell the tale of that healing. Now he tends to be kinda dry. And those people that come to faith healing most of them want to hear confabulatory-sounding stories, which don't mean they's confabulatory stories they ownself. It's just that when people come to be healed, they just likes to hear them confabulatory-sounding stories. And there's other folks that comes to them faith healings not to be healed but to be entertained, like it's a circus or a carnival rather than a faith healing. Them sorts you don't know whether there's true believers amongst them or not. And then, of course, there's the scientific-minded people that comes to some of them healings, and you see them jotting down in their notebooks, and questioning the people that claims they's been healed, even questions Nicholas—I tell them they can watch me heal, but I don't answer they questions—and most of them decides it's the people's own gullibility that's healed them. There ain't many true believers amongst the scientific-minded, though there's them that says that science itself is a religion, just another form of the modern world's religion. So you can't categorize all the scientific-minded as a skeptical people. I think I read that in the *People's Almanac*, that that modern science just supposed to be another religion. When I first seen that *People's Almanac*, though, I thought it was like the Communist Manifesto, but it ain't. You know, talking about its being the *People's Almanac*, like the People's Republic of China.

Still the wonder's in what happened, the wonder's in the healing, ain't in how it's told. It's the healing itself ain't how it's told that draws the folks like bees to wild nectar. Or like flies to honey. But I think bees is fonder of wild nectar than even flies is to honey. Course the bees makes they own honey.

But that's always been the procedure, though. Nicholas stands up in front of the people and tells them all folksy-like about the first time I ever healed someone, and then, after they's caught up in the tale, whether they thinks it's confabulatory or not, I begin the healing. I tell them a little about the first healing my ownself, and sounding more folksy than I naturally am, 'cause when you's doing the healing you's got to talk about the healing yourself, 'cause amongst some that lends as much credibility as the healing itself, but like I tell the scientific-minded people or them media people that wants to write up they own confabulatory stories about faith healing in America, I'm mostly there to do the healing. You's got to heal people to prove to most people that you ain't just talk. Course there's some of them disbelievers, even amongst them that ain't scientific-minded and ain't the media types, that believes it's the talk itself that do the healing. That all you's got to do is talk that healing talk and there's some gullible folks that is healed. Or they thinks that you's some kinda hypnotist. After one of them healings, somebody ask me whether I'm some kinda hypnotist. I don't even know the laws of hypnotism. Ain't all the scientific-minded cynics, though, and ain't all the mystical idealists true believers.

But she don't look like no preacher woman. I wouldn't want her in no roodloft of my church and no pulpit neither.

She ain't a preacher woman, she's a healing woman. And us church don't allow women to preach anyhow. They allows a woman to teach but they don't allow her to preach. You know that preacher woman that come here and they told her she couldn't preach. They said she could teach, but they wouldn't let her preach. And what if a woman is called to preach the same as a man? she asked. But us church don't believe a woman is called to preach, even if she herself believe she is called to preach, and one of the women, you know the one from Memphis, say, Maybe she called to teach and thought she were called to preach. Maybe the Lord say teach and she thought he say preach. So she give that little lecture. She referred to it as a lecture, but it sounded like preaching to me.

Same difference.

I can already hear 'em talking about me, those flibbertigibbets. She ain't no preacher woman or a teacher woman neither, she a faith healer, one of them others be saying. What's the difference? She look like she belong on a submarine or on a motorcycle. They don't allow womens on no submarine. On the modern submarine they do, 'cause this is the age of feminism. Her and that bum's jacket. It's what they call a bomber jacket. Anyway, I seen her heal someone in D.C. I seen her when she healed in Memphis and then again in Kansas City. She even healed folks in Milan, that's over there in Italy. Dottoressa is what they calls her there in that Milan. I seen this picture of her healing over there in Italy and she were surrounded by all these Italians who looked just liked colored people to me. Say she's even healed folks in Brazil. I know they's got colored people in Brazil. Curandera's what they call her in Brazil. She sent us them article clippings about that. And them looking at her like they believes in that healing, and others like they's sure that she's a shyster. And she don't just include them clippings that quotes the true believers but also them that say they think she's a shyster and a subversive. Seems to me like if you's going to advertise your healing powers that you'd just include clippings of them people that says you's a true healer. 'Cept it just she wants us to make up us own mind whether she a true healer or not? I don't know if she's healed anybody over there in that India, though, but they's supposed to have a lot of they own healers over there, you know them yogis and such fabulous people, like them healing monks, and they probably wouldn't want to import no healer from over here when they's got they own true healers. They's got they own true healers everywhere, shamans the Native Peoples calls 'em, but that don't mean they might not want to import another one. I don't know whether she's ever healed any white peoples, though, I mean true white peoples, even there in Memphis, 'cause somebody say she especially likes to heal people over there in Memphis. What you mean the true white peoples? 'Cause in one of them articles she's with these peoples from West Virginia and they's looking like true white peoples, but then when you read the article it says they's colored people, or they white people claiming they's colored and's prouder to be colored than a lot of the true colored people. That's 'cause they's got the pride of being colored and ain't the prejudice. They's gullible when it comes to they own healers, the true whites, though, and them evangelists, but I don't believe they'd be true enough believers to believe she could heal 'em, I mean a woman of us persuasion, I mean true colored women. Seem like in all them clippings and them brochures they's colored-looking peoples in them photographs being healed, or white-looking peoples claiming to be colored. Not to say that they's true colored, even them looking colored. You know they's colored-looking people in the world that claims to be white the same as they's white-looking peoples claiming to be colored. What were her first healing? She healed herself. Aw, girl, you don't believe that! Yes, I believe it, 'cause that's the proof of a true healer. They's got to heal theyself first. You's got to work your own salvation first, even us preacher say you's got to work your own salvation first. He say when he preach it ain't to work us salvation for us, we's got to work us salvation usself. He say he can tell us how to work us salvation or how us religion say work us salvation, but we's got to work us salvation usselves. He say that almost every religion say that, ain't just us religion. He say he don't like to compare them religious books to them how-to books, 'cause he ain't a sacrilegious man, but most of them is how-to salvation books. But ain't none of them religious books works your salvation for you. There's people that hides from they own salvation, but even they's got to work they own salvation first.

I take off my bomber jacket in the heat, roll it up into a pillow and place it in the crevice near the window. The mustard and sardines still gives off its pungent odor.

She really do do some powerful healing, though. And she ain't a root doctor neither. She don't need no root to heal. Some people say that that is a superior form of healing when you don't need no root to heal. When you just healing people by knowing that they is healed. You know, that Christian Scientific woman that Martha know was talking about that. That they just heals people by knowing that they is healed. Other people, they trust them roots and herbs and potions, though. This woman just heals by healing. I don't know if she claims to be Christianly Scientific, though, or a Scientific Christian. I know she heals by healing and don't use no roots or herbs or potions. Wait till y'all hears about that first healing she done. I don't rightly recall the man's name that witnessed it, who was there at that first healing, I mean. He supposed to be here too, tonight, though. Wait till y'all hear. Wait till she sees, you mean. She healed me. You don't say. What was it you had? I don't rightly recall what it was called, or even if she named it, but when I walked I felt like I was walking in chains. I felt like I was in the old days of slavery and walking in chains. Or like them men we seen in them chain gangs that they's trying to renovate down South, down there in Mississippi or Alabama, I think. One of them states in the Deep South. Said they had brought back the chain gang in one of them southern states in the Deep South. Ain't that how they got the name gangster on account of them chain gangs? Naw, a gangster's a gangster. Somebody said that they made that against the law, ain't it? Them chain gangs, I mean. I think somebody said that they made that against the law, that they can make them prisoners work, that that ain't against the law, but that they can't tie them together on no chain gang, 'cause that chain gang is cruel and inhuman. How come you don't see no womens on them chain gangs, though? In all the history of the chain gang, I ain't never seen no womens on 'em. They usedta say there ain't as many criminally minded women as the mens, 'cause they say it's always easier for the womens to find work than the men, even that domestic work, but now they say they's almost as many criminally minded womens as mens. You've got freer women, but you've also got more criminally minded women. I felt like I was walking in chains. Doctors couldn't do nothing or didn't want to. I would go from doctor to doctor and couldn't none of them heal me, or didn't want to. The women doctors or the men. Then she just looked at me and know my trouble. She said the trouble would end, and touched me, and it did. That's what I mean by she heal by healing. Now I moves easy as wind through trees. Sometimes she speak a word and it's done. Other times she got to lay on hands. She don't prescribe none of them herbs and roots and potions, though. She ain't that sorta healing woman. Well, I heard other vile things and notions about her. Say she was a gambler. Say she was loose-virtued before she become a celibate. You don't always begin on the right road. Especially saints and prophets don't. They says that saints and prophets always begins as sinners, even them minor prophets. In fact, I don't know a prophet or a saint—I don't think they's any minor saints, a saint's a saint, ain't they? they talk about the minor prophets, but I ain't heard them talk about no minor saint— that ain't began as a sinner. When you reads tales about them saints and prophets, whether you reads about them in a book or sees it on the Learning Channel or TNT, or even learns about the modern-day saints and prophets that appears on the talk shows, though, seem like they all of them begins as sinners. Especially them male saints. Seem like they demands more of they female saints than they do of they male saints. Seems like they allows they male saints to sow they wild oats, but not they female saints. That's why you's got so many criminally minded modern women, 'cause they believes they oughta be able to sow they wild oats the same as the mens. Naw, there is female saints that also begins as sinners. You ever heard of that Saint Mary of Egypt? Is that the other Mary? Or is that the same Mary as that Magdalene? Was a rock 'n' roll singer they also says. Naw, but she did used to manage one, they says, that were her profession, a business manager. One of them rock 'n' roll and rap singers business managers. I don't know if she sing that rap or not, but I know she sing that rock 'n' roll. That Tina Turner–type rock 'n' roll. 'Cept she ain't no Tina Turner. Talk about them minor saints and prophets, one of them minor rock 'n' roll singers. And nothing to glorify the Lord in none of that music. Talk about people hiding from they own salvation. One of the beautiful people, though. And somebody even say she usedta be a beautician or one of them makeup artist out there in Hollywood. Seem like she'd know how to beautify herself.

Martha, tell us what stuff you know.

I got my sweet cakes and strawberry pie to make. All this gossip about gossip. Ain't gossipmongering a sin? Seem like gossipmongering oughta be a sin. Y'all is gossips' gossips. Y'all learn all there's to learn when she get here. And when that Mr. Nicholas get here too. She ain't gonna tell you no more about herself than's in them brochures, though, and what y'alls read about in them clippings, 'cause she believe that the important thing is the healing. Who Mr. Nicholas? He the one that witnessed that first healing. I like to hear him talk about that first healing almost as much as to witness the healings.

Saint Nicholas. Ha-ha-ha. Is he a saint too?

I want everything to be so fine. I'm honored that she chose to stay with me. And Mr. Nicholas too. I remember when I got healed, he witnessed for her, and a fine specimen of a man. She don't just pause with anybody y'all know and Mr. Nicholas neither. Course Mr. Nicholas usually stays at the hotels or the boardinghouses, 'cause he's the reclusive type. But she don't just pause with anybody, especially amongst the skeptical-type peoples that just wants to test her healing powers, you know. She knows I'm a true believer. And I'm one of the first people that she healed in them old early days when she first started with her faith healing. And I fancied myself to be one of the skeptics myself. I didn't be-

lieve she could heal a flea myself. And then I witnessed it when she
healed her own grandmother. Straightened out her shoulders. Say she
have a hump in her shoulders just like a turtle's. In fact, there's people
usedta refer to her as a turtle woman on account of them shoulders.
Other say it ain't on account of them shoulders, that she usedta be a real
turtle, which is nonsense, ain't no real turtle turn into no human being,
not in the natural world, but I know them shoulders kinda look like that
turtle shell. They say she look like she have a turtle shell on her back and
the healing woman healed that. But that's a whole nother story. Mr.
Nicholas don't tell that one. He just tell the tale about her first healing
herself. I could witness for her myself, but I ain't as good at witnessing
as Mr. Nicholas. He one of them charismatic-type people. He more
charismatic than the healing woman herself. What charismaticism she
got come from them healing powers. When you heal, you creates your
own charismaticism. But you needs somebody like that charismatic Mr.
Nicholas to witness for you, though. If I was a healing woman, I'd sho
want a man like Mr. Nicholas to witness for me.

I first seen her picture in the *Louisville Defender* before she started
printing up them brochures. It talked about all the travels she'd done
over there in Africa, and somebody asked her whether she had learned
her healing powers from one of them Africans, whether she were a apprentice to one of them African healers, but she said she had never been
a apprentice to none of them African healers, but did say that she knew
of a African healing woman, but they didn't heal exactly the same way.
And the woman who were interviewing her said that maybe that African healing woman had transferred some healing powers to her without
her knowing it. I don't know, she said, maybe she put some healing
powers in some zebra stew or something, but I do know that I never ap-
prenticed myself to any of them healers over there. And then they did
this little tabloid story about her, "I Healed Kong's Daughter," and
made it so you'd think it's King Kong, you know with all that talk about
Africa, at least that's what I thought when I read that blurb, 'cause
there's only one Kong that I know about and that's King Kong, and then
it turn out it this little Chinese girl named Kong, you know, that famous

little musician prodigy she supposed to healed, so's she could continue playing her music, you know. Naw, she don't play the violin. I know who you thinking about, naw this little prodigy I think she play the flute. That's the healing that's supposed to made her world famous. I don't mean the little Chinese girl, I mean the healing woman. 'Cause that little Chinese girl she already famous. You know, that Chinese woman named Kong that's got all those Kong restaurants all over the world heard about her healing powers and hired her. That's her claim to healing fame. 'Cause if she was just healing ordinary colored people, I don't think anybody woulda heard about her at all or written about her in no tabloids. She mighta been written about in *Ebony*, but I don't think she'da appeared in no tabloid, and there's a lot of colored people that wouldn't want her to heal us usselves if she hadn't healed that famous Kong little girl, 'cause we's like that usselves. It's Kong that made her a star, at least in the world of faith healing. She don't look like she can heal a flea, though. Or them bees. You know, they's talking about them bees around here that needs to be healed, naw I'm not talking about them African bees, I'm talking about the native American bee, unless they's colonized bees, I mean originating in England, 'cause the farmers needs them to pollinate. Bees don't just produce honey, they pollinates. That's what they refer to as the ecological system. I wonder if she can heal them bees, if she can heal the human species. Do that Mr. Saint Nicholas heal? Is he a healer? A healer ain't necessarily no saint, is it, Martha? You can be healer and don't mean you's a saint. Bible say to be wary of folks of that sort. It warn you about them false prophets and them false saints. But the Bible also talk about them gifts of the spirit, and God don't give gifts of the spirit to looks. Tell her, Martha. Bible says Jesus was ugly, and He is the greatest spirit gift His ownself. Course the description they gives of him don't sound ugly to me. Sound like a man meant to be glorified. Supposed to have hair like lamb's wool and to be the complexion of brass. That sounds like a man meant to be glorified to me. If most of these people talking about Jesus see the real Jesus, though, they would probably run from him. These holy evangelists and religionists. I mean them that thinks he's supposed to have blue eyes and blond hair and them Nordic peoples from Sweden or them Germanic looks, I mean them Aryan-type Germans, not them dark-haired Germans, 'cause them pictures you see of that Jesus even in us church that ain't the real Jesus, that ain't the true Jesus that even the Bible describes. Like that little Buddha that Martha got that they make out there at that factory where she work, now supposed that little Buddha was to have blond hair and blue eyes? Suppose they made that little Buddha to look like them little blond Kewpie dolls they make out there? Now I ain't amongst the folks to say that Jesus is a African or even a North African, like that schoolteacher telling us about, you know Little Sal, but that ain't even a Mediterranean Jesus. Devil came as a angel of light. Ain't that what the Bible say? Aw, girl, I know that. I usedta belong to the A.M.E., the African Methodist Episcopals, before I joined y'all's church. That's what it says, don't it, Martha?

Yes, it does say that all right. It most certainly does. And Jesus is Jesus. I know there's folks who searches for the real, historical Jesus. But Jesus is Jesus.

That smells so good, Martha. What is it? Ginger. Will she be here one night or two?

Depend on how big the crowd is and how much healing need to be done.

Do she heal crazy peoples?

Yes, I do believe she do. Seem like I heard she healed some crazy woman in Memphis. Some crazy woman from over there in Memphis. Seem like that one of her first healings, some crazy woman, or at least amongst her first healings. I do know the crazy peoples do come to her healings to be healed the same as the sane peoples, them that knows they's crazy or has the suspicion of it. I know when she healed me, I think there was several crazy peoples there that got healed, at least they didn't seem to have no visible ailments. Yeah, that brochure do mention insanity as one of her cures. Yeah, that brochure do say something about insanity as one of her cures. I know that old brochure she usedta distribute when she first started advertising her healings don't say nothing about insanity, though, it just list the physical cures. I don't think a true healing

woman should advertise herself myself. I still know her to be a true healing woman, though. But that new brochure do mention insanity. She
don't refer to it as insanity, though, she refer to it as a ailment of the
spirit. She don't mention insanity at all in that brochure, or even eccen-
tricity, she just mention ailment of the spirit, which she say encompass a
lot of the metaphysical things.

Be here two days then, maybe three. Maybe stay the week. 'Cause
they's plenty crazy people round here to heal, ain't it, Zulinda? Ailment
of the spirit nothing. Metaphysical nothing. They's crazy. Big Sal is
crazy. I know Big Sal is crazy. Y'all know Big Sal. Now I ain't talking
about Little Sal, ain't that Little Sal, speak of the devil, I seen that bicycle
she rides around on, I said that looks like Little Sal's bicycle chained up
there, look like a little girl don't she, woman her age riding around on a
girl's bicycle, now that's eccentric, a schoolteacher, you'd think she's one
of her students, I'm talking about Big Sal. Everybody know that Big Sal
is crazy. She look crazy her own self, if you ask me. Looking like she belong in a comic book. Though looking crazy don't mean you is. Do
looking crazy mean you is? If that looking crazy mean you is, then them
psychiatrists and psychologists would have more work than they's got
now. Lotta people say us Wisdoms looks crazy us ownselves, but I know
insanity don't run in us. Maybe some of the New York Wisdoms is crazy,
'cause that's New York, and seem like I heard some of them has been
psychoanalyzed, but the Wisdoms from around here ain't crazy. I know
that for a fact, though like the poet says sometimes the facts about a
people obscures the truth about 'em. There might be some ailment of
the spirit people amongst the people she heals in her world travels, or
even amongst the New York Wisdoms, but around here the crazy
peoples that's crazy is crazy. Ain't they, Zulinda? Martha, you acts like
all crazy people is sane.

I get off the bus carrying a small overnight case made out of imitation
crocodile. To meet me at the station's three middle-aged women in a
Ford convertible. Martha's the driver and she's the slender one and
the tallest, the others are the proverbial stereotypes of plump church
womens. Cotton print dresses, pillbox hats, oversized vinyl purses that

dangles from their wrists or elbows. Zulinda and Josephine don't hide
their disappointment. I know they's expecting me to be more impressive, look less like some ordinary, common woman and more like a legend. More like some legendary healer. Even them pictures of me in them
clippings and in that brochure looks more legendary. But people always
say I don't look like my photographs. There's people look more impressive than they photographs, others look less impressive than they photographs. A lot of them models and movie stars, people say, looks more
impressive in they photographs. Or if they do still look impressive in
person, I know a lot of them movie stars people's always telling them
that they looks taller on the screen. They might be the shortest man in
Hollywood, but onscreen they look like the tallest. Now that rock star I
usedta manage, she look more impressive in reality than in her publicity
photographs and her album photographs. That's the same with them
movie stars, like I said. That's why they always insists on giving them
them screen tests, to test whether the camera loves them. The camera's
gotta love them. They's gotta be photogenic. Now she's making herself
them videos, that rock star, but them videos ain't half so interesting as
the woman herself. It's Martha who comes forward to greet me first,
bringing with her that odor of ripe strawberries and fresh ginger. We
shakes hands. Hello, Martha.

The other women step forward to introduce themselves. They're
staring at my blue jeans and bomber jacket, worrying that I'll appear in
church dressed so outlandish. Josephine gives me a look, then holds out
her hand. We shakes hands, then I shakes hands with Zulinda, but I
know they're eager to test my healing powers. Josephine Wisdom's already telling me about her sinus problem and Zulinda Tage's already
mumbling about her fear of cats. We walk together toward the car. I ride
in the front with Martha, while Josephine's in the backseat taking Kleenex from her purse, hawking into it, and Zulinda's glancing up at the
tattered ceiling and wishing they coulda borrowed the reverend's car,
the Cadillac or the Mercedes, but though he's opened his church to me,
he's one of them skeptical ones, and ain't about to lend them his Cadillac
or the Mercedes either for some fool calling herself a faith healer. Still,
she thinks that Martha oughta mend that tattered roof of that convert-

ible. Gifts of the spirit ain't modern gifts anyhow but ancient ones, he believes, that skeptical preacher, though the Lord Himself supposed to be the same yesterday today and tomorrow.

Martha, why don't you ever convert your convertible? asks Zulinda.

I prefers the top up.

I wouldn't have me no convertible not to convert it, says Zulinda. I wouldn't have me none o' these old reckless tops if I didn't use it.

Martha got style, say Josephine through her Kleenex. Them fast womens rides around in them converted convertibles. You know them fast womens always got them converted convertibles. Martha got class.

Well, I likes me them converted convertibles and I ain't a fast woman, nor a slow one neither, and I got as much class as Martha. Everybody says I gots class.

When I'm scheduled to appear? I ask.

Aw, you got plenty of time to rest and freshen up, says Martha.

And *change,* adds Zulinda from the backseat.

Josephine hawks into the Kleenex. The *show* don't start till eight, she says, making sure I hear her call it show. Martha turns on the radio. This is an old Memphis song, the singer announces. Do y'all guys feel funky tonight? Martha turns off the radio, then turns it back on, twists the dial, only to find more funky music, then some of that gangsta-type rap, then little D'Angelo. She listen to a little of that D'Angelo music, some love's melody, sophisticated-type rap, which she say sounds more like real music, like intelligent music, than some of that other music, then she cuts the radio off.

I'm really looking forward to tonight, says Josephine. I wants you to cure my sinusitis. You going to, ain't you?

I don't say nothing. To tell the truth, I don't like to say what I'll heal until I heal it.

I guess for you it's easy to heal folks now after the long time you been doing it, says Zulinda.

The first time is easy when you got the gift of the spirit, says Martha. It ain't like them learned things, things you got to master. It were easy the first time, weren't it?

Yes, it were, I admit. I wasn't trying to be no healing woman. In fact after that first healing, I denied I was a healing woman, that that healing was just a fluke, then I healed a horse, I touched a horse's phalanges and I healed it, somebody was talking to me about one of their horses and I touched it and healed it. I guess I coulda just kept healing horses, worked for the racing industry healing their horses, you know, and then I went down to Memphis and healed a crazy woman. I don't just heal physical ailments, I heal ailments of the spirit, like my brochure says. Anyway, someone heard about my healing powers and someone else heard about my healing powers and then I just started healing, but in the beginning I denied I was a healing woman. I know a lot of people are skeptical of my healing powers. I was skeptical of them in the beginning myself, but I just kept healing people. Like you say, one of them gifts of the spirit.

Zulinda's thinking of a furry ball and gray radar eyes perched on her lawn. Martha even give her a book of cat poetry to help her get over her fear of cats. But that poem about that galloping cat, even galloping about doing good, made her more skeptical of cats. She's thinking that if I'm a real healing woman I'd know what she's thinking and heal her right then and there. How do you know who to cure first? she asks. I just know.

The car turns a corner and climbs a hill. The narrow road's lined with duplex houses, green and white and yellow. Beyond them the land slopes down to a railroad track. Zulinda's thinking that if I'm a real healing woman, I'd piece out the deeper fears, deeper than the fear of cats, and heal them too. She thinking she just test me first to see if I can cure her fear of cats. I reach down and scratch my ankle.

You ever got lost coming to these little out-of-the-way towns? Martha asks.

Naw, not really, but then I always got nice people to meet me like y'all. And it's mostly in these little towns that there's true believers. Ain't too many true believers in the big cities.

Martha smiles, but that cynical Josephine just blows her nose. Or true fools, she thinking. Them big city people ain't such fools, she thinking. They say she healed people in Rio, though. Ain't Rio a big city? And maybe them true believers in Rio is actually from them little towns, and they just comes to Rio to the big city. Zulinda hums a jaunty tune then changes it to a more holy one. The car sloping down bumps into the railroad track, crosses it, then climbs another hill.

Didn't know the train came through here, I say.

It don't anymore. Depot's closed down. A lot of these little train depots around here have closed down. Just the tracks left.

The women in the backseat are still thinking how common I am, how full of chitchat, and my vocabulary sounds elementary, it don't even sound like that preacher-teacher woman that give that lecture, ain't that wondrous and fantabulous vocabulary them healers uses, and if I could really heal, wouldn't I already just know about them trains too? And I don't talk that revelation talk, that prophet passion. Just some ordinary woman, could be one of them, or one of their daughters, one of their own girls. They're staring at my bomber jacket, its gray fur collar, imitation fox, 'cause I wouldn't have a collar with no real fox, like I wouldn't have no real crocodile, and my greased and braided hair. I'm one of their own girls, they're thinking. "Except maybe more streetwise and jazzy," thinks Josephine. "Full o' all that city flash." I know Martha's told them grand things about me, 'cause Martha's like that. It's Martha showed them all them clippings about me. "She a regular boogie-woogie," thinks Zulinda, clucking. Josephine blows her nose almost into the back of my head. Then Martha turns into the driveway. We climb out among honeysuckle bushes and them maple trees. Inside, Martha's house is spotless and smells like lemon oil. There's two of those comfortable flowered sofas, a long beige coffee table loaded with them whatnots—wooden elephants, a brass Buddha, state fair mugs, a little glass tiger. There's some of them little Kewpie dolls she makes, even a few multicultural Kewpie dolls. They usedta just make them white Kewpie dolls, but I guess now they makes them multicultural Kewpie dolls, or maybe they's Martha's own inspiration. There's an upright Steinway piano, mahogany and shining, standing beneath a gilded mirror. I watch the women reflected in that mirror. Martha's the gingerbread woman, Josephine's a chocolate eclair, and Zulinda's a lemon snap. I'm thinking of the names of horses I would've bet on if I was still a betting woman: Regal Fawn, Box o' Chocolates, and Banana's Kin.

I take you upstairs so's you can get refreshed up after all that long ride, says Martha. It's a real great pleasure, though, to have you here. Ever since you healed me, I've been wanting to invite you here to do a healing, but they says that your schedule has always been filled up with that healing in them other little towns. Well, when you first healed me, I wouldn't've known that you'da developed into a healer to be known worldwide. At least amongst the true believers.

At the top of them stairs, I can hear the women downstairs just chattering. She got on mascara. Teal blue. Did y'all see that? Teal blue. And dressed up like a soldier. But we's God's army, anyway. Aw, girl, I'll have to see to believe. I'm a true believer, but that don't mean I got to believe in that bogger. Harm a flea, but cure one?

You can rest up here, says Martha, reaching into one of them drawers and holding up a clean towel and washcloth. I'll call you. We can have a light meal here, but they want to have a real supper at the church, after your . . . presentation. I mean, the healing. Bathroom's down the hall. Where you headed after here, up North again?

Naw, Tennessee. Memphis.

There must be more true believers in Memphis than anywhere, 'cause seem like you's always healing folks in Memphis.

And there's a group in London, in Brixton, who've heard about my healing powers too, and want me to come over there to Brixton to do some healing.

I've heard about that Brixton. I know some folks name Brixton. They might be at your . . . healing.

Performance, she'd started to say at first. The healing? She hands me the rose and cinnamon towel and washcloth, then heads downstairs. I go in her bathroom and toss water onto my face and rearrange my braids. Listening to those voices downstairs. It ain't a auditory hearing, I should tell y'all. I mean, to y'all their voices would be inaudible or merely whispers, but to me they're as clear as Martha's glass tiger.

Is she gonna change? whispers Zulinda.

Why don't y'all come back and help me pack the cakes and my strawberry pie, says Martha. I thought we'd have us light ham and potato
soup—for her—before we go on account of all that healing she be doing. Poor child looks weary . . .

If she were a true healing woman she wouldn't take no thought to
light ham and potato soup.

We can put everything into this straw basket.

I'll have to see to believe. Don't look like she could cure a flea. If it's
true, I don't see why God don't give such gifts of the spirit to good
women like you, Martha, and a woman with class, instead of who . . .
trollops.

Hush, girl. It ain't for us to judge. Zulinda, you hold my strawberry
pie right. Hold it up like this . . . The last time you held my pie . . .

I come downstairs wearing a plain-cut beige dress, plain beige
pumps, and a paisley scarf around my waist. Poised in front of the
Steinway, Zulinda frowns at the paisley but grins approval at the beige
dress and round-toed pumps. And Martha's palms are held up to dem-
onstrate how to hold a imaginary pie.

Don't you tell me how to hold no pie, now Martha, says Zulinda. If I
knows anything, I knows how to hold a pie.

CHAPTER TWO

Seeing him in the crowd. He look like he grown a little broader, even his facial features look broader, and there's more gray at his temples, and gray in his mustache, but other than that he look like the same handsome man, the same good-looking man. Seem like in all the men I know, there's something of the same man, or maybe it's just that women don't know men the same way that men know themselves; maybe we only know us idea of a man, and if we got us a certain idea of a man, then we see something of the same man in every man, 'cause it's us own idea of a man us own archetypal man that we think we see in every man, like maybe only all men know is their idea of a woman or they idea of the archetypal woman. Even that novelist that wrote that *Portrait of a Lady*, seem like that's just a man's idea of a woman or of a certain type of woman. 'Cept she a American lady in Britain and the American lady ain't the same type of lady as the British lady, 'cause in Britain you's got to be a true royal to be a lady. How I meet him? I met him one summer I spent up at the racetrack in Saratoga Springs, upstate New York. He was buying yearlings. After my show, he'll probably come up and whisper, A long time, and I'll say, Yeah. But for now I'm just watching him out of the corners of my eyes, pretending I don't know him, pretending I don't know him no more than the others come to the healing, pretending I don't even know his name, and listening to them flibbertigibbets.

She been celibate ever since the healing power came, leastwise they say that she celibate—aw, girl, you know what celibate is, you know I don't have to tell you what celibate is, what Big Sal say she is, but don't nobody believe her, that Big Sal, but Big Sal say she been to the moon too, ain't you heard Big Sal's tale of how she been to the moon?—but girl I could tell you stories, say one of them flibbertigibbets, and then she start telling stories about me I ain't heard my ownself.

Hush.

What she waiting for? Why don't she heal somebody? Heal.

Nicholas J. Love.

Who that?

Nicholas J. Love. I think that J. stand for Jess. They shoulda named him Jess Love, 'cause he look like it, don't he? He look just like Love, don't he? Well, he look like love ain't a jest with him. He supposed to testify. He the one witnessed that first healing. She don't heal till after he testify to the first healing. Anybody know anything about healing, you know you need somebody to testify. And can't just anybody testify, gotta be a true witness to the healing. Course them healings testifies to theyself, but you know healers, a lot of them they don't just heal, you's got to testify first.

Hush. That him now. That him. That big good-looking. . . . My, he's a mountain, ain't he, Josephine? Mountain of a man. What they call a man of impressive height. Nicholas J. Love. Who Mrs. Love? I wonder if he got a Mrs. Love. I know a man like him gotta have hisself a Mrs. Love. Look like he got plenty wanting to be Mrs. Love. I bet he got plenty womens wanting to be Mrs. Love. I know he got plenty womens wanting to be Mrs. Love. Martha, do you know if he got hisself a Mrs. Love? Look at Martha, looking like she wanna be his own Mrs. Love herself? I bet you could be his own Mrs. Love yourself, couldn't you Martha? Now, he look like he can heal somebody. Heal. I bet he can heal somebody. He remind me of a man I seen once at a carnival, though. They had him advertised as the tallest man in the natural world. The poster advertising him say he the tallest man in the natural world. Look like one of them Watusi. You know them Watusi. They's supposed to be naturally tall people. Men that is unnaturally tall to us is natural men to them. I didn't like the way they had him up there in that tent amongst them carnival freaks, though, like he were King Kong or the Mighty Joe Young or somebody—aw, you know the Mighty Joe Young, that's the other King

Kong—instead of a natural man. You's a free man, I told him. You's a free man, you ain't King Kong or the Mighty Joe Young and you don't need to be in nobody's carnival. Is you a Watusi from over there in Africa? I don't think he understood English, though, 'cause he musta spoken one of them Watusi-type languages. Then somebody, one of the carnival security guards, I think they call 'em security guards, come over and told me I wasn't supposed to be talking to their Tallest Man in the Natural World. He didn't say nothing to me, the tallest man himself, 'cause I don't think he speak us English language, but he seem like he appreciate the fact that I was talking to him even in my own language like he a natural man and not just the tallest man in the natural world. They musta gone over there to that Africa to get that man, though, 'cause even though they's got some tall men in America and they's supposed to have taller men in America than in Europe, they's supposed to have the tallest men in the world over there in Africa. They's supposed to have the tallest men in the world and the shortest men in the world. He ain't exactly the tallest man in the world, though, but he do look like he can heal somebody. Did they have the shortest man in the natural world? Naw, I don't believe they did. They mighta had the shortest man in the natural world, but when I seen the advertisement advertising the tallest man in the natural world, that's the man I wanted, so I didn't look around to see whether they was advertising the shortest man in the natural world. Heal. I've always liked average-sized men myself, though. Heal. The average-sized man is my ideal of a man. Not the tallest man in the natural world nor the shortest man in the natural world. Heal. He sho look like he can heal somebody, though, don't he? But her, I don't think she could heal a flea.

Nicholas comes down into the church basement, wearing khaki trousers and a white shirt open at the collar, and strides toward me, then we goes up to the front. I'm watching the other man while Nicholas is talking. Nicholas must notice him too, though he pretend he don't know him either. I've already heard and reheard Nicholas tale, so I don't listen to all of it, only the healing part. . . . I stabbed her, but the knife bent. Wouldn't go all the way in. Went in just enough to do some tiny damage but not what it coulda done. Then it bent. And I ain't talking about no rubber knife neither. I'm talking about a knife knife. Went in just enough to do some tiny damage but not what it coulda done. Then it bent. And you know I'm a powerful man.

Hush now, a woman shouts. Hush, hush now.

Can't explain it, Nicholas says. Some force beyond me. At first I thought it had struck a bone, that knife, and I'm a powerful man, and the bone bent it, that knife, and I'm a powerful man, y'all know I'm a powerful man, I know y'all know I'm a powerful man, but the anatomy ain't where a bone would be. She were as startled as I was, our healing woman. Hush. Hush now. The knife bent. And I'm a powerful man. Y'all know I'm a powerful man. A powerful man amongst powerful men. Hush. Then the knife just fell out. She put her hand to her chest, to the wound on her chest, took her hand away and the blood were gone. Right then and there it mended. I ain't seen it mend, I ain't witnessed it to mend, but I seen it mended. The first healing. I witnessed that first healing, but I can't explain it. She can't explain it neither. The healing woman can't explain it either. You ask her to explain how she heal that first healing, and she can't explain it. The healing woman can't explain it neither. Can't nobody explain it. I ain't met nobody that can explain that first healing. There's folks believe themselves to explain that first healing, even scientifically minded people, but they ain't explained that first healing to my satisfaction. Even the scientifically minded people ain't explained that first healing to my satisfaction. They even wrote about her healing powers in one of them scientifically minded magazines, but that didn't explain it to my satisfaction. They even wrote about her healing powers in one of them tabloid-type magazines, but that didn't explain it to my satisfaction. They even wrote about her healing powers in one of them slick magazines over there in Germany, translated it into English and resold it to one of these slick American magazines, but even that transcontinental explanation didn't explain it to my satisfaction. Maybe there's folks that can explain that first healing, maybe even ordinary folks that can explain that first healing and even explain that first healing to my satisfaction, maybe other healers themselves can explain that first healing, maybe other healing women themselves, or even other healing men, can explain that first healing, and even explain that first healing to my satisfaction, but I ain't met 'em. I ain't met anyone, scientifically minded, ordinary, or healers theyselves who can explain that first healing. It just healed. Y'all think only true believers try to explain that first healing? Ain't just true believers that tries to explain that first healing. Cynics and skeptics try to explain that first healing, and even they don't explain it to my satisfaction. That first healing. That first healing just healed. I wouldn'ta believed her healing powers myself if I ain't witnessed them. If somebody told me this a healing woman and I ain't witnessed her healings myself, I probably wouldn't believe 'em. I am not a gullible man. Nicholas J. Love ain't a gullible man. I am not a gullible man. I wouldn'ta believed her healing powers myself if I ain't witnessed them. And I'm the one witnessed the first healing. I told y'all I witnessed that first healing. Ain't I told y'all I witnessed that first healing? She were as surprised as I was, though. I seen that first healing, and that's why I'm here to testify. You can't falsify a healing like that. You can't falsify a true healing like that. I'm not the truest of the true believers, but I'm the one witnessed the first healing. I'm the one witnessed that true first healing. I'm the one witnessed that first true healing. You can't explain a healing like that, it's just pure wonder. A healing like that is just pure wonder.

Some look at me in pure wonder, others are looking at Nicholas in pure wonder, others are looking like they still gotta see to believe. Even if Nicholas a believable-sounding man, even if he a powerfully believable-sounding man. But a lot of them's looking at us like it one of them confabulatory tales of them UFOs, like it one of them confabulatory UFO tales that Nicholas telling. Like he telling them how he got hisself abducted in one of them confabulatory UFOs. And how one of them little confabulatory aliens that abducted him had them special and purely wonderful and powerful healing powers. You know they ain't gonna believe no tale like that. You know, they's too intelligent to believe a tale like that. And ain't none of them confabulatory aliens abducted them. If ain't none of them confabulatory little aliens abducted them, then there ain't no UFO and there ain't no confabulatory little aliens. But some others are in their own private world, looking like they themselves been abducted in one of them confabulatory UFOs, and would like to tell the people about them confabulatory little aliens themselves. Maybe some of them have heard the tale before about that first healing, or read about it in one of them tabloid-type magazines, but they've still got to see a healing for themselves. Nicholas is on a roll. He's on a roll. . . . And him? Perhaps he's merely looking like a man who knows the truth of it.

I thought she were a witch or something at first, says Nicholas. Even she didn't know what she were. And still she don't know. When she was healing some people up in the Dakotas, a few people started calling her the Healing Woman Healed Herself First. Maybe that's who she is. The Healing Woman Healed Herself First. And then when she's healing people in Memphis they just started calling her the Healing Woman. Maybe that's who she is. Well, I'm here to testify that she healed herself first. I'm here to testify that she healed herself first. I'm here to testify that this healing woman healed herself first. And now she trying to heal everybody that want to be healed. At least everybody that want her to heal them. I'm her witness. And that the truth. And I wouldn't trade truth like that for gold.

There's rumbles and hums and rustles, then Hush now!

Nicholas turns to me and smiles. He add that new thing about me "trying to heal everybody that want to be healed." And that new thing about "At least everybody that want her to heal them." He ain't had that in his witnessing before. Least he ain't said I'm trying to heal everybody. I come forward and take his hand again. I'm considered a tall woman, but beside Nicholas I just look average height. Yes! someone shout. Lord, today! exclaim another. A unbeliever mumbles, pirates, bandits, confidence people. A few snicker at a tale like that. Another starts singing.

I didn't even ask for the spirit gift, I begin softly. I weren't even pre-pared for the spirit gift. But it came, it came. I modulate my volume so's my voice grow gradually loud. It came. The Lord good. Yes. What can you do but claim what the Lord give. Hush. It's ain't me. It God who make you whole. A lot of y'all looking at me and just seeing just a ordinary woman, and asking y'allself how come a ordinary woman like me to be given a gift of the spirit, how come a ordinary woman like me to be given a spirit gift? Y'all thinks that just spirit gifts supposed to be given to extraordinary people, to extraordinary men and women, the kings and queens of the world, the princes and princesses. But that the point of them spirit gifts, the point of them spirit gifts, is that I am just a ordinary woman. I am just a ordinary woman, that is the point of the healing. The spirit gift extraordinary, but as for me, I'm just a ordinary woman. Come up. It God who make you whole. Praise the Lord, and accept his restoration.

And then I start calling names, like I've always known them:

Mr. Buster Gentry, Mizz Faustina Brixton, Mizz Gretel Loppie, Mizz Sheba Boss, Mr. Pete Menton, Mr. Bunyan Macheath, Mr. J. J. Ray, Mizz Sal Battle. . . . Come up and be healed.

Hush.

I lay my hands on a young woman suffering from a skin rash and immediately her skin become smooth and clear as a baby's. A elderly woman suffers from a bone ailment that make her lower back painful. I lay my hands on and she straightens, healthy, then bends forward and touches her toes. A baby's got chronic earache; I kiss both its little ears and they's made whole again. Gurgling and laughing, he don't wanna let go of my fingers. Then they's a young man who I'm unable to heal in public, 'cause it necrospermia he's suffering from, so before he comes forward I ask Nicholas to go inform him that we'll come privately to his home and heal him, and then he can expect that wife of his to have babies the very next year. Another woman's got psychic symptoms, restlessness, delirium, hallucinations, delusions: I hold her hands, stroke her forehead and kiss her.

I'm Mizz Sal Battle, she says. How you know my name? They calls me Big Sal. You said my name, so I figure you's a true healer. I got to believe in somebody know my true name. I figure anybody know my true name must be a true healer. Course you could just be going around asking

folkses' true name, and just be a faker. But most folkses calls me Big Sal,
they don't call me Mizz Sal Battle, and most don't even know my true
name is Sal Battle, so if you'da asked them my true name, they'da told
you Big Sal, so I figure if you says my true name, you's a true healer.
Then, Hush, she whispers her joy. Hush. Hush. Hush. Hush.

And then there's that smallish woman from the bus. I ain't think she
believed, but she come up. She ain't got no visible ailment either, but she
got what them psychiatrists refer to as "incipient insanity."

I touch her forehead and she cure.

It's after midnight before the session over. After the healings, we give
thanks, then gather around the table to feast.

A long time, he whispers.

Yeah, I say, turning.

But I know I ain't the woman he met up at Saratoga. I'm the one who
touched the horse's phalanges and healed them. I'm the one who
touched my own wound. I'm the one who healed my own self first.

He piles a plate high with fried chicken and potato salad and hands
it to me.

Come out to the farm, he whispers, his hand on my shoulder. I
haven't seen you in a long time, N'Orleans. You look regenerated. And
Nicholas is beaming. Is it you and him?

But I shake my head. And N'Orleans, that ain't my true name, that
just his sometimes name for me.

Then he whispers, He's free.

Who's free? Nicholas?

They freed Nicodemus.

Who's Nicodemus? Nicodemus? Oh, yeah, yeah. Nicodemus.
That's good.

He stands watching me a moment, thinking maybe I'll ask him some
more about Nicodemus, or how they freed him, or maybe—since he
helped free Nicodemus? or since it ain't Nicholas and me?—agree to
come back with him to his farm, then disappears up the basement stairs.
I feel like I'm standing in the tropics. I wipe sweat from my forehead
with the napkin. A tiny wind whips up.

I ain't breathed so freely in years, says Josephine, coming to me, touching her sinuses, marveling. He said we couldn't trade this for gold, and we ain't paid one cent over. Why, you must be a true healer, 'cause them other people they be demanding gold for this. Martha said we paid you little something, and for the transportation for you to come here, but ain't the gold that this is worth. Course somebody said you usedta manage one of them rock stars, and they is monied people, so you probably saved up a lot of money, mucho dinero, as the people say, and don't need to be greedy. Course monied people always wants mo' money. You don't look like you's monied to me, though. I don't know how you does it, though, being the ordinary woman that you says you is. How do you do it?

The Lord do it, corrects Zulinda, who's standing near the punch bowl, her phobia gone. It ain't no mystery. The Lord do it. It ain't no mystery at all. And if she were to demand gold for this, she might not keep them healing powers. That's probably the only reason she ain't demanded gold for this, so's she can keep these healing powers. I still don't think no gifts of the spirit to be given to ordinary womens, though.

Lord a mystery, says Josephine. His wonders do perform, and like Mr. Nicholas said we ain't paid one cent over.

When he say that? Where that Mr. Nicholas?

He just come to witness. He never stay to socialize. He one of them strange men.

That's 'cause he's amongst strangers.

I bite into a piece of fried chicken and smile at them both.

Mizz Battle think she dreaming. Look at Big Sal, she think she dreaming, and this ordinary woman, she got herself a mighty appetite to be so holy, ain't she? A mighty devilish appetite to be holy. They say you's supposed to hunger and thirst after righteousness.

Well, she the boss, if you ast me. Eat what she want. Us supposed to invite her here to heal us and then let her go hungry? And ain't asking no donations neither. Do that sound like a faker? Ain't even charged the people she done healed. She told them they could give Martha a little something for her strawberry pies. Something about Martha Gaines' strawberry pies. Martha say she likes making them Kewpie dolls. Heard her telling her she could start selling them strawberry pies they's so good. Ain't a healer supposed to be worth her hire? That make me a true believer even more than all this healing, though. Eat what she want is what I say. Ain't a healer supposed to be worth her hire? The gold that this is worth.

And that youngish woman from the bus, looking more familiar now. The one in the Gypsy earrings, riding that bicycle. I know her name now, but not who she is. Wondering how I knew what she had, didn't know what she had her ownself.

I thought I knew you, she's saying.

Know me? I don't say nothing, 'cause a lot of times when I'm healing, a lot of people claims they know me when they don't. Some of them knows me from the brochures, others from them clippings, but none of them don't know me. She do look kinda familiar, though.

I met you once in a beauty parlor up in Louisville. That's before you became a faith healer. I was reading in your brochure about you being raised in Louisville and originally being a beautician, and that's where I'm from, and then I realized that I know you. I was on my way up North to go to school, I mean when I first met you. I don't know if you remember me. It was my first time in a beauty parlor. It was my first time having my hair professionally straightened. Cornella and Jaboti's Beauty Shop.

Oh, yes. You that little girl. You don't look no older than you looked then, 'cept your hair's a little shorter. It's all those chemicals. Let me jot something down for you that you might start using, that is if you wanna keep straightening your hair. It ain't got no chemicals at all in it, no synthetic chemicals, just natural ones, made by a company in Brazil, and so harmless you can eat it, but it gets your hair just as straight. That is, if you want it straight.

Yeah, I heard them talking about that, that they was going to order something like that.

That's all they use in their beauty shop now, they don't use them synthetic chemicals.

I take out my notebook and jot the name of the product down for her and where it can be ordered. She can either order it from Cornella and Jaboti's Beauty Shop or from a wholesaler in Brazil.

I was looking at you and thought I knew you, I say. I was thinking that you look familiar.

I thought I knew you too, she's saying again, and then she cut herself a piece of that strawberry pie. She don't eat it, though, she just stand holding that pie and talking to me. I'm teaching school around here now, she say. I'm a schoolteacher. Harriet Tubman Junior High School, that's a new multicultural junior high school. I teach General Science but we emphasize multicultural contributions to science, as well as the sciences of different peoples of color. We even have a chart of the stars that has the different African names for the stars. A lot of people they don't know that Africans even named the stars, that different peoples, different so-called native peoples, have their own names for the stars, and have star charts just as accurate as the Chinese star charts, which are more ancient than the European star charts or even the Arabic ones or the star charts of the New World civilizations. Everybody's got their own cosmology. Everybody's got their own description of the universe. I helped them to form that school, though. Some people thought it should be a school just for African-American girls, "for colored girls only," you know, but I thought it should be a school for everybody and that we should teach about everybody, because to be a true citizen of the world, you've got to know about everybody. Of course, we've had people to be interested in the concept of Harriet Tubman Junior High but then to take their children out of that school, even though they're learning, and learning more in that school than some of the other schools, even some of the private schools, 'cause they just want them to know about themselves, you know, and telling us we're teaching too much about the minorities and women. But they just want you to learn about themselves. You might be teaching ninety-five percent about them anyway and they want that other five percent too. My name's Sally Canada. We're the other Canadas. I always tell people we're the other Canadas, you know, 'cause when people hear, especially people around here, 'cause you know she usedta work at one of the tobacco factories around here, the notorious Eva Canada, somebody said she tried to organize the first union in one of them tobacco factories around here, though that ain't the Eva Canada that everybody know about, but everybody that usedta work with her there likes to claim they know her, or claim they don't know her, but when they hear my name is Canada they think I'm kin to that other Canada, that notorious Eva Canada, you know, or they think that we're all criminally insane. I was a little girl when I first heard about that Eva Canada, when I first saw a picture of her in one of those *Police Gazette*–type magazines, and so a lot of the other little kids would tease me about that other Canada, and sometimes little boys would even be afraid of me on account of that other Canada, on account of what she done to that man, so I either don't tell people my name or I always make sure that people know that we're the other Canadas, that we're the other Canadas. Somebody say she out of prison now and a recluse somewhere. Maybe changed her name. You know when I told y'all that I didn't know I was supposed to make a appointment, I knew I was supposed to make a appointment, I mean for the beauty shop, when I come into y'all's beauty shop without a appointment, but I didn't want to tell y'all my name. I guess I coulda lied and give y'all a different name, like McCambridge or something—I've even heard that Eva herself is out of prison now and has renamed herself McCambridge, after that old movie star and uses that name—but I don't like to lie about my name. I didn't want y'all to hear my name Canada, even Sally Canada, and think I'm one of the other Canadas. That's one of those Canadas, I usedta hear people say. That's one of the reasons I wanted to go to school up there up North, up in Vermont, 'cause I didn't think Eva Canada's name as notorious up North, I mean in the Northeast. That's why when I got that scholarship to Bennington I went, because I was sure that nobody at Bennington woulda heard about Eva Canada. I was running from being identified with that other Canada. Even the Canadas that are the same Canadas don't want to admit it. I know Lulabelle Canada even changed her name and moved to Atlantic City. Or the Canadas that keeps their names they'll lie to you and tell you that they're the true other Canadas, when we're the true other Canadas. And there's another group of Canadas, too, that ain't any kin to Eva, and they claims they's the true other Canadas, and we just fictionalize ourselves pretending to be the true other Canadas. And there's even them that say that even Eva herself ain't a true Canada. Did I tell you I heard her name's McCambridge now? I usually don't talk this much, though, you know, even when I'm teaching, but you know, after you healed me, I feel so free. Anyway, people around here call me Little Sal on account of Big Sal, you know, to distinguish me from Big Sal. Of course, my students call me Mizz Canada. I know a lot of people around here because I teach their children. You know, I usually don't believe in faith healing myself. I'm usually kinda skeptical, being a science teacher, even though a lot of the early science, a lot of the alchemy is kinda mystical, but when I saw you heal Big Sal, who everybody knows is crazy, I thought you might be able to heal me. What craziness I have I've been trying to keep it to myself, to keep it a secret you know, to camouflage it. But when I saw you heal Big Sal, that's when I decided to come up and be healed.

She start to say something else, something about her healing, or Big Sal's healing, or some of them other healings, but then Martha join us near the banquet table. You must be tired, say Martha.

I am a bit.

Must tire you out so them healings, says Martha. Although she's made all that strawberry pie and all them sweet cakes, she's only got a little corn pudding on her plate. I healed her colitis years ago, but she still just nibbles.

I don't feel it while I'm healing. While I'm healing I feel energized. It's just afterwards that I do get sort of tired out.

While *He's* healing, corrects Zulinda.

Yeah, that's what I meant.

Martha stands in front of me like a shield, then leads me up them basement stairs. The teacher-woman looks like she wants to follow us, but she stays eating her strawberry pie. When I glance back, she's talking to Big Sal. Sane women again.

Then you shouldn't be tired, you, says Zulinda, from behind.

CHAPTER THREE

How did I first meet him? Not Nicholas, but the other one? The one come telling me Nicodemus free. Well, I'd come to the racetrack five o'clock in the morning 'cause they say you gotta come that early to watch them walk the horses and then most people have breakfast at the track restaurant. You can have breakfast at the outdoor part of the restaurant under one of them white and latticed canopies. The air smelled like lavender and fresh horse manure. Already a high-bred lady was sitting at one of them tiny breakfast tables. You know, one of them real wealthy-looking women, probably a racehorse owner. Somebody told me the way that you can tell wealthy people is they look well taken care of. Somebody told me that or I read it somewhere in a book. Mighta been a jockey's wife, that woman look well taken care of, 'cause a lot of them jockey's wives, especially them wives of them winning jockeys, them jockeys that's got they business managers and they talent agents just like they's movie stars or rock stars, them winning jockeys, looks well taken care of, but she look like a racehorse owner her own self, or the wife of a racehorse owner. 'Cause she look more well taken care of than even a winning jockey's wife. One of them wealthy husbands who bought her her own racehorse. I read about one of them wealthy husbands, maybe a racehorse owner himself, who bought his wife her own racehorse. She probably have all the diamonds and luxuries, and maybe even her own plantation-mansion 'cause she look like a woman of the South, or a southern belle wannabe, you know there's a lot of them northern womens that's got they ideas of the South before the Civil War from them romantic movies and storybooks and likes to vacation on them southern plantations, the ones that they convert into inns—I even heard of one woman that always insists on staying in the old slave quarters that they've converted into a guest house. Well, this southern belle wannabe, she got all the diamonds and luxuries and her own plantation-mansion and renovated slave quarters, but she still bored, so he buy her her own racehorse. She wearing a cucumber green dress and one of those green cloche. The dress look like it made out of layers of mosquito curtain. She just nibbling coffee cake and looking disinterested in them parade of thoroughbreds. Maybe that's how you can tell them wealthy people too.

But me and him was standing at the fence together. I wasn't sure what his nationality. He was wearing a business suit and I suppose he could be African American like me, but he had this other air about him, like a foreigner. You know, you seen them types of African Americans that got a kind of foreignness about them, some because they's spent years abroad amongst foreign peoples, like them diplomats and students and Army brats, others just has a natural foreignness, and people ask them what they are, 'cause you can't tell whether they's African Americans or one of them colored foreigners, and's always surprised when they say they's African Americans. And you know a lot of them colored-looking foreigners they don't want you to think they's African American, so I didn't know whether to ask him, Are you African American? 'cause he might be one of them colored foreigners that don't want you to think they's African American. Made me think of that Aladdin and his magical lamp. But he more dark-complexioned than that Aladdin, at least the Aladdin in the movies and the cartoons. I met me one of them Portuguese-type Africans once, though, that kinda remind me of him. One of them little Portuguese islands off the coast of Africa, where they's colored people, but they ain't as colored as the true Africans. What the name of that little island? I think it got a Portuguese-type name. Anyway, we was watching them thoroughbreds, and I don't want to ask, Are you African American? 'cause he might be one of them colored-looking foreigners. A handsome brown thoroughbred were led past. That's a fine horse, he commented. And there's some kinda accent. It ain't no

Portuguese accent, though, or none of them other romance languages. Ain't from Brazil or none of them Latin American countries. And that accent don't sound Mediterranean.

Yeah, I agreed, without turning, 'cause I didn't want him to think I was spying on him. He's a real challenger.

He looked at me when I spoke, though, on account of my own accent. People call it a Geechee accent. Don't sound like a accent to me, but other people call it a Geechee accent. Then some people tell me I got a blend of different types of accents.

Are you from here in Saratoga? he asked.

Naw, just visiting, and betting on the horses, you know.

We didn't say no more, just watched those horses. When they finished the parade, he asked me if I'd like to have breakfast with him. He himself he got some kinda foreign accent, like I said. It sounded kinda American and kinda foreign at the same time, though. Sound almost Eastern European, and I don't think they's many colored people in that Eastern Europe. But I know he ain't no Russian or nothing. Then his accent kinda remind me of that famous actor supposed to be from Austria. Maybe there's colored people in that Austria. Or maybe he one of them Dutch. I ain't as countrified as some Americans who think that the only colored people is in America, or that the only Africans is in Africa.

Where you from? I asked, when we'd found a table.

Germany.

Say what? But you's African-looking. You a real German? I was thinking you kinda sound like that famous actor from Austria. Austria, they speak German, don't they? Austria, ain't that the same as Germany? I mean, I know the only colored people ain't in America, I mean, I've seen Africans in Germany, but not any German Africans, I mean not any African Germans.

He just smiled and arched an eyebrow. Believe it or not, there are real Germans from Germany who look like me, he said. Real Germans in Germany who look like just about everybody in the world, like you Americans. Every time I meet an American, though, I have to explain who I am. Most think I'm African. Or from one of the former Dutch colonies. We've been in Germany for many generations, though, just like you Africans here in America. I'm an African German or a German African, to use your American way of defining who we are.

You speak good English, except there's a little accent.

Every American says that too. Of course, I speak good English. It's only you Americans who don't want to learn anybody's language but your own. You celebrate that in yourselves, but to us Europeans it's a flaw in the American character, one of the many flaws in the American character. You Americans are so good at pointing out the flaws in other "national character" but the flaws in your own "national character" you celebrate as virtues.

I glance at the high-bred woman, who bites into a rice cake, then holds it up like it's a tired moon. She looks toward us with curiosity, or rather at the African German with curiosity, then resumes her air of disinterest. It's a open-air restaurant, and we're sitting near a white railing. The railing's white to match the canopy. He's saying something about American culture. That American culture itself is a flaw, and even our own fascist tendencies, we celebrate as Americanism.

I'm real German, he says. But everyone asks that. Every American. I own a little farm in Kentucky now, though.

So how'd you get from Germany to Kentucky?

I kept being mistaken for an immigrant in my own country, you know, although we've been in Germany many generations, since the seventeenth century. Hottentot slaves, Ethiopian traders, you know. But to be mistaken for an immigrant in your own country? I came to your country once and we traveled through this area, I mean Kentucky, some German friends and I, we went to Keeneland and visited some of the horse farms, and I liked the country. So after being mistaken for an immigrant in my own country, I decided to come to a country where I really am an immigrant.

I was in New Mexico once and they mistook me for a immigrant, I mean a illegal immigrant. To tell the truth, I was kinda flattered myself. Course I had my passport to prove who I am. But if they'da tried to ship me back to Mexico I don't think I'da been that flattered. And I don't look like no Mexican to me, but there's Mexicans that look like me. I was in this little cantina, though, and they were raided by some immigration police, checking everybody's papers, you know. I know you need your passport when you're abroad, but that's the first time I had to use my passport in my own country. But they say whenever you're in those little border towns you gotta have your passport, like you's in a foreign country, especially if you don't look like their American idea.

During the war, the Second World War, being non-Aryans, we left Germany and settled in Zurich, in Switzerland. After the war, we returned to Berlin. I was born after the war and don't know all of that history, but I know we were exiles. But now we're treated like auslanders again, like foreigners, so that's why I decided to come to America. To be treated like a foreigner, I might as well be in a country where I am a true foreigner, where I am a true auslander. I spent some time in Alexandria, in Egypt. I thought I might settle there. But even there, everyone's dream is America, you know. The official governments won't tell you that. The ordinary people all over the world, they will tell you that their dream is America. Their politicians and intellectuals will complain about America, but the ordinary people themselves will tell you that America is their dream. They see the glamorous American movie stars, the glamorous American movies, and they think that's America. When I told some of my friends in Alexandria that I was coming to America, they all said that was their dream. My name is Josef Ehelich von Fremd.

That sounds like a German name. Alexandria, ain't that in Morocco? The only thing I know about Morocco is it's supposed to be a land without rivers. I remember that because that was one of our geography questions in high school. I don't know if it said Morocco's the only land without rivers, but Morocco's supposed to be a land without any rivers in it.

Alexandria's Egypt. Didn't I say Egypt? May I ask your name?

Harlan. Harlan Eagleton. Harlan Jane Eagleton. I usedta think I'd like to call myself just Jane, you know. But now I like Harlan.

Harlan? There's a Harlan, Kentucky. Are you from Harlan, Kentucky?

Naw, I was born in Louisiana, in New Orleans. My grandmother's from Louisville, Kentucky, though, and that's where I grew up. I don't know why they named me Harlan, though. Harlem, maybe. But Harlan. I guess Harlan Jane sounds better than Harlem Jane. You speak English very well. But I said that. And you said that was a flaw of the American character. One of the many flaws of the American character. But that ain't no different from most people, is it? Seem like most people turn they own flaws of character into virtues. They see other people's flaws, but they own flaws, they turn into virtues.

I grew up speaking English as well as German, you know. Most Europeans speak several languages. I speak English, French, German, Dutch, a little Portuguese. It's only you Americans who're stingy about language, who believe that your own language is the universal language. I guess it is the universal language. You've made it the universal language. You've made it so your language is identified with modernity, with internationalism. I even know some Americans, though, who've lived in Berlin for years, and in other European cities, and insist on speaking only English. Who insist on English only even when they're in other people's country. Most of you Americans. There are exceptions, of course. I have some American friends whose German is impeccable. Even some African-American friends who speak impeccable German.

I drink my coffee, nibble my coffee cake, and watch the high-bred woman. Josef's staring at me, though, then he's eating his cheese omelet.

Are you married? I ask. Your wife immigrate with you?

Yes, I've a wife, but she hasn't come over to the States yet. She's in Berlin. I don't know when she'll come. Right now, I've received threats, you see, and I'm trying to find out how seriously I should take them.

Threats? What kinda threats?

You know what kind of threats.

I'm wondering how seriously I should take him. All that business about being a Hottentot German or a German Hottentot. Like I said, I ain't so countrified that I don't know they's got Africans over there in Europe, even Hottentots, 'cause I've seen them on television, but maybe he's just jiving me, I'm thinking. But he's telling me again how he received threats as soon as he bought him some of that prime land for his thoroughbreds. They expected him to be one of them Aryan Germans, and then when he appeared, buying up that prime land, that I guess only Aryan Americans supposed to buy, he started receiving threats. After he'd bought the land for his thoroughbreds, he went to some of the local auctions, but some sort of consortium kept outbidding him, even though his bidding prices were pretty high, but his bidding prices weren't a match for a consortium, which he was certain had been formed merely to outbid himself—it wasn't conceit—so he decided he'd come to Saratoga, to the Fasig-Tipton sales.

When people think I'm German, an Aryan German, they don't have a problem. . . . Of course Josef Ehelich von Fremd sounds like an Aryan German, or what they believe to be a true German. I don't know our original Hottentot name because the original Hottentots changed their name to a pure German name or had their names changed to a pure German name, and there's nothing to distinguish my accent from that of any other German, but then they discover I'm an African German and not an Aryan. You know, in Germany I'm in arbitrage, but when I came to America and saw your thoroughbreds. . . . I remember once when I was in the city, at one of your restaurants, and I mentioned being German, the waiter thought I was "jiving" him, you know, as you Americans say, thought I was one of your locals only pretending to be German. He'd probably seen one of those American movies, I suppose, with the typical African-American jiver, the typical African-American Confidence Man, and he was certain I was playing some confidence game. My credit cards were suspect, and then he got the bright idea, some friend of his who spoke German said something to me. High school German, you know. But my real German, which he didn't understand at all, still convinced him that I was some local pretender. He didn't understand my real German, it didn't sound like the elementary German he'd learned in high school German, so he was convinced it wasn't real German. Do you think I'm a pretender?

No. I know they got splivs in Europe. I know they got splivs in Paris. If they got splivs in Paris, I figure they must have them in Berlin.

But that's not telling me who you think I am.

I don't know who you are, but I know they got splivs in Europe, 'cause I seen them on television. Even got splivs in Russia. I know some of them Afro-Communists in the 1930s went over there to Russia and some of them stayed over there, and I know them Russians they've always had they own history with Africa, even before the 1930s. The most famous Russian writer he got African in him, you know, though they don't think of him as African they think of him as Russian, 'cause I remember this Russian writer, this Russian poet was being interviewed on television, and this interviewer points out that this famous Russian writer he's talking about is part African, and he kinda looks embarrassed, you know, because you know he's not thinking of him as part African, but Russian, not Russian African or African Russian 'cause he's supposed to be Russia's greatest writer sorta like the Russian Shakespeare, you know, and maybe also because he knows of the prejudice about Africans in America, the interviewer's American, you know, they had that on television, and I know you telling the truth about them Germans thinking you a immigrant, 'cause I read about them, and I even heard a African American over there in Germany talking about leaving Berlin on account of being mistaken for a immigrant of color himself and he ain't even a true German like you and talking about all them neo-Nazis over there in Germany, them neo-Fascists in Berlin, and them talking about Germany for the Germans, and say that even in Sweden they's got 'em, them neo-Fascists, and Sweden supposed to be the land of racial tolerance. So I know you telling the truth about them neo-Fascists over there in Europe, but it wouldn't be honest of me to say I know you telling the truth about who you yourself are, 'cause I don't know you. Deutschland für Deutschländer—one of them neo-Fascists on television were holding up a sign that said that.

Deutschland für Deutschländer, he corrects my pronunciation, though it sound like the same German to me.

I know all over Europe it's supposed to be the same thing. France for the French. England for the Englishmen. All them former colonialists and colonizers wants they own land for theyselves. Why I heard somebody say that if all them Englishmen and French and Germans in other people's country had to return to England or France or Germany, they wouldn't have enough England or France or Germany even for theyselves, and they would start recolonizing again. Of course the colored peoples of the world would say they wouldn't let them Europeans recolonize them again, but now they's recolonizing each other, them that ain't economically recolonized. So you send for your wife when you feel things is safe?

He nods, then he explains how he don't want any dirty tricks with his wife around, then he's explaining again why he's at Saratoga, to buy him some new bloodstock.

Maybe you should just send for her in spite of the dirty tricks, I say. She German like you? I mean is she the same kind of German as you? Is she a Hottentot German?

Not Hottentot. She's Afro-German, actually African American and German. She's fairer than I am and so is often mistaken for a true German. No one mistakes her for an immigrant. Sometimes they think she's Jewish or Italian. Her maiden name is Wandervogel, her African-American father, a jazz musician, changed his name to a German name when he settled in Berlin after the war, but she's not at all a migratory woman herself. But a man knows how to handle dirty tricks better than a woman.

It depends on what kind of dirty tricks. And what kinda woman.

He says something to me in that German, but I don't know that German, except Deutschland für Deutschländer, so I can't tell you what he say. But what he say sound kinda like the universal language to me.

CHAPTER FOUR

And you, are you married? he asks, stroking my jaw. I half-frown. You
know, thinking that shoulda been his first question, whether I'm married or not. I'm wearing a wedding ring, but there's women who wears
wedding rings that ain't married, just so's they don't have to deal with
every joker. Least if you's a woman from the *Looking for Mr. Goodbar*
generation. There's jokers that don't mind a woman being married, but
at least the woman's got a wedding ring for a excuse. He ain't wearing
no wedding ring hisself, but that's my first question: Are you married?
Course a lot of you's probably thinking that this is the romance of a
roguish woman on account of my being with him and he say he's married. Maybe this is the romance of a roguish woman, or maybe it's just
him talking about protecting her from dangers, but me I'm supposed to
be the other type of woman. She supposed to be the mystical type of
woman and I'm supposed to be the common woman.

We're in the bedroom of his hotel suite, the furniture all gold and
beige. One of them real expensive–type hotel suites, you know the kind
you see in the movies, the kind I ain't seen except in the movies. I seen a
hotel suite like that in one of them movies where the people win the lot-
tery and then they go stay in this real expensive–type hotel. I think that
Nicholas Cage in that movie. He play the role of the good man in that
movie, and there's a good woman, and then there's the female rogue. Me
I think it be more interesting if the woman play the female rogue play the
good woman, and the woman play the good woman play the rogue.
Course I guess them moviemakers got they own stereotypes of good
womanhood. Ain't exactly the Plaza, though, but it's one of them

expensive-type hotels. Gilded mirrors and that gilded-type furniture. Might not be real gold. Might be fool's gold. I don't think even them most expensive hotels got real gold. They's probably all got fool's gold. But that's the America a lot of foreigners see in the movies, and a lot of them think that's the true America. They think that's everybody's America. Or even if they know it ain't everybody's America, they think they come to America and it be their America. Or they read about people like Josef, who maybe the exception that prove the rule.

No, I ain't married now, I say.

Even got a tray with all kindsa fruits on it. Even kiwi and them Caribbean-type fruits. I don't know the names of all them Caribbean-type fruits. I'm eating one of them kiwi. You usedta think of them kiwi as exotic-type fruits, but now a lot of people think of them as ordinary fruits. In the tiny refrigerator there's all kindsa drinks—wines and beers and liquors.

What happened? he asks, lifting up a banana and then one of them Caribbean fruits.

Jealousy. You know.

Yours or his?

I rear my head back and try to whinny, like one of his prime stallions. I wipe kiwi juice from my chin. N'Orleans, he whisper, taking a bite from my kiwi. He eat that kiwi, though, like he still think it a exotic-type fruit. I wonder if he think of American women as exotic, even African women in America? He don't call me Harlan or Harlan Jane. He say N'Orleans like he think N'Orleans more my true name than Harlan or Harlan Jane. He pull my hair back from my forehead and kiss me. I weren't wearing braids then, just straightened hair, though I was using that special cream from Brazil that didn't have all them harsh chemicals in it, and made your hair seem naturally straight. You're a charmer. And say something else in German. Must be saying You're a charmer, again, but saying it in German. I don't know the German word for charmer, though. Then he say the German word for pretty. I know that word 'cause I heard it once in a German movie. *Schönheit.* Or something like that. Or maybe that *Schönheit* stand for Beauty Itself and not just being beautiful. Then he say something to me in French, and that sound like a more universal language than that German. Least that French sound like the universal language of love. Course if you's Algerian during that war, or a Algerian in France after the war, you wouldn't think of that French as a lover's language. I met me one of them Algerians telling me about them French. Some of them languages might sound like a lover's language, but they ain't a lover's language to everybody.

When I stand in front of his mirror, arranging my hair, he say, Stay longer. You're quite beautiful, you know. And then he say that word *Schönheit*, which mean Beauty Itself. I know I ain't so beautiful to be Beauty Itself. But I know how men is. You know, when they's speaking lover's language.

No, I got to go bet on my horses.

Are you ever lucky?

Always.

Why don't you come home with me? My farm's just outside Lexington. I've got some of the finest thoroughbreds in the state. I'd wanted to buy a larger farm, but they didn't want to sell so much prime land to a "foreigner."

What about the dangers?

You seem like you're the kind of woman who can handle it.

Well, I ain't.

I bet you are.

You don't know what kinda woman I am, I start to say, but I just look at him. Men is always like that with me. I ain't met a man that ain't like that with me. A few might tell me I'm beautiful, might even say I'm Beauty Itself, which I know I ain't, others might point out my flaws, but they's all sure they know what kinda woman I am. Now his wife, he ain't sent for her, 'cause of them dirty tricks. Probably one of them type of women he don't even wanna get her panties dirty. But me I'm supposed to be the sort of woman who can handle dangers? Course the neofeminists what that man call the feminazis would say that they don't want the mens to be protective towards them, or the chivalrous type. 'Cause chivalry is prefeministic or some shit. But me I be wondering how come he talking about protecting his wife from them dangers, but me I'm just supposed to be that other kinda woman. And then you be asking with Sojourner, Ain't I a woman too? Least that high ideal of a woman. That's why I've always been kinda ambivalent about that feminism. Them women that don't wanna be on no pedestal or say they don't want to be on no pedestal, 'cause seem like to me a lot of them wants to keep the perks of womanhood, is kinda different from the women that ain't never been on no pedestal. Course Sojourner ain't mean exactly that when she ask, Ain't I a woman too? I just look at him, then I laugh, like one of his stallions again.

Why don't you come with me to the track? I say. I'll pick you a winner.

I think I've already picked a winner.

The elevator doors slide open. In the lobby, a huge African American is sitting in a leather chair, watching us. Now I know he African American, though he the same complexion as Josef, kinda that gingerbread complexion, like they could both be in the Original Adventures of the Gingerbread Man, but he ain't got that air of foreignness about him. When we step out of the elevator, he get up and walk toward us. He the sort of tall man who when he stands up keeps standing until he's a height you'd hardly thought possible. He dressed in dark trousers and a beige shirt, and wearing a tie but no jacket. He as dark-skinned as Josef, like I said, but his eyes and eyebrows slant up kinda like an Asian's, at least the stereotype of them Asians, 'cause the real Asian eyes don't all slant up like that. He ain't Asian, though. He pure African American, if there such a thing as pure African American.

Harlan, I'd like you to meet Nicholas Love, he's coming with us to the racetrack, say Josef. I thought Josef a tallish man, but next to Nicholas, he look like a average-sized man. Course he look more well taken care of than Nicholas Love. But a lot of them Europeans always looks more stylish than Americans.

I say hello.

He nod.

You a German too? I ask, though I know he ain't. And I know the name Nicholas Love sho ain't no German name, 'cause them Germans got they own word for love. Course there could be Germans got English-sounding names, like they's Americans got German-sounding names and every other kind of language–sounding names. The Americans, like he said, might not want to learn other people's languages, but they's got to say other people's languages when they says they own names.

No, he say. And say it like it the only word in the English language he do know.

Don't you recognize a fellow American when you see one? ask Josef.

I smile, 'cause I know all along he a American.

Nicholas walk beside Josef, not me. Neither of them converse. Nicholas seem like he one of them quiet-type men, like I said, one of them taciturn-type men. I don't think he inarticulate, though. I just think he one of them taciturn-type men. Outside, the three of us climb into the back of a chauffeured Lincoln Town Car, Josef in the middle. The chauffeur, he a little Italian-looking man. Somebody you got to speak the Italian language to say they name. Like them Italian movie stars. When you say DeNiro or Pacino or Aiello, you gotta speak Italian to say them names. Kinda remind me of that Danny DeVito movie actor, though, 'cept it ain't Danny DeVito.

She's coming back with us to the farm, say Josef after a while.

Nicholas didn't reply. And I'm wondering who this Nicholas suppose to be. And then I'm wondering if these men thinks they's supposed to form some sort of ménage à trois with me, or some shit, 'cause you read about that ménage à trois shit in them confessional-type stories in them confessional magazines, and I'm about to explain to them that I ain't that sorta girl, that I ain't no freak, and no trollop neither, and that's when Josef explain who Nicholas.

Nicholas is my bodyguard, says Josef.

And I'm thinking that just like in the movies. Here I am thinking about the movies and about my favorite Italian movie stars, when he starts saying what sounds like a movie. I ain't never been in the company of nobody famous or rich enough for no bodyguard. He didn't guard your body this morning, I joke. I meant at the racetrack. And I ain't been trying for one of them blue joke, you know, but it come out sounding like one of them blue joke.

I mean at the racetrack, I explain. I didn't see him at the racetrack.

Yes, he was at the racetrack. He knows how to be invisible.

Now that's a virtue for a bodyguard, but I can't imagine that Nicholas Love who one of the tallest men I ever seen outside of the *National Geographic* or maybe on a basketball court no invisible man, though. I remember when I was in high school we had to read that book about the invisible man. I couldn't even imagine the invisible man himself being the invisible man, though that was the name of the book. I told the teacher that I always felt too visible myself, but someone else, one of them little shy-type girls, said she felt invisible, but it were invisibility because of her shyness not because of the ethos of race. And then after everybody laughed at the word ethos even though most people didn't know its meaning and thought it was a made-up word and thought she meant ethics then people was talking about the virtues and the vices of invisibility, and one of the boys said that the point of the book was the paradox, that the invisible man was supposed to be a paradox, 'cause he's supposed to be visible and invisible at the same time, that he the visible invisible man or the invisible visible man. Then we started talking about whether invisibility was pertinent to modern African Americans, especially in modern America where there wasn't as much overt Jim Crowism, at least there wasn't as much overt Jim Crowism as covert Jim Crowism. Still, I ain't seen him, that Nicholas Love, whether he the visible invisible man or the invisible visible man.

I wanted you to meet him, though, say Josef. So there'd be no surprises.

I glance across Josef at that Nicholas Love, who sit impassive, but it a alert impassivity. And like I said, I don't think he inarticulate, I just think he taciturn. He gotta be taciturn 'cause he don't have the disposition of a shy man. And that probably in his job description, that he supposed to be taciturn.

Will he disappear again? I ask.

When we want him to, says Josef.

Nicholas frown, though it almost imperceptible. At the entrance to the track, we wait for a man crossing the road with a wheelbarrow, then roll into the racetrack parking lot. Nicholas and the chauffeur, who a little man, kinda look like maybe he a former jockey, though he middle-aged now, get out, while Josef extend his hand to help me out. As I step out, my dress climb up to my thighs. A peculiar look from Nicholas, but one I know. I ain't no whore, I ain't no trollop, if that what he thinking. Mens they's always thinking shit like that about a woman, and especially us womens of color. Don't care what woman of color, Asian, African, Native American, African American or one of them islanders, the first thing they think is you's a trollop. Even mens of color thinks that about they own women. And it don't matter what sorta woman you are. I might be a scavenger maybe and a gambler, but I ain't no whore. I ain't no trollop. I just pull my dress down and climb out.

Nicholas comes with us as far as the betting windows. I place a bet and when I turn he ain't there. Finally, I puzzle him out, like a chameleon at the edge of the crowd. It's strange. At his height he should be the most visible person at that racetrack, but that's probably why Josef had hired him, 'cause he's a big man but know how to be invisible when he need to be. Like them detective books say about being able to hide in plain sight. That the first thing them detectives is supposed to learn is how to hide in plain sight. They's the original invisible men. The best bodyguards like the best detectives is probably them that know how to hide in plain sight.

Josef lead me to one of them boxes. I ain't never watched a race from one of them boxes, you know with the wealthy people, them VIPs. I always sat with the anybodies in the stands.

This is really something, I say.

What? ask Josef.

I explain that I ain't never been in one of the boxes with the celebrities and the rich and famous.

You mean you haven't charmed your way in?

I say nothing. I ain't like the way he ask that question, you know, but I ain't say nothing. We watch the post parade of thoroughbreds to the gate.

Who'd you bet on? he ask.

Creole Beauty. Got to bet on my own people.

I look around, looking for my own people. A high-browed man, serving what looks like mint juleps. Must think this is Churchill Downs, Kentucky, not Saratoga, New York.

He don't say who he bet on. After the race, though, I go to collect my winnings. Creole Beauty had ridden unhurried from the beginning, like the man say, while them other horse outran early, then in a flash of speed Creole Beauty edged up and ran hard in a good position near the rail; Creole Beauty! I stuff my winnings in my purse, take out my sunglasses and autograph book, then shove through the crowds to the fence to get the winning jockey's signature. Thanks. Around back, under the trees, you can observe the horses up close. A groom's leading one of them horses around a copper beechwood tree. Which is number six and which is number seven? I can't tell six from seven, a woman complain. One of them wealthy socialite-type women. Then she pencil something onto a folded newspaper, onto the racing form. Look like one of them types who addicted to gambling. One of them prime candidates for Gamblers Anonymous.

Which one did you bet on this time? Josef ask when I come from the window.

Previous Condition. Not to win, just to show.

Josef ain't say who he bet on, 'cause he ain't bet on them horses. He owns thoroughbreds, but he don't usually bet on none of them horses. He just mostly likes to watch them run. And he likes to watch them horses to test his skills at judging good horses. Seem like he'd better test his skills at judging them horses if he bet on one of them horses. And I know people that don't bet on them horses, they bet on the jockey. They don't bet on them horses, they just bet on the jockey. They don't bet on the winning horses, they bet on the winning jockeys. When my horse—runs with a steady speed, but always follows the winners—show, Josef held my waist and laugh.

Do you always win? he ask.

On horses, I answer.

I bet you always win, he say. I bet you bet to win. You should've been with me at the Fasig-Tipton sales. Help me buy a winner.

Oh, yeah, I say. I coulda done you proud.

Guarantee me a Triple Crown?

At least one. At least a contender, I say. I like a winning horse, but I also like them that's good contenders.

Now you know I ain't never been to them Fasig-Tipton sales neither. Ain't even know what the Fasig-Tipton sales was when I first come to Saratoga. Then heard people talking about the Fasig-Tipton sales, where they sell them prime thoroughbreds.

Aged and aging jockeys sit on the leather sofas and oak chairs reading newspapers and racing forms. Upstairs in my hotel room I turn on my tape of Miles' "Bitches Brew" while I pack—a few clothes, my tapes, hiking boots, raincape, one of them poncho-type raincoats, souvenirs of Tropical Park, El Camino Real, Santa Catalina, San Vicente, Mountain Valley, Fountain of Youth, San Rafael, Swift, Florida, Remington, Louisiana, San Felipe, Tampa Bay, Bay Shore, Jim Beam, Rebel, Cherry Hill Mile, Santa Anita, Gotham, Garden City, Blue Grass. Mostly jockeys' autographs and pictures. I ain't been to all of them races myself, but jockeys and friends of jockeys and just other gambling people who met me in Saratoga would send me things for my scrapbook. Then I shower and put on blue jeans and a banana yellow sweatshirt. I struggle downstairs with the heavy bag, riding the boogey, as Michael Jackson sings. In the lobby, I turn in my key, pay the exorbitant bill. It a second-rate hotel, but in August, when the horses run, even them second-rate hotels take advantage. But I got my exorbitant winnings. I head toward the door.

You try your luck at the track? one of them old jockeys ask.

I pushed it.

Are you leaving town?

Yeah. I blow him a kiss. See you next year.

You're on the ball, he say, as I go out the door. He one of the few colored jockeys. African-American jockeys. But if you think of yourself as colored, ain't you colored? And tell me about how in the old days all the colored jockeys they usedta have. They's still got colored jockeys, he say, except nowadays they imports them from Latin America, from places like Colombia and Panama, and they don't call theyselves colored. Now you know they have got as much boogie in 'em as me and you have. But he said he knew a certain colored man from East St. Louis who went around the jockey circuit pretending to be Latino, 'cause he thought that would help him get more work. He's rode in a coupla races, nothing spectacular. He wouldn't tell me the name of the jockey, though.

Josef's car is waiting. The driver puts the bag in the trunk and opens the door for me. Josef, out of his business suit, sits in the back in blue jeans just like me. Except mine is them flea market blue jeans and his is Bill Blass. Nicholas in the front with the driver. But Nicholas look like he more the owner of thoroughbreds than Josef. When I get in, the wheels start rolling.

The bed king-sized and as luxurious as the Mediterranean. Ain't that Alexandria in the Mediterranean? I enter a land of the most ancient of rivers, and then I'm now lying toward the window. The shadow of a guard stand on the railing and beyond rows of black fences where them thoroughbreds graze at night and exercise in the mornings. Beyond that them fabulous black stables, and Kentucky bluegrass everywhere. Grass that was so green, the saying is, that it look blue. But I seen greener grass in Africa and wonder what color they could call grass beyond green and blue. I heard somebody say once that you could tell people that been to Africa and people who ain't. 'Cept all the time I told folks I been to Africa, they don't believe me. They say I don't look like somebody who been to Africa. He ain't got no expensive paintings on his wall, except he got a color printout of what he say is one of them holopoems by a avant-garde artist name Eduardo Kac. I think he a Brazilian, 'cause that name got a Brazilian-type pronunciation.

The shadow of a guard parade near the window. I give a short laugh. I kiss Josef's chin. He tell me that window of his is bulletproof, then he kiss the edges of my hair. I turn back toward the window and watch the moving shadow. Josef kiss the back of my neck.

I ain't never been in the company of anyone who needed bodyguards before and no bulletproof windows, or even thought he needed them. But I been with others, ordinary people, who played games of who do you trust. Perhaps in they own way, everyone does. I even know people who put other people on probation till they prove theyself. People you's got to prove yourself to. Maybe even I'm that sorta person. Why do I keep going to Saratoga? I told Josef that I always won. But I merely win enough to keep me hooked, to keep me in the game.

He kiss the back of my neck again and I wonder what tune I'm stepping to. I remember the first time I come to Saratoga I went to this dance hall, this little restaurant that had itself a dance floor, and some man asked me to dance, and I'm dancing, and he say, What tune you stepping to? 'Cause don't seem like I'm stepping to the music. I always like that modern music, but seem like I can't dance to it. Or when I dance to one modern music, they got them a new modern music. Were they ever playing my tune? When I was married, though, sometimes, sometimes it felt like they playing ours.

I win enough to keep me hooked, I say.

What?

You asked me whether I always win and I said yes. I lied. The truth is, I only win enough to keep me hooked.

I sit with my legs folded yogi-like, you know them yogis. Through his mirror I see myself. I look like one of them bottled genie. I spring up off the bed and stand in the center of the room. I watch the shadow outside the window watching me. That paranoid fool even got the guard watching me, I'm thinking. I ain't mean to call him a paranoid fool, 'cause I'm a paranoid fool myself, and they say a lot of people in the modern day and age is more paranoid, but that guard watching me. Josef too watching me. With that cold-type curiosity. Somebody say that the curiosity of a rational man. Then he hold out his hand and I enter the river again.

Do you want to go horseback riding? he ask when he come out the bathroom. One towel draped about his shoulders and the other worn around his waist and knotted. Remember the Mae West line when she asks Cary Grant, Is that a pistol you're packing or are you glad to see me? He seem still glad to see me. Look like he saluting.

I don't ride.

Come on, I'll teach you. I'll start you with the gentlest mare.

I reach onto the night table and turn on my tape player. I still used a tape player, not a CD. Rod Stewart sing about hearts on fire. Do you think I'm sexy? I sing along with Rod.

Is that how you make your living? Josef ask matter-of-fact.

What, sex? I ask. My feathers ruffle up like a pouter bird's. I look at him sideways.

No, he explain. The horses. Gambling?

Naw, I'm a business manager.

What kind of business? he ask. Maybe now he think I'm a madam?

I manage a rock star. Joan Savage. Her name usedta be Joan Sage, then Joan Savage. You know, one of them rock stars keeps changing her name. Her real name's Joan Scribner, or some shit like that, but she say that don't sound like a rock star. Her ex-husband is name Savage, so she uses the name Savage. He ain't in show business hisself, though. Don't believe in show business. Have you heard of her? Joan Savage, I mean? She says a lot of people think she's named after Joan Crawford, 'cause she kinda reminds people of the early Joan Crawford, her type of features, except she's African American of course. But she's kinda that type, you know. Maybe she's named after Joan Crawford and don't know it. I know she likes to watch them early Joan Crawford movies, says she's one of her favorite movie stars. Says she usedta be her ideal of the female persona when she was a little girl, says she even usedta pretend to be her when she was playacting. That's what she says in her promotional literature. I think it's all hype myself, though. I'm her business manager and even I think it's all hype. She sings rock mostly. Sorta like Tina Turner, except she ain't even a legend in her own mind. Sometimes she tries to sing that new music, that rap, you know, but she's mostly rock. She ain't really a rap singer, thinks the younger women are better at singing rap, though sometimes she mixes a little rap with her rock. But she mostly likes that classical-type rock.

He say he ain't heard of her. I slip out the Stewart tape and put on Joan singing "Kiss Me Till It's Good." Or some shit like that. She'll grow on you, I say. Some of her tunes are more witty, more obscure, then she's got more commercial-sounding tunes. They liked her in Europe when we toured there. Especially in Paris. And in Japan. Joan's good, you know. She don't think she's as good as she is, though, 'cause she ain't one of the top moneymakers, you know, and that's how she judges good, or that's how she thinks other people judge good, but she's really good. Sort of a singer's singer, you know. Like an artist's artist. To tell the truth, she's better known abroad than in the States.

I turn up Joan, let her do her brand of magic. Listening to "Lola," one of her new songs, free verse lyrics, kinda combining rock and rap. I don't know if Joan the first singer to use free verse lyrics. Listening to "Lola." Lola some new singer she heard on a talent show and wants to encourage by writing a song for her. He don't think she's that good himself. I mean Josef. But then he says he's never been that much for popular American music. He doesn't like pop music. He prefers Wagner, Beethoven, Mozart, the classical-type music, mostly the Germans, some of the French composers, some of the Russians, some of the more classical-sounding jazz, not the decadent raunchy-sounding jazz. He's heard the work of a few African-American classical composers that he likes, who remind him something of the Germans, but who sometimes mix jazz with classical. And he says he heard some Native American music that he likes, that he heard on the radio, and that sounds sorta like New Wave classical music, or rather New Wave classical music sounds something like it. He says he likes that. He says if he were a music promoter, he'd promote that kind of music. "But they don't allow some of it off the reservations, though. They don't want it to be heard by anyone but themselves. What I've heard of it, though, it sounds like superior music. I don't know if it can compete commercially, but it sounds like superior music. Some of it's traditional Native American music, but you also have Native American composers writing new music based on the traditional tunes." We listen to Joan sing "Rebel Years," then a song she discovered in Port-au-Prince when we were roaming about the Iron Market.

We tour most of the year and then she goes off to her farm in Minnesota, and I go up to Saratoga and bet on my horses. I did spend one of my vacations at her farm, but it turned out to be a bitch, you know. . . . In fact, when Joan made this rap-rock-type album, Joan was calling herself Joan "the Bitch" Savage, but we decided that that wasn't really the idea of herself that she wanted to promote.

I dig into a bowl of pomegranates on the night table, lean back on the pillow and listen to more Joan. The lampshades looks like they's stain-glassed windows. At one moment her voice is a porcupine, then it's butter.

I don't like modern music, he says. I don't like American music, and most modern music is American music. I like some of the African-American classical composers, some of the African-American avant-garde. You have a few British composers who are looking back to the pre-American pop influences of their own medieval ballads and folk songs. . . .

They like her in London too. The Londoners are really a wild bunch, not like I used to imagine them as being, you know. Well, I guess now with all them tabloid tales of the royalty you got a different idea of them British. Joan was reading this article about where they used to always depict the British in books and movies as kind of the moral center, you know, something like that, but now they just depict them as fools like everybody else. Or villains, or just ordinary boggers, you know. I usedta think all Europeans were pompous types, but they ain't. Joan made her first record in London, and there's folks who thinks she's British. She's big in Japan, as the song goes. She's got a sort of cult following here in the States. You know, them that don't judge their music whether or not it's on the pop charts. She ain't well known here at all, like I said, 'cause she don't make the pop charts, you know. And that's what American music is all about, whether or not you make the pop charts. Of course you can be on the pop charts and not be making any royalties. You can be heard on the radio and still be poor as shit. Lotta people think 'cause you're on the pop charts or they hear you on the radio or that you have a record deal, that you've signed a contract for a record deal, and even made a record, that means you got money. I usedta think that myself till I met Joan. You can be heard on the radio, but that don't mean you's making royalties. But a lot of them they're still paying back their record company. And people thinks they're millionaires. Or they'll see them singing on TV and think they're millionaires. Joan said when she made

her first record, and lot of people thought she was a millionaire, 'cause
those the only people they knows about that makes records, you know.
They hear about Michael Jackson's millions or some of them others and
they think anybody makes a record must got millions. Joan's real sensitive about that. You know a lot of them starlettes they wants you to
think that they's got millions when they ain't. Course a lot of their logic
is that if people think they got millions, it attracts millions. They might
be on unemployment or some shit. I usedta think that myself, about
them millions, till I started managing Joan. This little record company
in London, one of them little independent labels, you know, is the one
that recorded her first album. Joan says you don't make it till you make
it in your own country, though. That's her logic. Then she's the sort that
sabotages herself, or lets other people sabotage her. She's got more good
gigs since I've been her manager, though, than when she called herself
managing herself. Now she's got a few more recording contracts, a little
more lucrative, and she don't just sign for any record deal the record
company wants to give her. I got her out of one of her early contracts.
But the fool is still trying to make it in her own country, though. I don't
agree, about you got to make it in your own country, I mean, but we
never agree. She says that every entertainer wants to make it in America,
so why shouldn't she? I get her booked in a nice club in Paris, where they
like her music, or I get her on a London television show, and the fool's
asking me how come it ain't New York? Course if Joan was making it in
New York, she'd probably get herself a new manager. That's when they
get themselves new managers. Joan says she ain't like that. But most
people don't know what they're like.

I sit on the edge of the bed, shuffle a pack of Turkish cigarettes, take
one out and light up. My back hunched like a cat's, I swivel to stare at
him, one knee up on the bed. I look at them lampshades. Tiffany glass?

Should I pack up and go? I ask.

What do you mean?

Since I ain't what you thought I am.

You don't know what I think you are, he says. Then he say again how
he don't like American music, but he likes American women. He thinks
American women are racier than European women. Then he ask me if

I knew what he meant by racy. I say yes. I ain't say that I ain't never thought of myself as racy. That I ain't never had the word racy applied to myself. Or maybe I am racy. Maybe I've grown into racy without noticing it. Maybe since I've been managing Joan I've grown into racy without noticing it. I puff my cigarette, watch the rolling smoke, tilt my head back and listen to Joan. Sometimes when I listen to her I don't know what she is either. Her music don't explain her altogether, but I feel that it's good. I wouldn't manage her if I didn't think her good. She must be good. She ain't at the top of the charts, but at least she got the music. And me when I ain't managing her, all I do is gamble. Racing in Saratoga, blackjack in Vegas. I don't gamble a lot, 'cause I ain't got a lot to gamble.

But when she played Vegas that other time, I didn't go near the tables. I sat in the hotel room with a former showgirl, an old woman who used to be a showgirl, a dancer in a chorus line. She said, I stopped dancing before they made me stop. I stopped dancing before they made me. When I started feeling like a fool I stopped, before I started to look like one. Her earlobes were stretched from wearing gold and brass earrings, kinda like them African women that wear them heavy earrings. The skin on her hands looked like a newborn baby's.

We watched the soaps, then a news story about these townspeople collecting all their rock 'n' roll albums and destroying them. I thought of that time in Africa, them Sonjo tribesmen. That Sonjo tribesman who used to test people for crimes. They'd form a circle around this one man, all them accused, and then he'd gyrate in the circle, and he'd pick out the one who'd committed the crime because he smelled wrong. Because when one is guilty one has the smell of guilt, the crime solver explained. It sounds silly, but maybe the body would emit odors. Sweat and nerves. Maybe no different from the lie detector principle, except the technology.

There was one woman, though, who gathered everything that her neighbors might destroy and hid it. She said she didn't like some of them albums herself, but she wasn't going to destroy them. Her neighbors in the background taunted her while she hugged a tattered album to her. For all I know, it mighta been a Joan Savage album. She hugged it to her, stared into the camera, and dared the world. "I don't like this album my-self," she said, "and it ain't one that I would buy, but I ain't going to de-stroy it."

Josef, getting dressed, puts on olive green corduroy trousers and a light blue shirt. I'm thinking of how sometimes it takes someone else, a stranger, to point out what you've become.

Should I get up too? I ask.

If you want me to teach you to ride.

I get up, pull on my panties and jeans. Put on my bra and sweatshirt. What's that attached to your phone? I ask, pausing in front of it. One of them answering devices? I peer close. Why does it say Silent Conversation?

Actually, it's a telephone scrambler. It scrambles conversations. So the wrong ears won't hear. I always like to know about the new technology. That's a rather primitive device, though. They have even smaller scramblers now.

Paranoid bastard, I'm thinking, but, That's fantastic, I say. That's really fantastic. I love stuff like this. Technological stuff. I love the new technology myself. I've always liked stuff like that. But what's really spooking you? I push my sweatshirt down into my waistband and stand waiting for his explanation. What's really spooking you? What wrong ears?

He stands with his back to me, facing the window. I've seen only his guards, but none of the dangers he's been talking about. Maybe he's just a paranoid bastard, some rich lunatic from Germany. Maybe not even from Germany. Maybe he's from Germany, Kentucky. There's a Ger-many, Kentucky, you know. He keeps his back to me.

I put on the tape player again, softly. This is my scrambler, I say. It don't scramble conversation, though. Scrambles thoughts.

What sort of thoughts? he ask, turning. He scratches his jaw.

What sort of conversations? I ask.

Outside, the stable boy leads out his stallion and my mare.

So is this the monster mare? I ask. So what do I do first?

First you get on, he replies.

CHAPTER FIVE

I peek over his shoulder to see Joan standing in the doorway. She has a handful of yellow hair sticking up, looking like Don King's. She's wearing faded green gaucho trousers and a bright purple tank top and a purple bandanna, worn like the cowgirls wear. Chewing a pear, she watches us with an air of nonchalance and tepid curiosity like you'd watch reruns on an old TV. Make me wonder whether she's watched him with other women. She'd told me about his other infatuations, but said she didn't know any of his other women. She ain't exactly looking at me like she think I'm one of his new infatuations, though. She looking at me like one of us is a fool. Then she chew a little more of that pear. Which one of us is the fool? I whisper, There's Joan, at the same time that she close the door and he come.

What? he ask, rising up. Say what?

Joan was standing in the doorway watching us. Your ex-wife was watching us.

I don't know why I call her his ex-wife, 'cause he know that. Unless I'm telling myself she his ex-wife. Reminding myself that she his ex-wife and he her ex-husband. And thinking about that movie about that ex-husband and ex-wife, and him saying something about that being the first time he felt like a ex-husband when he heard about her being with some other man. I didn't feel like an ex-husband until now, said the man in the movie.

He look freak, like she ain't his ex-wife caught him with another woman, turn, look like he doing one of them yoga postures, look just like one of them yogi, you know one of them posture them yogi do, then dig his elbow into my shoulder. Not now. Before. I'm telling you about them old days, when I first started being Joan's business manager. Joan, the rock star. You know, like them flashback scenes. Lotta readers say they don't understand them flashback scenes. You got to always explain them flashback scenes. They just understand that chronological order. Seem like to me anybody seen a modern movie, even them old-time modern movies would understand a flashback scene. Or if you listen to jazz, seem like you'd understand them flashback scene. In them modern movies, though, they even got them parallel scenes, and seem like anybody can understand a movie can understand the flashback scene, and not just them modern movies. In them early movies they got them parallel and flashback scenes. Even them comic movies.

Anyway, he get up, dress hurriedly, and go downstairs. Seem like I hear him say Joan Darling. Just like he her now husband. Or maybe it just my imagination hear him say Joan Darling, like it her true name. I'm still laying in the bed, looking like a fool and rubbing my shoulder, then I get up and get dressed. Unhurriedly. When I go downstairs, Joan in the living room, sitting with her long legs thrown over the arm of the sofa and still looking nonchalant. Still got her hair sticking up looking like Don King's. Or looking like a character in one of them comic movies. You know that Laurel of the comedy team. And she even scratch the top of her head, looking like that Laurel of the comedy team. Except James play the Hardy to her Laurel. She looking at me, though, like I'm one of the Stooges. I look around for James, but he musta gone outside. Or maybe she told him to leave, I don't know. Maybe he'd made promises to her to be with other women only when she was on her tours. And ain't just with any other woman, but her own manager. Still that sounds more like a now husband than a ex-husband. Then she finish her pear and toss it into a ashtray. Then she scratch the top of her head, looking like that Laurel again. Then she open up one of them paperback novels she likes to read and pretend like she reading it. A Amanda Wordlaw novel. *Don't Let Cowgirls Fool Ya*. Not one of them Great Novels. She likes reading them Great Novels, 'specially the Russians, but she also

likes them popular novels, and for nonfiction she reads both the popular
nonfiction and them obscure, intellectual-type nonfiction. Maybe she
signifying. *Don't Let Cowgirls Fool Ya*. That novel supposed to be
about a colored cowgirl. 'Cept she say that novel ain't true popular fiction, it just satirizes the popular fiction. She say it uses the techniques of
the popular novel to satirize the popular novel, but she also say this
Amanda Wordlaw thinks that African-American writers oughta be able
to write "the popular novel" and not just the Great African-American
Novels. You know, like some book reviewers think that African-
American writers are only supposed to write the Great African-
American Novel. So this Amanda Wordlaw thinks why shouldn't they
write a whole range of different types of novels, from trash novels and
popular fiction to the Great African-American Novel. But this Amanda
Wordlaw supposed to even satirize the Great African-American Novel.
I think that Amanda Wordlaw a confabulatory woman myself, though,
'cause I ain't never heard of her. She must be a confabulatory woman or
maybe that a pseudonym for one of them other literary womens, but one
who want to maintain her anonymity. Maybe she write the Great
African-American Woman's Novel under her true name, but them trash
and popular novels under the name of Amanda Wordlaw. When I come
in, she look up from that novel, still looking nonchalant. Then she look
kinda sullen, then she look curious. That same curious I told you Josef
look. But that before I met Josef. 'Cept I don't really think of that Joan
as a rational woman, though. I look at her, then my eyes take a running
turn about the living room, looking for James again, then I look at her
again. She pretends like she reading that paperback novel again. On her
coffee table are some other books: *The Dictionary of Clichés*, *World
Treasury of Love Stories*, *Alchemy: The Medievalist's Royal Art*, *The
Women Savantes*, *Modern African-American Sculpture*, a biography of
Jim Thorpe, and a novel by Ishmael Reed. Now I know that Ishmael
Reed ain't a confabulatory author 'cause I've read some of his books myself. She always include them Ishmael Reed novels on her shelves with
the Great Novels, though in the bookstores where we buy her paperback
books, when she's got a gig in different part of the world, they ain't on

the shelves with the Great Novels. And them mail-order bookstores where she order some of her books, they don't list them with the Great Novels, neither, though we seen *The Autobiography of an Ex-Coloured Man* listed with the Classic American Novels. Joan think they would list *Invisible Man*, but they list *The Autobiography of an Ex-Coloured Man*. Joan say that's on account of them Ishmael Reed novels don't use the techniques of the traditional Western novel, she say that because they use the techniques of they own tradition, but when I ask her what they own tradition, she just look at me like I'm a fool. *Hermione?* Ain't that the name of one of them novels. Seem like one of them novels got the name Hermione in it?

I guess this means you're going to fire me, I say. I don't know why I ask that. Make her think that's all I'm thinking about, whether she fire me or not. I know when I'm negotiating one of her contracts, she tells me I'm crude haggling about the dollar bills. "Maybe I just want to make the record," she'll say. "Maybe I don't care how much they'll pay me up front. I'll just have to pay 'em back anyway. The important thing is getting the record made." And then I tell her about the history of them record companies screwing them Negro entertainers, and not giving them all they royalties and them recording companies making all the money on they recordings, you know, them race recordings before Motown, when they usedta call Negro music Race Music, and she still tell me I'm crude haggling about the dollar bills, and using that history of them record companies screwing them Negro entertainers as a excuse to be crude. Or maybe she thinking I should apologize for letting her catch me with her ex?

Why should I? she's saying. It ain't like we're still married or nothing, Jamey and I. She look at me, trying to look nonchalant again, or disinterested like that wealthy woman I seen at the racetrack, but it look like lightning sleeping in her eyes. She put the paperback novel on the coffee table on top of *The Dictionary of Clichés*. I start to say something, but can't find a way to say it, though I could mention the fact that it her exhusband she just caught me with, and that ain't the same as sneaking around with somebody now husband, even if he still do call her Joan Darling like it her true name.

I . . .

Darling, I don't care who you screw, or who he screws either, as long as it ain't me. James can screw you all he wants, or any other of his little infatuations, or get him a harem of girlies as long as it ain't me. He knows not to screw me. He knows better than to screw me. Jamey and his little group of serious thinkers. I shouldn't say that. When we were in grad school I usedta be one of his little group of serious thinkers. Or at least I thought so. He knows better than to screw me, though.

I know she ain't just meaning screw screw. I don't know the tale of they divorce, and I ain't ask the full tale. And don't know who precipitated the divorce, and don't ask. I sit down on the opposite arm of the sofa. She continue with her back to me for a while, then she turn to face me. My eyes take the same running turn about the living room, looking for James again, then I meet her look.

Of course I'm going to keep you on, darling, she say. You're my manager. You're the best. You're the best manager I've had. Trying to manage myself is a bitch, bitch. I like that. Trying to manage myself is a bitch, bitch. Then she narrow her eyes; the lightning in them ain't sleeping. You just ain't welcome to come here no more, that's all. You can manage me, but you ain't welcome here.

Then that lightning sleeping again. She ain't curious or even nonchalant. She stare away from me. No expression I can name. Then she thumbing through that book, *Don't Let Cowgirls Fool Ya*. Ain't she said something about that Amanda Wordlaw? Seem like once when she reading one of them confabulatory novels, she say, She my alter ego. I think she my alter ego. I think she my other self. I don't know why she say that, though. Seem like you wouldn't want a author of trashy novels to be your other self. Seem like she would pick one of them Great Novelists to be her other self.

What about him? I ask.

She shrug. The lightning still sleeping, but she wave her hands in the air. Then she looking at me like I'm one of her Stooges again. Don't be stupid, she say. And then she wave her hand in the air again like she brushing away my stupidity. And then she scratch the top of her head like Laurel. I guess she mean to say how can she tell him he ain't welcome. But that's what they always talking about on them talk shows. How when them women catch they man with the other woman them women go after the other woman and treat the man like he innocent. Not that he her now husband. But I guess they's even them like that about they ex-husband. Some women is probably possessive like that about even they ex-husband. Seem like on some of them talk shows, they's even women possessive about they own ex-husband, that stalks they ex-husbands and they ex-husbands other women, and more possessive about they ex-husband than when he their now husband. And then I'm imagining Joan on one of them talk shows:

So I went upstairs and opened the door and there they was screwing each other, my husband and my business manager, Harlan Jane Eagleton. I don't know if I can say screw on TV. Can I say screw on TV?

Yeah, sure. I don't think you can say Jane on TV, though. I'm just kidding ya. Four-letter word, you know, Jane. But you say he's your ex-husband he ain't your now husband, says the talk show host.

Yes, he's my ex-husband. He always felt like my ex-husband until I caught him with her, I mean I've known about him with his other little infatuations, but then I caught him with her and suddenly he felt like my now husband. You know, I always thought of him as my ex-husband, 'cause he is my ex-husband, you know, but when I caught him with her, I felt like he's my now husband.

Girl, you know you a fool, don't you? says the talk show host. The women that write to me, millions of women from all over the world that watch this show, always tell me the same thing, that my talk show helps them to realize that they ain't the only fool. They might be the fool that they know themselves to be, but at least they realize they ain't the only fool. Girl, you know you a fool, don't you, Hermione?

My name ain't Hermione, it's Jane, I mean Joan.

I thought you told me your name Hermione?

Naw, it's Joan.

It says here that your middle name is Hermione.

Naw, it's Joan. And what about the other girl? she ask. I ain't the only fool.

That's what I said, but girl, you ain't got to worry about the other girl being no fool, you just got to worry about you yourself being a fool. The other girl might be a fool too, even the very archetype of a fool, maybe even a fool's fool, maybe even a photogenic fool that I'll have my production assistant invite to be on the show, maybe Business Managers Who—Can I Say That on TV?—Their Client's Ex-Husbands but it's your own foolery that you got to recognize and ameliorate. If there's one purpose to my talk show, though personally I believe my talk show is a multidimensional talk show and not just one-dimensional–pop psychology–tabloid journalism like some of them other talk shows, but if there's one definable purpose to my talk show, it's for you fools to recognize you's fools and to stop being fools. Especially the female fool. Especially y'all Hermiones. And I'm talking about the female fools of every race and creed, Hermiones of every race and creed, not just the colored female fools, not just the colored Hermiones. Geraldo or Montel gotta deal with male fools. All the Hermans, Geraldo or Montel gotta deal with them fools.

How come you call them Hermans and us ain't Hiswoman's? ask Joan.

'Cause Hiswoman ain't nobody's true name, and Hermione is.

Anyway I come to Saratoga to bet on some horses. I went upstairs, packed my bags, and went to Saratoga. Then when I was staying in one of them little hotels in Saratoga, one of them little hotels with a Dutch name, I telephoned Joan from my hotel room.

Joan?

Yeah, what? What's it?

This is Harlan.

I know who you are. What is it?

About New York?

Yeah, so what? What about New York?

Do you still want me there?

I reminded her that she supposed to go into the recording studio in a month, then on tour. We're supposed to go on tour.

So, what's changed? she ask, and hang up.

As for now, mostly, we get along, except sometimes I'll catch that look of sleeping lightning, or maybe that lightning ain't sleeping. Maybe it just playing possum. Are you sure you want me to hang around? I'll say. You're the best, she'll say and grin, you know, the joker's grin that don't reveal nothing, or maybe just the entertainer's grin, the one that masks it all. Anyway, she keeps me on as her manager, and I ain't been to that farm of hers, and I ain't seen that James of hers. Tell me he's her ex-husband, and then acting like he's her now husband.

Like once after one of her gigs, I reach onto her dressing table and take out one of her cigarettes. I lit a match and then the cigarette. She don't smoke, but keeps them cigarettes in the dressing room for different folks. Joan's putting on mascara and peering at me out of raccoon's eyes.

Girl, you're a bold bitch, she say.

I say nothing. I ain't sure if she say bold or not, but I don't want her to repeat it. I don't know a woman like to be called a bitch, less they call theyself one. I've heard women brag on theyself as a bitch. Like when Joan were calling herself Joan "the Bitch" Savage. But me I ain't think that the right idea even for her to have of herself. Enough men to call women bitches than them start calling theyselves bitch. 'Cept Joan say the difference between the men and the women is that the women know how to call each other bitch without exactly say the word bitch. Like she could say, Girl, you bold, and still be calling me a bitch.

What would you have done if he was still mine? she ask, putting the mascara down. Then her hands fly into the pockets of her robe like they's nests. What'd you have done then?

I woulda sure stayed clear of him, I answer. I don't fool with other people's husband. Them that I know is married. I've fooled with husbands that I didn't know was husbands. I ain't a husband diviner like some women are. Course the age I am now ain't too many that's free. And them that say they's free ain't free. But you're the one told me he was your ex-husband and that. . . .

One of her hands fly out its nest pocket and fly backwards. She scratch her cheek and then put on her little orange cap. To tell the truth when she wear that little orange cap, she kinda remind me of one of them organ grinder's monkey. She a attractive woman, but in that little orange cap, she still remind me of a organ grinder's monkey. Especially when she got her hair straightened. When she wearing it natural, she don't remind me of no organ grinder's monkey. That little orange cap, you know, it's one of them deerhunter's cap, though, but she always wears it turned backward. It for her antihunting song. She wears the bib backwards, so you don't see the bib—I mean bill—and from the front it round and remind me of one of the organ grinder's monkey and his little round cap. But she's watching me. Like she the hunter. And I'm the deer.

CHAPTER SIX

There's one of your people looking out for us, I say as we ride along the fence. A man on a roan stallion hang back, away from us. It ain't Nicholas, but one of the other guards. I don't know how many security people he got besides Nicholas. I know Nicholas his chief security person, but he got men he claims is former policemen and former soldiers and former members of different countries' CIA, or different countries' equivalent of the CIA. I know one of them security people is Vietnamese, said he usedta fight in the tunnels of Cu Chi, or maybe that his own way of bragging about hisself, but I don't know the nationality of them others. And I don't know if he's truly employed former members of different countries' CIA or not, or if he just saying all that to be bragging. And one of them men look kinda like a Gypsy that Joan and I seen when she was singing in a nightclub over there in Paris. I think he a Gypsy but Joan say he a Turk. Or maybe he a Turkish Gypsy. We pause under a oak tree. The guard, a muscular, dark-haired man with disheveled eyebrows, pause under another oak. Some of his other guards are sitting on the veranda eating lunch. Brown bag lunches, lunchboxes, thermoses, like ordinary workingmen. They's all rugged-looking men, some with that rugged intelligence that you might associate with different countries' CIA, others look just like ordinary men, but maybe they know all that kung fu and karate, that martial arts, and don't need to but look like ordinary men.

Are you a spy? Josef ask.

I pull back on the reins of my horse. Horse want to lead herself.

Spy? What do you mean spy? Maybe he ask that 'cause he notice me spying on his security men. You know, maybe he just jealous seeing me spying at his security men and especially that Turkish-looking Gypsy or that Gypsy-looking Turk, and thinking maybe I'm more interested in his security men than in him, so he just ask me whether I'm a spy. I think he's joking, you know. Naw, I ain't no spy, I says. Then I realize he ain't joking about me being no spy, and it ain't even jealousy at me spying at his security men, and to tell the truth that Turkish-looking Gypsy or Gypsy-looking Turk also kinda look like that Steven Seagal, ain't it Steven Seagal the one supposed to study them martial arts in Japan? that spiritual kung fu—but who am I a spy for?—and I'm about to call him some paranoid fool. If he's got men that's truly former members of some countries' CIA maybe they's the true spy. Maybe one of them's spying on him for his government or us government or the Thoroughbred Breeders Association or maybe that arbitrage if he the sorta man to be spied on. But if he just a paranoid fool, then a lot of people is paranoid fools, 'cause them pop psychologists and even them ordinary psychologists say a lot of modern people is paranoid.

I steady them reins again. Horse still want to lead herself. I try to make that sound the jockeys make, but just sound like I'm clucking.

I think you're a spy, he says. And then he says something about how we met, as if I was deliberately watching to encounter him when he was standing up there watching them walk and exercise the horses. And that maybe some of them people wanting to play dirty tricks on him mighta hired me. They didn't want him acquiring the best Thoroughbreds in the state. They had a consortium to outbid him locally and then when they seen he was going out-of-state to acquire some Thoroughbred they sent me up there to spy on him. Especially since I'm telling him I'm from Kentucky just like himself, or rather that's the same state that he's immigrated to. Don't that sound like a paranoid fool? If I was a spy I wouldn't be telling him I'm from Kentucky just like himself. I'd be from Kansas City or someplace like that, or maybe even from New York. And seem like if they consortium could outbid him in the state, they just send they consortium up to the Fasig-Tipton to outbid him. I don't think that Fasig-Tipton got laws against consortiums of Thoroughbred owners bidding for they horses. Seem like them Fasig-Tipton people just wants to sell they horses to the highest bidder. Course ain't many splivs bidding on them horses unless they's sports stars or entertainment personalities. Seem like somebody say though that there's a wealthy colored woman that's in the Thoroughbred business who ain't no sports star or entertainment personality and that she bids on horses at that Fasig-Tipton. Maybe I seen her at the Saratoga racetrack but just thought her a ordinary woman.

Naw, I ain't a spy. 'Cept a spy in the house of love, I say, remembering one of those song titles. Or it a book title? I think I seen Joan with a book with that title. Seem like on her shelves in the midst of either the Great Books or the popular novels, she got a little paperback book called *Spy in the House of Love*. Ain't that Anaïs Nin? Seem like that Anaïs Nin got a book called *Spy in the House of Love*. Seem like that one of them Anaïs Nin books. I think she mighta even published that book her ownself, 'cause seem like Joan say a lot of them books she collect the authors have to publish they ownself, you know. But it's also a song title. I am a spy in the house of love. Something about a spy in the house of love. I look at him. I'm about to call him some paranoid fool, again, but he reach over and touch my jaw, his horse trotting sideways. Mine nibble grass.

What are you? he ask. Who are you?

A spy in the house of love.

Who are you?

I'm just Harlan. Harlan Jane Eagleton. I manage a rock star. Joan Savage. Joan "the Bitch" Savage. I think her middle name is Hermione. She ain't told me that her middle name. Or maybe that her maiden name, but I think that her middle name. I know there's a Hermione in her favorite book—that's *Steppenwolf*. Her husband name Savage, so she use that for her stage name. Sorta like Tina Turner, you know, except she ain't no Tina Turner and her husband ain't Ike, I mean her husband ain't in show business, you know. He some kinda scientist. But Joan a rock star. Well, she ain't exactly a star. And ain't exactly a bitch. She just likes to call herself a bitch, you know. She likes being a woman, you know, but she doesn't like women being judged by different standards than men are judged, you know. I think she means even colored women, but you know when she talks womanhood, she just says womanhood, you know. Like we were watching this politician who was talking about this female politician and so he says, And she's a attractive young woman. And you know, like that was a compliment. And Joan says, Now what's that gotta do with anything, but like this male politician that's like his highest compliment for her, you know, not that she's a good politician but that she's a attractive young woman. Joan's a attractive woman herself. And I'm a charmer. You said so yourself. Why don't you hire yourself a detective and find out who I really am if you're so paranoid about everybody? They's even got electronic detectives now, that just works using computers. All them guards and shit. You don't need all them guards. Well, I guess you gotta have your security people. I guess you ain't no different from the rich and famous they have on TV. They're always talking about the different security people they have. Every one of them stars and starlets has got they security people. Even the rich but not so famous got they own security people, and the famous but not so rich that can afford they own security people got 'em. It's probably better to be rich and not so famous than famous and not so rich, 'cause if you famous and not so rich people think you's rich when you ain't, 'cause they don't know it's possible to be famous and ain't be rich, 'cause they think if you's famous you gotta be rich. I just ain't never been around nobody that needed themselves so many security people, though. I mean, I manage Joan but she's nobody. I mean she ain't nobody, but she ain't a diva or nothing. She's neither rich nor famous. I mean, she's famous amongst the people that know her, but she ain't famous famous. Course with me managing her career she's a little more famous than when I met her, and a little richer, but not rich rich. She tells me I'm preoccupied with wealth and fame. That's her idea of me, you know. You know how someone can have a idea of you and even convince you that that's the true you. She say she don't judge good management by how rich and famous I make her, though that don't make no kinda sense, do it? I mean, how else do you judge good management? Do you think I'd be a good manager if as soon as I started managing her she become less rich and less famous? Not that she's truly rich or famous. She don't even have herself a entourage. All the rock stars got entourages, and even the wannabes. I ask her who she know that we can hire for cheap to sorta be her entourage, you know, but she say she don't want no entourage, or tell me I'm enough entourage.

Josef eyes as black as pepper. My horse try to lead herself but I pull back on the reins. I try to steady her. I ain't no experienced rider, y'all know. Josef reach out and steady her, and make that clicking sound.

Naw, I ain't no spy, I say. Then I imagine lighting up a cigarette and blowing rings of smoke in the air above him. My horse leads herself. I start to ask Josef more about them dangers he talking about, and why he thinks I might be a spy. And maybe he mean some other German word that mean the same thing as spy, but ain't exactly mean spy. Maybe there's a German word that mean the same as spy but ain't spy. Since I've been at his farm, though, I ain't seen any of them dangers, or heard any of the locals threatening him. Or maybe that was before he got all the security people, and now all the locals have heard the rumors about him having former policemen and former soldiers and former CIA-type people working for him. Or maybe they think he's some kinda gangster, just camouflaging hisself as a Thoroughbred owner. I've seen all these guards but I ain't seen what they's guarding him from. Unless it's hisself. A lot of them paranoid fools the guards they need is to guard them from theyselves, and to guard other people from them, more than to guard them from other people. When I ask him to tell me some more about that Germany, he starts talking about Prague, which I know ain't Germany. I know that Prague ain't in Germany. He's from Berlin, he says, but he say that Prague have always been his favorite European city. Most Germans prefer Paris, that's why Paris was one of the few European cities the Germans didn't destroy during the war, even when they occupied Paris they didn't destroy Paris, but he prefers Prague. Maybe my imagination as good as a tale he could tell me, though, about that Germany and what made him to be a paranoid. I'm thinking about some scene in Germany where some of them neo-Nazis mistook him for one of them immigrants of color, maybe a African or a North African, and he running from them neo-Nazis, and maybe that when his paranoia began, where he got his first security guards.

He ain't tell me about when he first got mistook for a immigrant in his own country, and I ain't ask, but years later when I dream about it we're riding them horses again and I ask, Tell me about when them neo-Nazis mistook you for one of them immigrants of color. Did they look anything like those guys in the movie *The Wanderers*? Did you ever see that movie *The Wanderers*? Joan say the same guy wrote the screenplay for *Sea of Love*, you know with Al Pacino, wrote that movie that *The Wanderers* based on, I mean wrote that book that the movie *The Wanderers* based on, that's Joan's hobby reading works of literature, you know, 'cept they seemed kinda innocents compared to the neo-Nazis they talk about on television.

That's when I hired Nicholas. He was there. He rescued me. It was in Berlin. . . .

You first met Nicholas in Berlin?

In my dream he start talking kinda like me.

Berlin, yes, Berlin. He was roaming about Europe a musician I think a musician, you know, he couldn't get any "gigs," as you call them, in America I think a musician I know he plays the French horn so he comes to Europe to Berlin and I, well I suppose I was roaming about my own country, I'm in arbitrage, you know, deciding whether I should leave Berlin, on account of all this Deutschland für Deutschlanders, you know, perhaps go to Africa or Prague, perhaps come to America. . . . Nicholas thought it was a fellow African American he was saving, you know. . . . And I thought he was a fellow African German saving me. . . . There's something about him that makes him seem more like my culture than his own, though I've never thought that I've anything like your culture, though people say my way of speaking English has something of your accent, your easy colloquialisms, and something of the German. . . . Then I hired him. It's not like he's a hireling, though. I still allow him to be his own man. I mean, he's still his own man. I mean, he works for me but he's still his own man.

CHAPTER SEVEN

Joan grabs my arm as I enter the recording studio. I wink at the guitar player who's leaning against the wall. Name's Jimmy Cuervo. I first heard him play in a cantina in South Texas and introduced him to Joan. They even started talking Spanish to each other and I heard her call him Caballero. His name ain't Jimmy Caballero, though, it's Jimmy Cuervo. Or maybe Cuervo the way them Mexicans pronounce Caballero, 'cause them Mexicans ain't supposed to pronounce Spanish the same way them Spaniards from Spain pronounces Spanish. Theirs is American Spanish. And them Mexicans, they's got they own music, it ain't that flamenco in Mexico, it's that mariachi music. Or maybe that mariachi music a Americanization of that flamenco. But even in Spain you's got two kinds of flamenco. You got that flamenco they do for them tourists, and then you's got the true flamenco, the flamenco that them Spaniards do for each other. Sometimes just the men do that true flamenco, and sometimes you's got men and women do that true flamenco. But for the tourists you's always got to have them women to do that flamenco, or you's got to have the men and women to do that flamenco, and them tourists they see and hear that flamenco, and they think sexuality, but that ain't the same as that true flamenco.

Maybe in Spain his true name be Jimmy Caballero, though, that Jimmy Cuervo, but in American Mexico or in Mexican America his name Jimmy Cuervo. And that Jimmy ain't his true Spanish name. Maybe his true Spanish name is Guillermo. Naw, Guillermo ain't the Spanish for Jimmy. What the Spanish for Jimmy? Jaime? Ain't Jaime the Spanish for Jimmy? Ain't Jaime Mexican for Jimmy? Anyway, that

Jimmy Cuervo, I call him a guitar player's guitar player he's so good.
He's the kind of musician Joan likes to call a "working musician" 'cause
he ain't preoccupied with stardom. One of them African-looking Mexicans from South Texas. A friend of mine from New Mexico, who first
told me about Jimmy Cuervo and his music, and who I first heard
perform in her cantina-type restaurant in Cuba, New Mexico, calls
them kinda Mexicans "chitlins con carne Mexicans." Anyway my ex-
husband Norvelle and I were playing pool in her cantina restaurant
when Jimmy Cuervo comes in. It a cantina-style restaurant but she got
one of them pool tables in it, you know. He's got his guitar and he asks
whether he can play for free, and then if the people like him, he might get
him a gig there. So he plays for free and the people like him, so she hires
him to play there. That's the first time I heard him play, and then when
Joan hires me to be her manager I think of that Jimmy Cuervo and tell
Joan that he one of the best guitar players I've heard since Hendrix. Ain't
Hendrix, ain't no guitar player that's Hendrix, but still one of the best.
Joan say if he one of the best guitar players since Hendrix, he be famous
and she woulda already heard of him. I tell her that's 'cause he don't
really know how to market hisself, just plays the clubs and cantinas
around South Texas. I remember when that Joan had her a gig in some
town, seem like Seattle, Washington, or one of them towns, and so she
takes me to this pawn shop and tells me that the pawn shop where Hendrix's daddy bought him his first electric guitar. And there's this big
painting of Hendrix over the pawn shop and I figure it's a true tale and
ain't none of them confabulatory tales. So anyway he sends us some of
his tapes, that Jimmy Cuervo or Jaime Caballero, and Joan likes him
and wants to make a record with him. Anyway, he gives me a approving
look. Ferocious red bangs hang across Joan's forehead. Every time I see
her she's got a different hairdo, different-style makeup. And she's wearing her favorite sweatshirt, one by the African-American sculptor-
designer Catherine Shuger but purchased in Amsterdam, called Monkey Puzzles. Putting her hands onto my shoulders, she hug me close. She
the best of pretenders. So who'd you win this time? she ask.

She put her foot up on a straight chair and pull up her socks. Painted figures make the socks look like they been tattooed. She's wearing the same gaucho pants she'd worn when I'd peeked up from behind her husband's shoulders—her ex-husband's shoulders.

I don't answer.

You were in Saratoga?

Right.

Who'd you win? Her eyelids are purple. So what gigs we get? she ask. I tell her.

So tell me who'd you win? she asks. Maybe you should get me a gig in Saratoga. I know they got clubs in Saratoga.

When I don't answer, she goes into the recording booth. Jimmy Cuervo follows, strumming his guitar. Well, if Josef can be German, Jimmy can be Mexican. 'Cept ain't the sorta Mexican you see in the movies. Look more African than Mexican, like I said. Chitlins con carne. My friend from Cuba, New Mexico, say she first seen a Mexican look like him in one of them French movies, said that surprised her 'cause she ain't never seen no African-looking people in Mexico, not in them American movies. You know, 'cause in them American movies they's always got white people playing the Mexicans at least in most of them early movies or they's got them Spanish or Native Americans or Italian-looking Mexicans, but not no African-looking Mexicans. This little Mexican boy in that movie, though, look just like a little African, she say. 'Cept my friend from New Mexico telling me about how they had slavery in that Mexico before they abolished it, so I guess there's as many Africans in Mexico as anywhere. And there's little towns in Mexico where all the people look like they's Africans, she say. Is that true, Nadine? I'm asking. She the one own that cantina-style restaurant, Nadine. She a African American herself, except her husband a Mexican. I think she say he from Chiapas or somewhere in southern Mexico. I think he one of them illegal aliens myself, or usedta be one of them illegals. He look more Native American than Mexican hisself, though. Nadine say he look like a Aztec prince. Sure, it's the truth, she say, about they being whole towns of Mexicans that look African. I ain't been to any of them little towns myself, but I've heard about 'em. Some of them

Africans when they escaped slavery settled in them little towns. When I was in Texas City, before I come to Cuba, New Mexico, with my Aztec Prince—sometimes she don't even say his name she just call him her Aztec Prince—and then she start telling me a lot of confabulatory stories about Texas City, Texas, and how she use to drive a truck in Texas City, Texas, then she met her Aztec Prince and they come and settled in Cuba, New Mexico. The way she tell the tale, she supposed to have smuggled her Aztec Prince across the border her ownself when he escaped from that little revolution they had down there in Chiapas. Somebody else mighta smuggled him across the border, but I don't think Nadine smuggled him across the border her ownself.

In the recording booth, Jimmy Cuervo's singing with Joan one of them Mexican *corridos*, one of them Mexican ballads. They're jazzing or bluesing or rocking it up, though, so that it don't sound exactly like a pure Mexican *corrido*. Something about a man and all his different women, or a woman and all her different men. And then they sing some of the new songs: "Big Dick from Boston," "Phoebe, Little Phoebe," "Captain Hicks, Captain Jimmy Hicks of the Marines," "Ada Ross." Then they sang some songs she'd previously recorded: "Remora," "Randy Dandy," "Xingu" and "Kedgeree," and then she sang songs whose titles I think were from literary works she'd read: "The Odyssey of a Nice Girl," "The Map of Love," "The Clown and His Daughter," "The Hermit and the Wild Woman," "Mina Purefoy in Puritan City," "Wolfe Tone and the Wandering Scholar," "Aldonza del Tobosa," "Younghy-Bonghy-Bo," "Le Roman Experimentale" and "The American Song."

When she come out of the recording booth, Joan stand watching me.

Jimmy's always excellent, he's like caviar, she says. How'd I do? How'd I sing? Did you like the new songs? Did you like the *corrido*? He's teaching me a *canto hondo*.

Yes. Very much. You sounded real good. You know you always sound good. And your songs are always intelligent.

You're just saying that. You know I like to hear you tell me that I'm good. Jimmy's always excellent, though. He's like caviar. You'd think he'd be better known. Jimmy, could you return Mr. Calandrino's keys. You're like caviar. She hands Jimmy the keys to the rented recording studio. Sure, he says. He bows to me gallantly, then bows to her, then heads toward Mr. Calandrino's office. Then Joan says, Let's go have Chinese. You can help me pick an album title. We can go to one of Isabel Kong's restaurants. The elusive Isabel Kong. They've got the best food, though. I went to school with her, you know. Isabel Kong. You know, when we were in Paris I took you to Isabel Kong's. She has an Isabel Kong's in Paris. She says everybody thinks she's a gangster. A woman like her ain't supposed to have so many fine restaurants all over the world if she ain't into something illegal.

I don't know if I can trust you, I say.

Trust me, she say.

When we get to the street, she's still holding my arm. I slide my arm out of hers as we walk down the windy street. Few people look at her, 'cause she's dressed like a fool, but they figure she must be some sorta theatrical person. She almost slender enough to be a fashion model, though. Sometimes you see them fashion models on the runways dressed up to look like fools. They say them ain't the sorta dresses that real women are supposed to wear. The designers just make them to give their shows a little flair and make them more entertaining. You know, something for the fashion journalists to write about. For a while them fashion models got more famous than the movie stars, on account of they had more of that glamour. Then them movie stars started getting glamorous again. 'Cause for a while you didn't see a lot of glamorous movie stars. Even at them awards shows, you didn't see the glamorous-type movie stars. A few of them rock stars turned movie stars would look kinda glamorous. Then they started bringing glamour back to Hollywood, which some people call Glamourtown anyway. Joan walks like she onstage, anyway, doing a little jig, then she touch my jaw. She move her hand up to my jaw, quickly, like she going to strike it, but she don't. She touch it gently instead.

Let's go somewhere where we can have some champagne, Ashley, I hear a woman say as we walk down the concrete stairs into the Chinese restaurant. As always, I feel awkward navigating through the tight spaces between tables, but Joan move like she own even the tightest space. And she ain't a small woman neither. Neither one of us is small women. She a slender woman, but she ain't a small woman. We're led to our table. The waiter, a tall man who look more Indonesian than Chinese, pull out her chair first, 'cause he can tell by her behavior I guess that she the VIP, or maybe because she the more attractive of the two of us, but when he turn to me I'm already seated and reaching for one of the fried noodles.

Joan say something to him in Chinese and then order shrimp and fried rice in Chinese. I know that *ni hao*, that the only Chinese I know. And what's that other Chinese I picked up from Joan? *Ni shi neiguo ren?* That mean, Where do you come from? Seem like people need to know that in everybody language. And to ask them what they name? *Ni jiao shenmo minzi?* In her gigs in different countries, she always like to sing at least one song in that different language, and to say a few words and phrases in them languages, so she know how to say a little in a lot of different languages. And she know how to order food in almost everybody language. I order sweet-and-sour pork in plain English, 'cause I ain't learned how to order food in nobody language but my own, or the language that supposed to be my own. Joan say that's why she like to learn different people's language, 'cause she ain't never felt like English her own language. She say the language that feel most like her own when she speak it is Italian, but she ain't got no Italian in her that she knows about. I thought she would say Swahili or one of them African languages, but she don't, she say Italian. We sit in silence until Joan kick my shin under the table.

What do you want me to do? I ask.

She don't answer. She slide off her pumps and rub my hurt shin with her toe. She move her foot up under the hem of my skirt, like she think she in a X-rated movie. She punch at the hem, but don't go no further.

So what do you want me to do? I ask.

Do you really think we're birds of the same feather? she ask. You said once we were birds of the same feather, that I only imagined I was different.

I ain't never said that.

I take a bit of that Chinese pork. Joan always coming out with things like that, things I'm supposed to have said. She either dreaming I'm saying a lot of that shit, or her memory playing tricks on her, or she overheard somebody else saying that shit and thought it was me, or maybe it's some lyrics to some song she's writing or heard, 'cause I ain't said half the shit that Joan ascribe to me as saying. I mean, if it Joan telling you this tale, or her version of this tale, she probably be telling you all kindsa shit that I ain't said. And I ain't never imagined that me and Joan anything alike. I don't even think of her as my alter ego. She ain't even the sorta woman I imagine myself to be anything like. You can like someone and it don't mean you want to be anything like 'em.

You said you wanted me to help you pick an album title.

The Floating World?

Sucks.

The Spear Maker?

Sucks.

Alter Ego.

Too elite.

Remora.

No.

Do you know what a remora is?

No.

It's a little sucker fish that attaches itself to a bigger fish. Fable has it that—

Sucks.

Our Nig Joan?

Stupid.

Queen Joan's Songbook?

No. What about Queen Kong?

Isabel's name is Kong, I can't use Kong. But that's good, I like that. I'd like to do an album and do something with Kong in it. But I know Isabel Kong, and she'd think I meant her.

Stupid.

La Femme Pensante? "*Je ne suis qu'une femme, mais je suis une femme pensante.*"

Say what? Sucks anyway. Why don't you go with one of the song titles. I kinda like "The American Song."

Sucks. Anyway, I think there's already an album named *The American Song* or *The American Songbook*. What about the name of some of those horses you bet on? What about Creole Beauty? When I played that gig in New Orleans, somebody thought I was Creole.

Doesn't sound rich enough for an album, you want something that sounds rich, you know. I don't mean rich rich, not elite, but rich. A marketable title. Not something obscure. Not something you'll have to explain in liner notes. A rich title, but not rich rich.

When you first met me did you think I was rich? she asks. I mean rich rich.

I don't know.

When you first met me did you think I was rich? she repeats. Did you think I was rich rich?

I don't know. I musta thought you musta had some kinda money. You look well taken care of, so I figured you must have some kinda money. Plus, you never like to talk about the amount of money that you getting for this gig or that contract, and somebody said it's only rich people that think money talk is crude. . . . Poor people talk about money all the time.

You know, you have never even asked me where I'm from. You have never even asked me anything about myself.

I never ask people about themselves. I figure people tell you as much about themselves as they want you to know. You want me to ask you where you from? So where you from? Detroit? Kansas City? St. Louis? Atlanta? I know you got a farm in Minnesota. Are you from Minneapolis? Your bio says that you're from New York, but I know a lotta jokers in the business say they're from New York when they ain't. They're from some little tank town, but they tell people they're from New York. I know your passport says New York. Maybe you're from some ghetto in Kansas City? Maybe you're from East St. Louis? West Virginia?

She get up abruptly. I see her talking to the Chinese woman at the desk and then she walks outside. I pay the bill and follow her out. The woman I pay the bill to is a short, round woman that remind me kinda of Thaka, that Masai woman, except she ain't Masai, she Chinese, say something to me in Chinese, 'cause maybe I speak Chinese too, but I tell her I don't speak Chinese, it's just the other one speaks Chinese. Then I ask her if she's the famous Isabel Kong. Isabel Kong? she ask. No, no I'm not Isabel Kong. Isabel Kong in Hong Kong. She's starting one of our new restaurants in Hong Kong. I just manage restaurant for Isabel Kong. I not Isabel Kong herself. You think I'm Isabel Kong? Everyone thinks I'm Isabel Kong. No, no I'm not Isabel Kong. Don't believe the stories you hear about her. She is a good woman. She is for the Chinese people. She is all the time helping the Chinese people. A good woman. I a good woman, but I not Isabel Kong herself. When I get outside, Joan's walking with her hands in her pockets. I catch up with her.

Look, I don't see him anymore. It was just that one time, I say. Look, it was stupid of me, but you were divorced. It was you making the big deal about how you was divorced, and how you didn't mind if he saw other women. Bragging about how y'all's divorced and how you don't mind if he sees other women, as if it's your business to mind.

What do you mean bragging?

I mean, I didn't even ask you. Did I ask you? Maybe I did ask you, but then you started bragging. You said that you and he were divorced, that was the first thing you told me. Certainly I didn't ask you about him and other women, about his other infatuations. The way I figured, the way you were sounding was, if I was interested, then it was okay, 'cause y'all was divorced. And if he was interested in me, then that was okay. And you said said y'all didn't have no claims on each other, and you were talking about some of his other women that you'd heard about, some of his other infatuations, but. . . . But you were divorced. You both said you had no claims on each other. You seemed like . . . You for really seemed like. . . . You seemed like you wanted us to like each other. And the way he was acting, he was acting like he wanted me to like him. You know how men act when they want a woman to like them, that's the way he was acting.

Your own conceit. I don't think we know the same Jamey.

Well, I thought it was wonderful, you know, I mean the two of you still being good friends, you know, being divorced and all and still being good friends. I thought it was the most wonderful thing. . . . Being able to be divorced and—

So you had to test us.

Test? No, I admired you, you and Jamey—

You haven't a right to call him Jamey. He's my Jamey.

—how you and your Jamey both keep track of each other, are on friendly terms. More than friendly terms. How you care about each other. . . . I admire that, and I was thinking that must be the most wonderful way to be divorced. To be divorced like you and James are divorced. I mean, if you gotta be divorced, then to be divorced like you and James are. I've heard men brag about their ex-wives like that, telling you how them and their ex-wives are still friends and how even their ex-wives is friends with each other, that's nice, but that's just to brag on themselves more than their women, but you're the first woman I met to brag about her ex-husband, to truly brag about him, as your ex-husband, not just bragging on yourself. . . .

I'm trying to explain what I mean. And should I tell her that I started not only thinking the way they divorced wonderful, but then started thinking him wonderful. That he must be the most wonderful man. Or maybe it was just my own conceit. Was I testing them or myself? But she wave for a cab. When it pull up to the curb, she climb in without inviting me. The driver shaking his head at her orange hair and purple eyelids. Looking at her like she some freak. A trollop? Bitch, she mumble, slamming the door.

CHAPTER EIGHT

He had tiptoed into the room, and now he digging into my shoulder like a wrench. At first I think it one of his security guards, even Nicholas. That maybe they don't recognize me and think I'm some secret agent hired by the local Thoroughbred Owners Association or whoever Josef think playing dirty tricks on him. But then how did I get through them security guards? Maybe they think I'm some kinda Ninja or something. Most of the Ninjas you see are men Ninjas, but I seen this television show that had women Ninja. Maybe they think I'm some kinda woman Ninja, hired by the local Thoroughbred Owners Association. He even got security people working for him who claim they former KGB, and former security people when Germany was still East and West Germany. One of them security guards say he was with the East German police, but then when East and West Germany united he come to America, because they was putting a lot of them East German police on trial for crimes against the state, or something like that, except when they was working for East Germany it weren't crimes against the state, 'cause they was obeying the laws of the state. He one of them dark-haired Germans, though, he ain't one of them Aryan-looking blond-haired Germans that that Hitler describing as the superior race. That always seem curious to me, Hitler and his ambivalent aesthetics, 'cause even he himself weren't that blond-haired aesthetic ideal that he say supposed to be the aesthetic ideal of that Germany. A lot of them little countries he invaded have them stories about him separating the blond-haired people from the dark-haired people, and saying the blond-haired people the superior people, and the people didn't even have to be Jewish or Gypsies, they just supposed to have dark hair. And even a lot of white people ambivalent about they aesthetics. The same people that celebrate the suntan celebrate Snow White. You'll hear women selling that suntan lotion and talking about being too white till they put on that suntan lotion, and then you hear the same women saying they ain't white enough and trying to sell you another lotion that give you a fairer complexion. Joan say that that the influence over there in Europe when them Moors invaded most of Europe. That that's why a lot of them Europeans is ambivalent about they aesthetics, 'cause when the Moors was the rulers over there in Europe, the aesthetic ideal was to look like the Moors, and then when the fair-haired Christians won back most of Europe from the Moors, the aesthetic ideal was to look like the fair-haired Christians. 'Cept them original Christians wasn't fair-haired, amongst the Mediterranean peoples. They mythologizes that Christianity. So them Europeans have always been kinda ambivalent about they aesthetics. I don't know whether she read that in one of them nonfiction books and if that the truth about why them Europeans is ambivalent about color and does all that suntanning or just one of them confabulatory truths. Like that psychologist that wrote that book on the psychology of color. Maybe it him, that former East German policeman, or that Nicholas. Anyway, I jerk my hand out of the desk drawer.

Spy, he say. It a German accent, but it Josef German accent. I'm barefoot, in a Chinese silk nightshirt. Couldn't find my Moroccan sandals. I'd climbed out of bed and wandered into the study.

I'm searching for scratch paper, I explain. Moonlight across his jaw. I can see his black pepper eyes.

What d'you want with scratch paper? he asks. To write up your report on me? Who hired you? Who do you work for? The Thoroughbred Owners Association? Your government? Mine?

I start to tell him I work for the Thoroughbred Breeders Association not the Thoroughbred Owners Association, or Our Nigs, International: Spies in the House of Love and that he our prime suspect in love arbitrage, 'cause he always talking about that arbitrage, that he in the arbitrage business before he become a Thoroughbred owner, but you can't joke like that with no paranoid fool. Especially a paranoid fool that's got former KGB and former CIA and former soldiers and former policemen and former policemen for the former East Germany and former Vietnamese soldiers who fought in the tunnels of Cu Chi—either that or they's all confabulatory storytellers. Or maybe they all just told Josef them confabulatory tales just so's they could get hired as his security people. Seem like I seen that former East German policeman on television, though, telling them about the reason he was interested in coming to America, 'cause in East Germany they considered him a hero, or at least a good East German, but in the reunited Germany they considered him a villain, and that he'd rather be a first-class citizen in America— 'cause they didn't know one German from another in America—rather than a second-class citizen or even a criminal in the reunited Germany.

Naw, to write down a song, I explain. I got a idea for a song. Anyway, if I was a spy, I'd be using the new technology. I wouldn't need to write up a report on you. I'd have one of those miniaturized cameras or some shit. Those miniaturized recorders. And you wouldn't even think I's a spy 'cause they'da trained me so well. Therefore, you should know I ain't no spy, 'cause if I was a real spy you wouldn't be suspicious of me at all.

You write songs for your Joan? he ask, letting go of my shoulder. Do you write some of her stupid music?

No, for myself. I don't show her my lyrics. They ain't her type of music. The type of romantic music I write she ridicules. She likes satire, wit, what she calls intelligent music. Intelligent and satirical rock 'n' roll. I like romance. I even like country music if it's romantic. The only country singer Joan likes is John Prine. She thinks he's the only intelligent country singer. She likes intelligent music. She thinks all African-American music is intelligent whether it's intelligent or not. You know, musical intelligence.

He don't say nothing. He's looking like her music don't sound all that intelligent to him, or much African-American popular music. Then he starts kissing me, nibbling me. You want romance? he asks. He draws me down on the carpet, kissing me, nibbling me, pulling up my night-shirt. Then there, beneath a leather chair that face away from us toward the Dutch windows, I can see shoes and trouser legs. He drops the core of an apple on the carpet, then scoops it up. I push up to get up, but Josef thrust harder. I watch the shoes and trousers. Josef rise up and kisses me again, nibbles me, then he pad out of the study. I turn on the desklight. Nicholas don't stand up and reveal himself, but I know it's him. Hiding in plain sight. I watch Nicholas' shoes and trousers, and think he going to say something, but he don't. I can hear the apple core plop in a nearby ashtray. Then he rise and leave the room. I keep searching for scratch paper, but have forgotten whatever song I intended.

CHAPTER NINE

This how I first met Joan's ex-husband James Savage. She introduced me to him her ownself. Harlan, I want you to meet my ex, she'd said, as he opened the door of the farmhouse. Honey, this is our lady lodger. I told her I'd show her how I spend my summer vacation, she said, sounding like a little girl, but a little girl in a confessional. Except I don't think a little girl in a confessional would call a priest honey. We shook hands, James and I. He'd been eating breakfast and there was a crumb on his lip. Joan reached out and scraped at it, then licked her finger. Um, banana bread. You smell like banana bread. Yummy. She sniffed under his chin then kissed him. He gave me a steady look before he said, Pleased to meet you. He was dressed casually in a blue workshirt with rolled sleeves and gray cotton trousers. He was wearing tennis shoes. He a average-sized man. He got a high, broad forehead and high, broad cheekbones, but a narrow chin. It narrow, but it still kinda square and prominent. His lips is sorta full. And he got a mustache with little bits of gray in it, though the neatly trimmed hair on his head is dark brown. His big brown eyes look like curiosity is they leading characteristic. And he got little dimples at the wings of his nose. I think they's dimples. Maybe individually his features is kinda strange, but put them together they make up a handsome man. I ain't say he a Denzel Washington or nothing, though he kinda got his self-possession, but he still a handsome man.

Harlan's my new manager, Joan explained. He nodded as if he already knew me, but didn't say anything, then we went inside and put our bags down on the living room carpet. He was puffing on a cigarette which he put out in one of them crystal tray. He mumbled something about giving up the nasty habit, that he ought to know better than to smoke, then he carried our bags upstairs, but when he came back down he was puffing on another cigarette. Joan had settled on the couch, reclining, with her legs thrown over the worn arm, facing the mantel and the fireplace. I sat in an armchair with my legs folded under me. Some of the furniture was old-fashioned, the couch and the chair of unmatched fabrics, and other of the furniture in the modern style. Look like the kind of furniture you might get in a flea market, mixing styles and fabrics, not the kind of furniture you'd think a rock star would have, even a not-so-famous rock star. Or maybe the furniture remind me of Joan's music, 'cause her music do mix different musical styles and textures, though it supposed to be rock 'n' roll. The couch was upholstered in a sort of woolen fabric, a plaid mixture of browns, whites, oranges and beiges; the armchair had silky upholstery of blue, purple and wine-colored stripes, its arms frayed and worn.

The farmhouse, though, looked larger inside than it did from the exterior. The living room was rectangular and had a sprawling chaotic look, the furniture not just a mixture of styles and fabrics but arranged haphazardly, catty-cornered as my grandmother Jaboti would say, except for the couch and armchair that faced each other. There's several of them leather chairs, and there's a rough-hewn wooden coffee table in the center, decked with albums of Joan's favorite singers, not including her own, 'cause she always say she ain't her own favorite singer, which surprise me 'cause I'm thinking seem like most singers would have theyself as one of they own favorite singers, 'cause seem like if somebody a singer they'd have that conceit of being they own favorite singer, even if they favorite songs is songs that other singers sing, but she say she ain't her own favorite singer, and even the songs that she herself sing ain't always her favorite songs. Now that don't make no sense, though. That not being your own favorite singer make more sense than the songs you sing not being your favorite songs. Seem like you'd just sing your favorite songs, don't it? 'Cept she explains that sometimes a singer don't have the range to sing they favorite songs, that other singers might sing their favorite songs better than they can sing 'em, and that they favorite songs might not be they own style of singing. 'Cause can't all singers sing in everybody style. They's some singers that can sing in everybody's style and every type of singing, so you can have favorite songs that other singers sing, as well as having other singers be your favorite singers. Still seem kinda crazy, you have the conceit to be a singer and ain't have the conceit to be your own favorite singer singing your own favorite songs.

She ain't tell me who her own favorite singer or what her favorite songs, but them albums mix assorted styles of singing, and not just American music, but Continental music, popular and classical, Caribbean and African and Latin music. And in American music it ain't just African-American music, it everybody's American music, even including country music. I remember reading a short story called "Why I Like Country Music" and written by a African-American writer, and seeing Joan's country music albums make me think of that short story. I don't remember, though, why he say he like country music in that story, but I don't think his reason for liking country music the same as Joan's reason for liking country music, and Joan ain't even from the country. Well, her farmhouse is in the country, but that don't mean you's from the country.

Joan glanced at her ex-husband. He's always such a mystery to me, she said. But he's so sweet. Ain't he sweet?

No, I'm not sweet, said James.

I'm thinking I'm in some stupid movie, you know, them talking that silly talk like that, ain't that lovers' talk, talking about whether he sweet or ain't sweet—looking at him, though, I bet he is sweet maybe even Sweetness Itself—then he put out his new cigarette before he'd half-finished smoking it. He have a high, lined forehead; his dark complexion, though, make you hardly see the lines. In fact, except for that little gray in his mustache, he look kinda younger than Joan, though she say they the same age. I guess that's why some mens likes to get theyselves younger women, so's they don't look younger than they wives. I think it's just a power thing myself. Though they ain't gonna tell you it got nothing to do with power, they'll just tell you that younger women fascinating. Which might be the truth. Maybe them younger women is more fascinating to a man. That's why they's got laws, though. 'Cause you's gotta have laws to help some of them men to decide who's too young. Course when them womens gets power, they tries to play that same power game theyselves, 'cept with them older women, you's still gotta look like you's a younger woman. You might be a older woman, but you's still gotta look like you's a younger woman. You can't be no Sean Connery if you's a woman, you's gotta be Cher. I think it's just a power thing myself.

You were sweet to carry our bags up, but we'll be no further trouble, will we, Harlan?

I said nothing. James puffed on yet another cigarette and rolled his sleeves farther up. Joan apologized for something, but I didn't understand it—some private matter. I thought of the Ring Lardner story in which the man can't go to bed without apologizing for something; he apologizes even to his shaver before shaving.

Joan kept kicking her legs back and forth. He gave her a couple of irritated glances. He looked at me again. And looking at me like I'm somebody he think he already know. He flicked ash into the tray. Joan told me you're a good manager, he said, the cigarette in the corner of his mouth. There was still a bit of crumb of banana bread on his lip. To tell the truth I wanted to wipe that bit of banana bread from his lip myself, or lick it from his lip, or kiss it from his lip, and then, Say what? I asked. Joan told me you're a good manager, he said. He took the cigarette out of his mouth, licked at the crumb on his lip, then put the cigarette back in the corner of his mouth.

I try to be.

Are you or aren't you? he asked with impatience, the cigarette dangling.

I am, I said. Yes, I am. I don't think I could manage anyone but Joan, though. I don't understand how these managers can have more than one client and call themselves managing, you know.

Yeah, Joan is enough to manage, isn't she?

And then I'm thinking, he every man I know. He ain't just hisself, he every man I know. But then men, they's supposed to talk like that. Is you or ain't you a good manager? They's supposed to have the vocabulary of command, it's women supposed to have the vocabulary of suggestion or innuendo. They say even little boys at play are always commanding each other, whereas little girls at play are always suggesting. Course there's bossy control freak little girls, and you's gotta have little boys that takes commands from other commanding boys. And then I feel like they got me in their stupid movie, and he almost as handsome as one of them movie stars. To tell the truth he a handsomer man than Joan a good-looking woman. I bet he is sweet, I'm thinking. Then he ain't looking at me. He staring at Joan's feet, which rotating clockwise, then counter-clockwise. He put out the new cigarette.

I've stocked the refrigerator and the bar, he say swiftly to Joan, but still looking at her feet. He pick up a brass tray from the mantelpiece, look at its content of butts, put it down.

You're sweet, she said.

It was good to meet you, he muttered, staring at me finally. But then he looking at me like he ain't so sure we know each other. I'll probably see you before you leave, he says.

Stay for dinner, Joan say.

I would, Joan Darling, but I got to go over some lab reports.

Joan say you some kinda scientist.

Yes, I am.

Yes, he is some kinda scientist, say Joan. The language of innuendo.

Yes, I am, he repeat. But he don't tell me what kinda scientist, like a scientist a scientist. He take a package of Camels from his breast pocket, examine it like it a lab report, then put it back.

What are you working on now? Joan ask.

That new book I told you about: *Symmetry, Matrices, and Molecular Orbital Theory*, he say, and that Joan looking at him like she know exactly what symmetry, matrices, and molecular orbital theory mean. He start to say something else about that book he working on, but he don't.

Have dinner with us tomorrow then? I ask.

Okay.

Joan purse her lips together and frown. Looking like I ain't supposed to say nothing to him, her ex-husband, and it her introduced us, and even telling me how sweet he is, and even telling me he more sweet than even he think he is his ownself. Anyway, he nod to me, walk by her, behind the couch, pause for a moment, glance at me, then hug her head and whisper, Be happy, and left. Joan ran her hands through her thick hair, and pouted. Then she picked up one of James' half-used cigarettes, lit it with one of them antique cameo-type lighter, one of them real expensive-looking lighter, and puffed.

So what's the story? I asked.

What do you mean? she asked, then she combed her hair back with her hands. She took a long draw, then put out the cigarette.

You're on friendly terms. Maybe even loving terms, I said. Do you think you'll work something out? How long have you been divorced? I mean, are you legally divorced? Do you think you'll get married again? I mean, you're divorced, but you don't really give me the impression of being divorced, and he still calls you Darling. I know people who get divorced and get married again, and I ain't even heard them call each other Darling. And I ain't never been called nobody's darling myself.

That's when she laughed and told me that he'd stay her ex. He'll stay my ex, darling, if that's what you mean. Anyway, he's got his little infatuations now. Younger, sweeter women.

But like I said they didn't behave with each other exactly like any ex-spouses that I knew about. So what's going on? I kept asking, and suggesting that maybe they'd get married again. I just kept suggesting that maybe they'd get married again. And Joan kept looking at me as if I was overstepping my bounds, asking and suggesting that maybe they'd get married again, but then she started telling me again that he had other women, other sweet young women. That's why I always find that Prince Charles so curious, you know, 'cause all them other men's other women is other sweet young women. I remember me and Joan seeing that Prince Charles on that television and Joan she say something about respecting his choice in women, and I ain't know what she mean by that, 'cause it ain't the opinion of them media people. I ain't ask her what she mean by that, and that Joan it seem like she's always liking the people that ain't the media darlings better than the people that is the media darlings, when most people likes the people that is the media darlings, or the people that is at least photogenic and charismatic. And then she have me sitting there watching that Prince Charles talking about architecture. And then she say that thing about respecting his choice in women. And then she say something about American culture being a immature culture, which didn't seem to have nothing to do with that Prince Charles. And what America being a immature culture have to do with Prince Charles? Then she say again about respecting his choice in women. And what that got to do with architecture? But maybe it just 'cause he the exception that prove the rule.

Why you so preoccupied with us? she asking, and I forgot about asking her about that divorce 'cause I'm thinking about immature American culture and Prince Charles. Girl, I ain't even as preoccupied with us as you are. Why we divorced or getting married again or staying divorced or ain't staying divorced or wanna be lovers again and people you know that's got divorced and got married again? You don't even know us. You don't know us. Well, you know me, or think you know me, or know me about as well as I know myself, or know me about as well as I think I know myself, but you don't know us. I know us, but sometimes I don't know him. Or I know him about as well as I know me. Girl, I ain't even as preoccupied with us as you are. Anyway, he's got his other women, his other little infatuations, his young sweet things. All that talk about a lab report. It might be a lab report, or his book on symmetry, matrices, and molecular orbital theory, or one of his little infatuations, one of his young sweet things, she said, picking up one of his cigarette butts and looking at it, as if she thought he was as addicted to his other women, his little infatuations, his young sweet things, as he was to his cigarettes.

I didn't keep asking questions, though. I studied the patterns in my armchair. And then she told me how they have joint ownership of the farm, how she bought it when she got her first money from her first real gig. Then it seem like after she had her first real gig, they got divorced and all.

At first I thought we'd work things out, you know. I guess I thought it. I don't even know why we got divorced. Well, I know why we got divorced. I guess I know why we got divorced. It wasn't catching him with some other woman, even a younger woman, or shit like that, or him catching me with some other man. Certainly no younger man. What's there of interest? You know, like that Pepsi commercial. No stupidity like that. One man's enough for me. Somebody once said I'm like the woman in that poem—I forgot what poem—where the poet asks, What does a woman want? Why, her own sweet way. Course a poet would say, Her own sweet way. Maybe the bitch who wants her own way ain't sweet.

Shakespeare? I ask. I mean, the poet.

Naw, not Shakespeare. He knows what a man wants, and what a man thinks a woman wants, even the best of women. He's good at portraying bitches, but even they're a man's idea of a bitch. You know, even Shakespeare's sweet bitches are still a man's idea of a sweet bitch. Chaucer's the only old bard who seemed to know what a woman really wants, at least the Wife of Bath—and she ain't really a bitch, she's just who she is—but I don't think that's Chaucer either. Then she start saying something that sound like it right out of that Chaucer, you know what that woman say about all them husband she have, but saying it like it right out of that Chaucer, and then she say, A woman wants to be her ownself, just like a man wants to be his ownself. Anyway, I guess you can't have a marriage where both people want their own sweet way, want to be too much of their ownselves, and won't negotiate. We're friends, still. We're both friends. Anyway, he looks after the place when I ain't here. He stays here when he wants, keeps a lot of his research papers and projects here, has what women he wants, his little infatuations, his little sweet bitches, I suppose, or bitches in training, and then I come here after my tours and recuperate. Do you remember *Carnal Knowledge*? I was just thinking of those women in *Carnal Knowledge*, and the way those men would talk about those women? You know, I was wondering if men really talk about women like that, you know. Jack Nicholson and that other guy? Garfunkel? You know of Simon and Garfunkel, I think he played that other guy. He had a few roles in movies then. I guess people thought he was more interesting than Simon in those days, I mean for roles in movies. I was a bitch in training myself I guess when I first saw that movie. I remember thinking that's sorta like the stereotyped idea that women have of men, that they talk about us like that, like we're things, you know, when they're talking to each other about us, but then there was this movie, and there were these men talking about women like that. White men, but men are men. I couldn't imagine Jamey talking to some man like that about me. Of course I hadn't met Jamey then. I don't think I'd met Jamey then. But the Jamey I imagined. So it's like that, you know. I don't bring any of my own infatuations here. In fact, I haven't had any infatuations since we divorced. You'd think I'd taken a vow of celibacy or some shit.

She nuzzled back against the pillow. Yes, I suppose he even brings other women here. I haven't asked him whether he's had other women up here. I just suppose. He hasn't said as much, but I know he does. He ain't celibate. Even if he ain't in love, he's got to have some infatuation. He's a passionate man. I suppose he doesn't seem so, but he is. And men's ideal is always the harem, ain't it. That's the ideal of every man I know, even the monogamous ones. Who do you think invented the harem? Woman's ideal is always the one great love. Most women.

Some men's ideal is the one great love.

Maybe. But he still wants his concubines. I always let him know when I'm coming up here, anyway.

That must bother you, I said.

No, we're divorced. Why shouldn't he have other women? Maybe I'd mind if it was more than a fling, more than a little infatuation. But we're divorced. Why shouldn't he have other women? Why shouldn't he have younger women even? I don't own him, but sometimes I think he still thinks he owns me, though. Did you hear him call me Darling? Yes? He still calls me Darling. He still thinks he owns me.

He doesn't act like he thinks he owns you.

What?

I was going to say he acts like he thinks you still own him. But he doesn't act like that either.

Yes he does. I mean, like he still owns me. He's not the sorta man you can own. I mean, himself. She massaged the tip of her nose, then swung her legs down. How about a drink? Bourbon? Scotch?

Scotch, with some soda.

She was up and at the oak bar. It was rough-hewn like the table, but well stocked. Rocks? She glanced over her shoulder.

Yeah.

He's handsome, I said.

She gulped her bourbon. Yeah.

I like your house too. It ain't like a rock star's house. You know, how you'd imagine a rock star's house. . . .

Thank you.

. . . . Except the high-ceilinged rooms. . . .

What about a rock star's husband? Or ex-husband, I should say.

He seems secure in himself. He seems to know who he is. He doesn't seem like a harem maker to me. I bet you're his great love. Anyway, I'm talking to the Schacter people—

Let's not talk shop. Or love. Or even great love. Why is it when I say it it doesn't sound like love? Anyway, you settle those questions. That's what I hired you for. Not the question of love, or great love, I mean my career.

She got up, danced over to the bar, carried the bottle of bourbon back and set it on the table. She gave me a sullen look. Then she reached for another of James' unfinished cigarettes, lit it and puffed.

Just let me know when the deal is made, okay? Though I do want to hear that new guitarist Jimmy Cuervo, the one you said's from South Texas. What's his name?

Jimmy Cuervo.

But no shop talk, let's agree, and certainly not when Jamey's here tomorrow. I don't know my own mind when Jamey's around.

I don't believe that. You call him Jamey. That's nice.

Does he look like a James to you?

What?

A James. Rather than a Jamey?

Yeah, I suppose.

Maybe that's my way of still calling him Darling. Actually he's a Jim. He was named after Jim Thorpe, you know the Indian. . . . the famous Native American athlete, the one they called the top athlete of the first half of the century. You know, that movie we saw about Jim Thorpe, in the days when they didn't get real Indians to play real Indians.

There's real Indians in that movie.

Extras. Minor roles. Not Jim Thorpe. But in America you don't know who's a real native. I don't know why he was named after him, though. Jamey, I mean. He ain't got no Native American in him that I know about. And he ain't never been too fond of sports or athletics. I think his daddy or granddaddy's just a great fan of Jim Thorpe's. He looks athletic, he works out, even does yoga, Jamey I mean, but he ain't fond of sports himself, though. Jim, that's his name. He don't like it, though. I think it reminds him of that Nigger Jim in Twain's book. You know, Nigger Jim. Ain't you read Twain? Girl, I know you read Twain. That's high school. Elementary school. You can't be a American and ain't read Twain, girl. Talk about un-American. Girl, you ain't a true American. That oughta be the test for Americanity: Have you read Twain? I'm just kidding, girlfriend. I wonder what that book'd sound like if Nigger Jim had told that tale? I bet Twain couldn'ta imagined Nigger Jim telling that tale, you know, or if he'da imagined it, I don't think they'da published a book with Nigger Jim telling that tale, even the Nigger Jim of Twain's imagination. People don't think of Jim Thorpe when they hear Jim, they think of Nigger Jim. Twain's Nigger Jim. So he calls himself James, and I call him Jamey. If they wanted to name him after Jim Thorpe, I think he'd've preferred Thorpe rather than Jim. Thorpe Savage. That sounds like a soap star. You know that guy on the soaps with all those braids, the fine-looking one, you know that fine-looking young man with all them braids, the one on that soap, naw I ain't talking about A Martinez you know A Martinez ain't got no braids and he ain't on the soaps now anyway, they oughta put him in the movies. . . .

He looks kinda like Nadine's husband.

Who Nadine? That Kim Basinger movie?

Naw, I mean my friend Nadine. This woman name Nadine from New Mexico. Well, she ain't originally from New Mexico, but she own her a little cantina-style restaurant in New Mexico. Ain't I told you about Nadine? Her husband from Mexico, though, I mean the real Mexico, look kinda like him. She think he better looking than even A Martinez, though.

. . . .did you see that made-for-TV movie with him in it, you know that good-looking, that African-American actor with all them braids what's-his-name, now he could be a Thorpe Savage, but not Jamey.

She poured more bourbon, spilled some on the coffee table, dabbed it with her sleeve.

I promise you'll be bored, she said.

No.

This ain't Vegas. Jamey ain't as flamboyant as the kinda guys I know you like. He's a passionate man, but he ain't a flamboyant passionate man.

You don't know what kinda guys I like. I only go to Vegas sometimes. It's mostly Saratoga, the races.

She poured more bourbon while I nursed my old glass of Scotch.

Well, I meant, Jamey ain't like your gambling buddies, he's into microbes. He's too sweet for you. But maybe you like 'em sweet. I bet you like yourself some sweet, don't you? Have you got a sweet tooth? I've never had much of a sweet tooth myself.

Yeah, you told me he's a scientist.

A microbiologist and a chemist, a researcher. Generates ideas for some sorta research company. He partly owns the company, so it's sorta his own company. Anyway, they generate ideas in biology and chemistry, mostly, for other companies, you know. Then the other companies do the more practical research, but then he has his own research, independent of the company. Both practical and theoretical. To tell the truth, I'm not really up on what his research is now. I used to always know what he was researching. Now he prefers a lot of theoretical stuff, you know, pure ideas. So that's sorta like the ideal company for him, you know, just generating ideas. A lot of his ideas are somewhere in the stratosphere. Whatever's the highest sphere. I think the highest sphere's the stratosphere. I don't understand a lot of his theories myself. So I was just telling you it ain't Vegas. Or Saratoga, or whatever. Jamey and I ain't as flamboyant as your gambling buddies and jockey friends. We'll bore you.

She puffed the cigarette down to its filter. I was silent.

Here I just rest up and take things easy, and Jamey's. . . . he's passionate about his work, his research, but otherwise. . . . Well, this ain't Vegas.

That's cool, I said. I like him.

Now you see how I spend my summer vacations. She picked up another unfinished cigarette and puffed.

He didn't seem to me like a unpassionate man. I wondered if they still made love, but that wasn't a question I'd ask.

I know we ain't supposed to talk about it, but do you mind if I give the Schacter people a call from here? I asked.

Why should I mind? You're looking out for me, right? Do you think I'm too old to be a rocker? Jamey thinks I'm too old to be a rocker.

You're too old to be a rapper, maybe, but there're rockers older than you.

Yeah, we're the true rockers, ain't we? Our generation. The best rockers are us.

CHAPTER TEN

One evening in the dressing room, after one of her shows, I'm rubbing Vitapoint into her orange hair and brushing it. This orange shit is shit, I say. You oughta cool it. Why don't you just look normal and let the music. . . . let the music. . . . like Aznavour says. . . . He ain't rock 'n' roll, but you remember when we were staying in that hotel in Paris and saw Aznavour on the television. . . . I don't think you oughta try to be Madonna or Rodman. . . .

I was doing this before Rodman or Madonna, changing the color of my hair. The fans that know me expect me to change the color of my hair all the time. I was changing the color of my hair when I was singing in the little clubs in Rhode Island. I told you when I was going to grad school in Rhode Island, that's when I first started singing professionally. . . . Well, I didn't want to be a singer, I just wanted to help pay my way through grad school. . . . You didn't even see colored people with blond hair in those days, I mean colored people my color with blond hair. . . . Anyway, what's normal? she asks. I mean, even though rock 'n' roll now is considered a mature music. . . .

What do you mean mature music?

I mean when you got classical rock and modern rock you got yourself a mature music. You know when Billy Joel usedta sing it's still rock 'n' roll to me. Well, in those days I couldn't even imagine a music beyond rock 'n' roll. But rap ain't rock. That's what I admire about the young singers is that they could imagine something beyond rock 'n' roll. . . . I don't really like all the rap I hear, and I think a lot of the music could use some maturity, but I admire the fact that they could imagine something beyond rock 'n' roll. I mean, now that rock 'n' roll is pretty music, Establishment music. Except my rock 'n' roll. I think music should be kinda controversial, I mean popular music. . . . I don't want my music to be the Establishment's Darling. I don't wanna be the Establishment's Darling. But I don't want it to be just decadence either. Though I think modern music has gotta be a little decadent, otherwise it isn't really reflecting the decadence of the modern world. You know, except my music kinda satirizes decadence. Like Madonna and the Artist Formerly Known as Prince, or some of the rappers. Sometimes you don't know whether they're satirizing decadence or decadence itself. I like the bubblegum rappers myself, you know the sweet rappers. Intellectually I know what Public Enemy and those other rappers, the gangsta women and the gangsta men are doing, but I like listening to the sweet rappers myself, the healing-type music. . . . I don't want my music to just be decadence itself.

I say nothing. I watch her through the mirror. I brush. I don't dig you, she say. On her dresser there's a paperback book of Freud's. I think it's got something to do with sex, but it ain't. It's got something to do with wit. I mean the title of that book says something about wit not sex. I didn't know that Freud wrote about wit. Seem like whenever people talk about Freud, they talking about sex. I thought the only thing he wrote about was sex. Sex and dreams and even dreams of sex. Maybe that book got to do with the wit of sex or the sexualization of wit.

I thought Freud only wrote about sex, I say. Sex and dreams. I didn't know Freud wrote about wit.

That's the Freud of the popular imagination, she says.

You mean of the sexual imagination, I say.

She don't say nothing, then I think she going to start saying something about catching me with her ex. Her sweet ex. I'm always thinking she's going to say something about that, even when there ain't any mention of sex. When I seen that Freud, I'm thinking she signifying about me and her ex. But it ain't a book about sex, it's a book about wit. I don't know what sort of degenerate game you were playing in my house. That's my house. That's what I imagine her saying. Or calling me a self-

indulgent little bitch, or some shit. I keep thinking she's going to say
something like that. 'Cause that sounds like Joan. She's even got a song
about a self-indulgent little bitch, except she wrote it before she met me.
Or maybe it's a song about herself. Maybe it's her idea of herself when
she wrote that song. But she don't say nothing about that, about me and
her ex. She just look at me through the mirror.

I apologize, I say.

What? For Christsakes, girl, you still thinking about that? You still
chewing on that old chestnut. How the hell was I to know? I wouldn't
have opened the fucking door if I'd known you two were bumping
boody like a couple of bonobo monkies or some shit. . . .

What do you want? I ask. Do you want me to leave? What's a bonobo monkey?

It's you still chewing on that old chestnut, not me, she say, thumbing
through that book of Freud's. When I want to fire you, I'll fire you.
You're a good manager. In matters of love, you might be a fool. . . .

I pull at the tangles in her hair, knots and pieces that look like fishnet.
I massage her hairline. This shit is really destroying your hair, I say.

She pull at a piece of fishnet.

What's a bonobo monkey?

You. Well, I suppose even you've got more morals than them. Do you
think animals have codes of morality? I don't just mean sexual morality,
I mean. . . . well, the higher codes of morality. Do you think animals
have a higher moral nature?

CHAPTER

ELEVEN

May I borrow your phone? I ask. We're on the veranda. Beers and pizza. My treat. He said he'd never had pizza. Unbelievable. I start to say something about them Germans and Italians during the war. Lotta Americans think of that pizza as American food as much as they do Italian. But he say he ain't never had none of that pizza. So I'd ordered us some. Eating his he said he knew why he'd never had pizza. And then I know he mean he ain't never had that American pizza. He say he had the true Italian pizza that got a taste that distinctive from American pizza or Italian-American pizza. He say he like the true Italian pizza better than American pizza. I'll reverse the charges, I say.

Go ahead, says Josef, sipping his Budweiser. And no need to reverse the charges.

I start to tell him that ain't the way you drink Budweiser. He drinking his Budweiser like he think it supposed to be champagne. Course maybe that's better than them people that drink champagne like they think it Budweiser. What's this new contraption? I ask, picking up the phone from the table just inside the glass doors.

The same odd honeycombed device attached to the receiver as at the hotel.

If the red light goes on it means our privacy's been invaded, he says.

On the table are some papers. Some look like contracts, but they's all in German. And there's a few handwritten letters, also in German. Maybe there're from that wife he's spoken about, but he ain't got no photographs of her, at least none that's visible.

Oh, yeah? I dial.

The red light does not go on, but Joan's voice says sleepily from the other end of the receiver, Hello?

This is Harlan. Are you set for tomorrow? We're supposed to meet the Schacter people.

Where the hell are you? Do you know anyone named Norvelle? Anyway, someone named Norvelle called you from Africa. Zanzibar, I think. Ain't that in Africa? Norvelle? At first he thought I was you. A message? No. Ain't that that new promoter you were telling me about? You were talking about some African promoter for my music. Zanzibar? Ain't rock 'n' roll against the law in Zanzibar? Oh, that Norvelle. Yeah, your ex-husband, you told me about him, but you didn't exactly tell me his name. Norvelle. Is that his name, Norvelle? I don't know how he got this number. Maybe he put a private detective on your ass. He told me where he was staying over there in Zanzibar. He thought I'd already written the name of the hotel and I asked him the name of the hotel again, but he already hung up. So I didn't get the name of the hotel. Naw, I didn't get his phone number. I thought it was that promoter you were talking about. I thought you already had his phone number. Girl, if he anything like his voice, you a fool.

BOOK

TWO

CHAPTER TWELVE

When my husband started following around that Masai medicine woman, I told him I was going back to the States. I'd followed him all over Africa while he recorded the medical lore of various tribal doctors. He said that there was a lot of traditional African medical lore that had never been recorded or collected. For him it was exciting, but I was exhausted. Let him follow the native doctors from Korogwe to Morogoro, from the Rufiji River to the Great Ruaha, from the Uluguru Mountains to Meru, in the Eastern Rift Valley. Actually, I found the African cities— Nairobi, Lumbumbachi, Kampala, and Douala—more interesting than the little villages or the African bush. On television and in the movies you always saw the little African villages and the African bush, or the people on safari, or the native African medicine men and women, but you never saw the cities with their modern buildings and the bustle and automobiles and rumble and bicycles and mixtures of type and dress. My husband referred to these city Africans as "detribalized." But I liked them, the African businessmen I saw in the hotels, the market women, the college students, and I liked the tastes and sights and sounds and smells of the cities, but especially the islands off the coast of Africa, the islands of Zanzibar and Pemba.

Although Norvelle, my husband, had books on modern, urban Africa and the detribalized African he still behaved himself as if Africa was all bush or highland village or damp river valley. And the minute we got to the tourist hotel, before I could rest up from the previous expedition to meet some new African medicine man or woman, he'd rent a jeep or a Land-Rover or a van and head toward the next wilderness. I used to wonder what women did when they got trapped in the wilds without their tampons or SNs. Did they use leaves? I didn't have to find out, though, because after the first expedition I developed amenorrhea.

Still, near Lake Eyasi when we watched one famous medicine woman perform, it was no magic hokum-pokum like I'd expected. It resembled some intricate surgical procedure, but a makeshift one. Like when she pushed the reed into the man's belly and sucked out gallstones.

Why ain't the man showing any pain? I whispered.

Because he trusts her, said Norvelle, standing beside me with his notebook in which he scribbled notes and drew sketches. It looked like those naturalist's notebook you see in the library, except he's what's called a medical anthropologist. To show pain would be a sign of disrespect, he explained.

But he feels it? I asked.

Yes, but she's given him. . . . he gave the name of some natural herb, though I don't remember the name of it. Anyway, when she finished making the man well, she spit on him behind the ears. Norvelle explained it was another sign of goodwill and respect. But while Norvelle stood talking with her in Masai, or whatever the language, some Bantu language, I contemplated her bald head, brass earrings, and bare hanging ashy breasts. She smiled at the man she'd just cured, then she spat behind his ears again. A lot of respect, I mumbled, wondering if she could cure my amenorrhea. But just as well. Ignoring me, Norvelle and the woman continued talking.

Ain't we going to what's its place? I asked, back at the hotel. Ain't we supposed to go to some Gamba village?

And he had also promised to take me to some volcanic crater, the Ngorongoro, and he had planned to meet a highlander medicine man near Tabora. And afterwards he'd promised we could return to Zanzibar or Pemba, not to collect any lore, but to have a real honeymoon, to eat coconuts and lie on a beach or go to the markets not to query where such and such a medicine man or woman could be found, but to buy ornaments of coral or ebony. Not ivory, Norvelle said, because of the elephants.

He wanted to stay with her, he said, the Masai medicine woman. He wanted to go to the next village she decided to go to. He'd learned more lore from her than any of the others, so he'd already arranged to meet her the next morning. So I told him he could follow her to Kingdom Come, but I was going back to the States. I was still hot and funky from the last expedition, and even my Extra Power deodorant stick hadn't been made with the African bush in mind. I went and took a shower.

In the morning I boarded my plane. I ain't the kind of woman who'd follow a man anywhere. I decided that a long time ago. I'll follow a man just so far and then. . . . Well, you ain't heard my grandmother Jaboti's story yet. She claimed that she followed a man so far that she turned into a human being. Me, if I wasn't a human being yet, I wouldn't follow a man so far, even if his intention was to turn me into one. Or if that was his conceit, that by following him I'd turn into a full human woman. But that's another story, and most people think that she's a crackpot anyhow. But like all little girls, you hear how the older women, mothers and grandmothers, handle their questions of romance and love, and you make your own resolutions, mostly what you won't do. Listening to their tales is as close to a initiation ritual as you get in the New World.

Anyway, so when I look back on it now, of course it was jealousy, plain and simple. Jealousy, I guess. That Masai medicine woman with all her charms hanging out, and all his looks of admiration for her knowledge. And me dragging along behind, carrying the Nikon camera, and fighting mosquitoes and dragonflies and tsetse flies and funkiness and the heat and not knowing which way was up. . . . I'd have preferred to have been in one of the nightclubs in the city drinking palm wine. And do you suppose, though, if I'd been the anthropologist and told him I'd planned to follow some medicine man that he'd have come along carrying the Nikon? I think not.

And it wasn't that I didn't like that Masai woman. Thaka, I think he called her. A small, round woman, round head, round body, beautiful by the standards of her tribe. I liked her, but following him following her? No thank you. But once she'd surprised me by speaking English. And I found out that she'd actually studied European medicine, that she'd been a top student in one of the mission schools and had won a scholarship to study in London, and when she returned to the Rift Valley, she'd worked as a sort of medical liaison and interpreter between the Tanzanian villages and some international medical organization, Doctors Without Walls or Sans Frontiers or one of those organizations. She herself, though she knew the European medicines, used traditional medicine because the people themselves whom she worked with responded more favorably to that. Sometimes the traditional medicine worked where the modern, European drug didn't. And when there were parallel medicines, where a certain herb or root for instance contained the exact same chemical compounds one found in a synthetic European pill, she'd use the traditional herb or root. In fact, Norvelle said many European medicines had and have herbal beginnings, such as the malaria cure. When she used European medicine, it was introduced within the African context. Least that's what Norvelle said about her in a article he wrote on the subject. Actually, Norvelle published a series of papers on her in a medical anthropology journal, and then collected them into a book on traditional Masai medicine.

Are you a medical anthropologist, too? she'd asked, her accent British. I tried to picture her out of her traditional Masai clothes and in European, but I couldn't. Norvelle was making a sketch of her, and she'd glanced at me and asked that.

No, I said. I didn't even know what medical anthropology was until I met Norvelle.

You're just with him? she asked, sounding like I was some sort of groupie or hanger-on.

Yes, I said.

Norvelle kept sketching her and I took photographs.

So when I said I didn't want to follow him following her anymore, he drove me to the airport in the van. He kept looking as if he thought I'd change my mind, you know, but I didn't. And his own pride, I suppose, kept him from asking me to stay. Or did he feel relief? Did he want to be free to be with her? Not just to study her, but to be with her? But he said he'd stay at the hotel until I arrived in London, before transferring planes, in case I changed my mind and gave him a call. But when I arrived in London, I merely transferred planes. If I'd called him, would he have kept his promise to be at the hotel, or would he already be with her?

At first he sent me postcards on which he scribbled bits and pieces of new medical lore he'd picked up. He sent translations of songs and chants he'd collected, because he thought I'd like them, or just to fill in the empty spaces. He even sent me some love magic chants from a Kikuyu medicine man, and told me about a special tree they have called the Mote wa Ombani. Mothaiga wa rwenda, he said it was called. Love magic. Just to fill in the empty spaces. He didn't speak of Thaka, the Masai woman, in any of his postcards, but I knew he still followed her. Then the postcards came fewer, then stopped. I went about for a while feeling as if I'd made a mistake, that I shoulda stayed with him in Africa, but I'd thought and acted for myself. I don't know how much was fatigue and and how much jealousy. Or how much was simply wanting to be my own woman. Anyway, I kept saying to myself, if it was a mistake, then it was my own. And I acted like the woman I imagined I'd become, not like the woman that perhaps Norvelle or any other man imagined for me.

Still, there was times I thought of going back to Tanzania to hunt up that Masai woman, for I figured finding her would find where Norvelle was. If he kept writing articles about her, then she knew where he was. The journal he wrote articles for claimed not to know his whereabouts. So I went to Saratoga and bet on a horse, and to my own surprise, I won.

When I got back to Louisville, Grandmother Jaboti told me, He been here.

Who was here?

Norvelle.

Didn't you tell him where I was?

I tried to. But he jumped to his own conclusions. You know how mens is. Thought you was off with some lover. I give him your address, but he didn't want to catch you with some lover.

So, did he say where he was going?

Couldn't get no word outa him edgewise after he thought he had done got your story. He think he know you, don't he? He brought me some palm wine. I never had it before, but I likes the taste of it. And a can of zebra stew. Now you know I wouldn't eat stew made from no zebra. And dressed up looking just like a African. And braids in his hair. I wouldn'ta recognized him if I didn't already know him.

I said nothing. I climbed onto a wooden stool and started cleaning brushes.

Maybe he be back, Grandmother Jaboti said. If he know you as much as he think he do.

I just cleaned brushes.

THIRTEEN

And no, there weren't any lovers, not at first, not till Josef. The first time, though, I spent with someone else it was this old jockey. We just talked and talked. I didn't meet him at the racetrack, though, but on the porch of a little hotel I was staying at. We both had racing forms. I collected old racing forms, so the one I was reading was one I'd just purchased, an old Saratoga race. He made a joke of that old racing form, then I told him I was a collector of them. So first off we started talking about horses and racing, then we started talking about anything and everything. We spent the whole summer talking and talking and then when it was time for me to leave he got all strange-sounding, like it had been more than talk for him. Like he thought he'd been courting me or something. So I went to bed with him. It was stupid. I told him I didn't want it to happen again, though. Then it won't happen again, he said. Then I told him about Norvelle and the Masai woman, and showed him some of the articles that Norvelle had written about her. He said nothing. He just looked at me. I don't know what he was thinking. He had long eyelashes for a man and this made him look exotic, but he still looked very masculine, a little man, you know how jockeys are, but still very masculine, and them long eyelashes made me call him Bird of Paradise or simply Paradise. But his name's Nathaniel. From West Virginia. He'd grown a little pounchy around the middle, he said, but the rest of him was still as trim and solid as when he won his first race.

Bird of paradise. I used to think that they were mystical birds—mythical birds, I mean—but they're real, them birds of paradise. Norvelle had this book about this man who went on this trek to New Guinea to discover them, and it was full of their pictures. Dancing on the ground and in treetops in their courtship dance. Norvelle said that was the sort of book he'd like to write, a pure naturalist's book. The man who'd written this pure naturalist's book had also formed a foundation to protect these birds, these birds of paradise, because they got the most beautiful feathers, and so they's hunted, and it's becoming harder and harder to find them. I guess that's why a lot of people don't know that they's real birds. Norvelle, of course, sent in some bucks to this foundation to protect the birds of paradise. Then he sent in some bucks to another foundation to help protect the human species. He didn't think it was right protecting birds and not protecting humanity. But he'd wanted to be a naturalist before he'd decided to become a medical anthropologist. He was in college during the 1960s and becoming a naturalist didn't seem "relevant" and certainly he didn't know of any African Americans who were naturalists, not pure naturalists, so he decided to become a medical anthropologist instead. He could've been a naturalist in Africa, but in those days people wouldn't have considered it relevant, the young militant students who were his schoolmates and who once took over an administration building. He wasn't one of the spokesmen for the group or even a mediator; he went back and forth bringing them food and water and made sure that they had enough to sustain themselves while they kept the administration building. The situation he said was resolved peacefully, though, and they got certain of their demands: an African and African-American Studies Department, more "teachers of color"—not just African-American teachers, but other teachers of color, more students of color, and assorted other demands that seem trivial now. From Oklahoma City, Oklahoma, where all the African Americans he knew had always been self-reliant, he'd felt ambivalent about some of the demands himself. He'd wanted to be relevant, though, so he made sure they had enough food and water.

Pretty-eyed birds, them birds of paradise, though. And of course it was the males who did the courtship dance, and like most bird species, it was the males who were the brightly colored, attractive ones.

When I told Paradise about the birds of paradise and why I was calling him out of his name—Nathaniel Bower—to call him a better name, he told me about the bowerbird and its nest of shells and fruit and feathers. He'd been searching for the meaning of his name once, like we all sometimes do, and discovered the bowerbird. It built a nest of shells and fruit and feathers to attract female birds. But the female birds didn't even use the nest. They were attracted to the male birds that built the best nest. They'd allow themselves to be mated in that nest, but then they'd lay their eggs in their own nest somewhere else. But he liked Paradise better. Or that I called him that, though most people just called him Nat.

So you want to travel the road back to him, he said when I told him about Norvelle. We were sitting on the porch of the hotel where both of us was staying there in Saratoga. A hotel with a long porch.

The road back to him got twisted, I said.

Then untwist it. But I don't think his bower is better than mine.

I didn't answer. Paradise said he liked to see me at the racetrack. At the racetrack, I sprang to life, and I was fun. And when I talked of Keeneland or the Kentucky Derby or the Santa Anita Derby or the San Felipe Stakes, or some new Thoroughbred or even some new jockey, or who won what race by what length victory. . . . But when I talked about Norvelle I just sounded like a fool.

Let's have dinner, Paradise suggested.

Sure.

He seemed surprised.

Look, I don't want you to have any illusions about me, though, I said.

Old jockeys ain't got no illusions. Old black jockeys got fewer than none.

Pictures of celebrities decorated the walls, movie stars like Clark Gable and singers like Billy Eckstine. And there was the other Billie, the Holiday, in her gardenias. So young then. The woman who owned the place said it was from an advertisement of her for her first performance in New York. In the thirties, she'd taken a train from New Orleans, the woman who owned the place. She'd seen the movie starring Clark Gable and Carole Lombard—no, it was Jean Harlow. The one that had put Saratoga in the limelight, or on the map, and so she'd opened a restaurant specializing in southern cooking.

I always look forward to seeing you, he said after we'd ordered. He had a way of talking that surprised me. Sometimes it was what you call proper, I guess from being around West Virginia bluebloods—or did they have bluebloods in West Virginia or just Virginia? He was born, though, he said, in New York, in Harlem, but his family, unlike most families in those days, had migrated south to West Virginia. While other people were moving north to the promised land, they were traveling south. His father he said had an obsession with trees and wanted his children to grow up around trees and not concrete. When he'd thought of West Virginia, though, he'd always thought of the mountains, of the West Virginia coal mines. But his father worked on farms, mostly, in tobacco and racehorse country, the part of West Virginia near the Virginia border. He stayed small, and around horses it just had seemed natural that he'd become a jockey. But his father would talk and talk and talk and talk about trees and being able to ride for miles and see nothing but trees and green. He taught his children to appreciate the green. Not the green of the dollar bill, but the green of nature, of the countryside. But then he stopped talking, because he was making the South sound like a paradise, and it wasn't no paradise.

I bit into a spicy chicken wing. I thought he was going to tell me some southern nightmare that his father had encountered, some southern nightmare like in that Billie Holiday's song, but he didn't. So I ate my chicken and looked at Billy Eckstine, then at Nathaniel. Then at Billie Holiday.

She says that's the very first advertisement of Billie Holiday's very first concert, I said. I wonder how much a collector would pay for that. She didn't have it framed or anything. I'm the one told her to frame it. I wonder if Billie Holiday ever come to Saratoga to bet on the horses. Did you see that movie *Lady Sings the Blues*?

Yeah.

I seen it two or three times. Read the book too. It's based on her autobiography. The book moves back and forth in time, though, more than the movie. You think you're in one time and the next chapter you're in another. Joan says it's kinda like jazz. That that's what she's trying to do in that autobiography, kinda suggest the improvisations of jazz. Joan says she sing like her voice is a horn. You know, try to do with her voice the same thing them horn players do. Like what Satchmo would try to do with his horn, she would try to do with her voice. That's why her voice ain't like no other woman voice. On account of that horn. I don't know if she ever been to Saratoga, though.

Seem like once I was here, somebody said "the lady" here. And there only one lady so I know who they talking about. I didn't see her myself, though, but somebody said "the lady" here and that the only lady I know anybody to be talking about. I remember when there were black jockeys up and down, though, he said. Now I'm 'bout the only old spook around. Oh, plenty of us come up here to bet on the horses, but ain't none of us riding them. I heard a man to say that if we weren't riding 'em and owning 'em we shouldn't bet on 'em. But you know we'll bet on 'em anyhow, 'cause that's how we are. I don't ride the horses anymore, though. I don't bet on 'em much myself. Sometimes I escort folks to the track, show them around the city.

I tried to imagine him as a young jockey, but I couldn't. When he retired he stayed in Saratoga, I guess for the green. There was still some green here. I looked at Billy Eckstine again, and then at Billie Holiday, and then at Paradise. I thought of that story by Carson McCullers about the jockey. I wondered if anybody had written any tales about jockeys like him.

The waitress set a shot of whiskey on the table for him and a sloe gin fizz for me.

Were you ever married? I asked.

Naw. In those days I wasn't taking any chances with a woman. I was too intent on being the best jockey around, you know. I had a few girls. You attract girls. No one like you.

I said nothing. I grabbed an ashtray from another table and lit a cigarette.

Is this your first time in the States? someone at a table behind us asked. Yes. I was in San Francisco first. I thought all Americans were like that, without values. Oh yeah? Is that Jean Harlow? Jean Harlow or Carole Lombard one. Carole Lombard? I wouldn't be knowing that one. Clark Gable married her. Oh, that one. I'd be knowing that one for certain.

Bird of Paradise gave me a large, warm smile. I tried to picture him in the winner's circle.

You still wear his ring, he noticed.

Yeah.

I did have a woman I almost married, once. I'd just had me a good season, my best season in the world and I was making a whole lotta bread, you know, and it turned out to be the bread and not me the girl was after. She'd take me for sure as long as I was dressed like a king.

Statuettes of saints crowded the shelves in my mother's and grandmother's beauty shop. They were my mother's saints because my grandmother thought it was merely entertaining to have them. No one in the family was Catholic. But a customer and a Catholic, pleased with a new hairdo, had given them to my mother and she'd kept them. Though a Southern Baptist, she was convinced they were holy. There was a little Peruvian saint who was our complexion, but the other saints were white. At least the one who'd imagined them had painted them white. Every time they got dusty, she'd diligently take them down and clean and polish them. Grandmother called them whatnots.

My mother attended church regularly and believed in the Bible passage which said: Whatever you do to the least of my brethren, you do to me. Something like that. She interpreted it to mean that you should treat everybody as if they were Christ. Whenever you're about to do something mean or disrespectful to someone imagine they're Christ, she'd say, and then decide how to treat them. That was superior, she felt, even to the Golden Rule. So, among some, she got the reputation for being a good and wise woman. Among others, she was considered a fool and a pushover. Needy people crowded to her door. So, as a child, I grew up thinking the whole world was needy, except for blue-haired and blue-veined Mrs. Smoot, who somehow kept above need. When I discovered there were other kinds of people in the world, people who weren't needy, though, I found them more interesting because less familiar.

When I got a chance to leave Louisville, even to go to beauty school in Cincinnati, I took it. But I had aspirations beyond beauty school. I audited a few courses at the University of Cincinnati. I remember once I went to a lecture on Nietzsche. At the reception I was standing at a table eating cheese and one of the girls in one of the classes I was auditing spotted me and came over.

I didn't know you were interested in Nietzsche, she said. She said something about our reading assignment, Camus' *The Rebel*. She didn't think Camus' book was genuine philosophy—literature but not philosophy.

But you'll probably ace it, she said.

I explained that I was just auditing the course, that I wasn't a regular student but studying cosmetology at the local beauty school. She laughed, picked up a piece of cheese and an oyster cracker and moved toward others, glancing back at me, whispering, laughing. "She's a beautician," I thought I heard her say. "I thought she was a philosophy major." I stopped auditing the university courses and concentrated on beauty, though I wasn't too sure what beauty was.

When I returned home one summer vacation my mother was entertaining some visiting African Baptists. Sometimes she rented rooms above the beauty shop and several of them were staying in those rented room, for free, because she wouldn't take money from visiting African Baptists. I knew there were Catholics in Africa, because there were Catholics everywhere, but I didn't know that Africa had any Baptists. Anyway, my future husband was escorting them and acting as their guide and interpreter. But since they spoke impeccable English themselves, his duties were mainly to interpret for them our curious idioms, colloquialisms and peculiar southern turns of phrase. They'd just been on a trip to Mammoth Cave, Kentucky, and it was all their talk—not of religious things. They kept talking about the transparent fish that swim in the underground streams at Mammoth Cave, what the tour guide had called spirit fish.

Norvelle and I watched each other before we even said a word. But it was only when the group was about ready to leave—still talking of the cave fish—that Norvelle spoke to me.

I enjoyed our stay very much, he said, as we stood together in the supply room where rows and rows of cosmetics and hair care products were stored. He'd seen me come back there and followed.

I'm sorry I didn't really get a chance to talk to you.

Well, I'm shy as the devil too, I said.

I lifted a jar of Ultra Sheen hair dressing. He smiled, reached into his pocket and took out a pad.

I'm an anthropologist, he explained. It's my first year at Bloomington, I mean the university there. I teach during the year, but in the summer I escort various African groups.

Mom says you know a lot of African languages.

A few. He kept both eyes on me, but I kept peering from him to the jar of Ultra Sheen. Well, I've always been good with languages. I just seem to pick them up, especially African languages. I just seem to pick them up. Anyway, here's my address, if you're ever in Bloomington.

You a real professor? I asked, looking at the card.

Of course I'm real.

You don't act like no professor.

He laughed. How's a professor s'posed to act?

Not like you.

I prefer fieldwork to the classroom, though, he said. I've never much liked the classroom actually. So I'm in blue jeans most of the time. I collect folklore, medical lore from different African tribes, to help to preserve it. You know, I'm what they call a medical anthropologist. But I'm boring you. Well, if you're ever in Bloomington. . . .

One rainy day after I'd finished beauty school and had worked for a couple of months in the family business as a licensed beautician, I appeared on the porch of a little stucco house in Bloomington. When he opened the door, I said, Surprise.

When I got inside he hugged me. I kept looking around. There was nothing but books and papers piled to the ceiling and photographs and sketches of Africa and Africans and masks and sculptures and drawings. I recognized none of them then, of course, except that they were African. Only later under his tutelage could I distinguish an Igbo mask from a Bambara, an Ife sculpture from one from Benin. And I thought the painted calabashes were also sculptures. And I had no idea who Skunder Boghasian was, but I thought the name sounded Scandinavian, not African. Nor had I heard of Lamidi Fakeye or Yemi Bisiri. I didn't know a Ashanti sculpture from an Anyi.

What are you looking for? he asked.

Another woman. Maybe you married or something. Maybe you got yourself a wife I ain't know about. I just remembered, you might be married or something.

Naw, I'm not married. He was wearing blue jeans and a light green sweater over a polo shirt. Except for the blue jeans, he looked kinda like a professor.

Ain't you surprised I'm here? I asked.

I'm happy.

I bet you angry I didn't write and tell you I was coming.

No, I'm just glad you're here.

I wasn't sure I'd show up. Didn't want to tell you I was coming and then not show up. You know, chicken out, or something. And then I wasn't sure if you really wanted me to look you up if I ever came to Bloomington. You know, how some people tell you that, just to be polite. *Mi casa es su casa*. But they don't actually mean it. Then I was thinking you couldn't really be interested in me, because if you're a real college professor then you'd want yourself a professional-type woman.

I don't say what I don't mean, he said. Then he kissed my jaw, then my mouth, then he took off my coat. And I ain't always been a professional-type man myself.

CHAPTER FIFTEEN

I was a turtle before I became a human being, said my grandmother. She was taking a new order of beauty products out of the boxes and restocking the shelves. The beauty products were from a wholesaler in New York. She thought New York beauty products were superior to local and regional products, even when the beauty products were manufactured by the same company and only distributed by a local or regional company. Perhaps she believed that the beauty products which they allowed to be distributed by local or regional companies had inferior ingredients. She didn't seem to notice the contradiction: that if those products allowed to be distributed by local or regional companies contained inferior ingredients, then wouldn't they sell her products with inferior ingredients? She said, though, that she could get a discount when she ordered the products in bulk from New York, whereas she didn't get a discount when ordering them from a local distributor. She even had the ambition of manufacturing her own beauty products, but said she would only manufacture them if she could make a better beauty product than those already on the market. And the beauty products that she herself manufactured would all contain superior ingredients no matter to what region they were marketed. Her beauty products marketed out West would have the same superior ingredients as those marketed to the Northeast or the South. She was however negotiating with the wholesaler in New York so that Cornella and Jaboti's Beauty Shop, Inc., could become a local distributor of their products. But wouldn't they sell her inferior products? Again, she didn't seem to notice the contradiction. Cornella and Jaboti, though, would advertise their New York connection, which would make them the superior beauty shop. In fact, they would advertise their international connections, for she was always sending to different parts of the world, wherever there were colored people, for samples of their beauty products. She was certain, though, that other nations wouldn't ship beauty products with inferior ingredients to America.

Then I saw this handsomest young man and took a liking to him, she said, as she put the superior beauty products on the shelves. Do you want to know how far I followed him? She chuckled. I followed him until I turned into a human being. Is that far enough for you?

Mother, rinsing brushes in the sink, said nothing, like she always did when Grandmama told her turtle stories. As soon as Grandmother turned her story into fantasy, Mother always brought it back to reality again.

She was a Turtle Woman in a carnival, explained my mother. She played the Turtle Woman. You know how them carnivals got them the Bearded Lady. Well, they's got Turtle Women and Crocodile Women and every type of freakish womanhood. They had her in one of them carnival tents and people paid their money to come and see the Turtle Woman. In those days, I think it only cost them a nickel or a dime to see the Turtle Woman or them other freakish women. Mighta just cost them a penny to see those freakish women, but that was considered good money in those days. They put a nacre shell on her back. A fake shell to pretend like she was part turtle and part woman. I don't even know if they paid her good money to be their Turtle Woman, but I guess they paid her better money than they were paying domestics in those days, but not as good money as they paid them factory workers, you know. You go up North and get you a job in one of them factories, that's good money, or even around here working in them tobacco factories after the war, that's better money, you know, than being a domestic. Or you could be a schoolteacher, but a schoolteacher ain't no kinda independence, and in those days, you know, all the schools were segregated, but that still ain't no kinda independence, and even the colored schools had to be obliged to the white superintendents, you know. The colored

schools could have their own principals, but only the white men could
be the superintendents, and not even white women in them days, just the
white men. I don't even think they have white women superintendents
these days. They can be principals in the schools, but not superintendents. Daddy saw her and fell in love. He knew the shell wasn't real, and
that's the truth, but he kept coming to that carnival till she up and left
the carnival and followed him. She said that he were the first man enamored of her among all the men that would pay their good money to see
the Turtle Woman, and that them other men just thought of her as
freakish, as one of them freakish women, whether or not they believed
in the reality of that turtle's shell. Now that's the truth. That the truth.
You can tell all the turtle stories you want to tell, but that's the truth. She
say Daddy say that a fake turtle shell don't make her a fake woman, and
that he more interested in the woman than the fact that she played a fake
Turtle Woman in that carnival. She say that he could see the genuine
woman behind that fake turtle shell. She say he say that she a more genuine woman than any woman he know, a category which he say ain't just
limited to colored women, which some mens do. You know, how some
mens do. They'll compare you to other colored women, but not to
Womanhood Itself, and prefers every other man's woman to they own.
You know, like that television show we were watching, and they were
asking them men about they women, and all the other men complimented they women on their beauty, but when they asked the colored
men didn't none of them say nothing about beauty, they complimented
they women on everything but beauty, exceptin' those that had them the
other men's woman, or them of us that most resembles the other men's
woman. Ain't that right? Well, I noticed what them colored men said.
She got them hunched shoulders, though, from wearing that fake turtle
shell. That the truth.

I was five and sitting on the counter. When Grandmother finished
putting them new beauty products on the shelves, she braided my hair.
In the long mirror, I could see her. I could see her hunched shoulders that
looked as if they had really gotten hunched like that from wearing a fake
turtle shell. I couldn't imagine her, though, as fitting the description of

"freakish women," like the Bearded Lady, although others might've seen those hunched shoulders as a sign of freakishness. She smiled like she knew that her tale was the true one, or that a tale could be true and not be a true tale—that perhaps her Turtle Woman stories were truer than any carnival tale. I didn't say whose tale I believed, though. I only squirmed as she twisted my hair into braids.

And spose I wasn't really a real Turtle Woman? she asked. Spose I wasn't? Spose I'm just a rogue in disguise. They had some real ones, though. Had a fake Bearded Lady but they had them a real Unicorn Woman, I know that for the truth, a woman with a real horn just like a unicorn, I mean a real horn just like a unicorn's and not a fake one, though some people swore it was a goat's horn that they just glued on, and a colored woman too, I mean a real colored woman, and that's the truth. A lot of people when they would see that sign advertising the Unicorn Woman, they'd think she a white woman, you know, 'cause all the unicorns in the storybooks is white, 'cause that's supposed to be a sign of purity, you know, and even the colored people that come to see the Unicorn Woman, they's as surprised as the white people that she ain't a white Unicorn Woman, 'cause even colored people thinks that white's a sign of purity, and she is a genuine Unicorn Woman, but a colored one. 'Cause ain't none of them seen no colored unicorn in none of them mythology books or storybooks neither, so colored people usselves thinks they's only white unicorns. Of course I heard someone say that even if she a real Unicorn Woman, she still a fake one, just by virtue of being colored. But I know that horn real and I know she a real Unicorn woman. And her horn as real as this braid. She lifted a braid in the air and waved it. She pulled it out like a horn, she did a little dance, and shook the braid again. At least I think that horn was real. I can't testify to the reality of that horn, but I believe it to be real. I mean, I know that horn to be real although I can't testify to the reality of it being a real horn. I mean, there wasn't nothing that Unicorn Woman said or did to make me disbelieve the reality of that horn.

Hush, said Mother, running water in the sink. She'll grow up and won't be able to tell truth from truth. You can't know the reality of that unicorn horn and not know it's reality at the same time. That ain't logical in nobody's book of logic. It ain't inductive reasoning and it ain't deductive reasoning. I don't know what kinda fallacy that is, but it sounds like the fallacy of contrary propositions. It ain't classical logic.

I don't know whether it a contrary fallacy or a logical proposition, say Grandmother Jaboti. It might not be classical logic, but it's Jaboti's logic. Ain't it, Possum?

Well, she'll grow up and won't be able to tell truth from truth. And look like she don't know how to tell truth from truth even now.

I don't say nothing, 'cause I don't know nothing about that logic. I know she ain't meant truth from truth, though, but she didn't correct herself and Grandmother didn't correct her either. And maybe she did mean truth from truth? And suppose she mean truth from truth? Then how that any different from Jaboti's logic. But truth from truth can't be the fallacy of contrary propositions, can it? Ain't truth and truth the same thing? What the opposite of the fallacy of contrary propositions? The fallacy of equivalent propositions?

Tell me some more about the Unicorn Woman, I said, 'cause I ain't know nothing about that logic. Did she follow a man anywhere to turn her human? And how come a woman got to follow a man to turn human? I start to ask, How come a woman can't follow her ownself to turn human? I ain't know nothing about that logic, but I know enough to know that that don't sound logical, and that maybe they's got a fallacy of impossibilities. Later, when I'd be reading through one of them books of Joan's, it would say something about logical truth, and seem to distinguish logical truth from true truth, that is that something could be logically true, that is, fulfill all the requirements of classical logic, you know, them different syllogisms and still not be truly true. I ain't sure that's what that book on logic mean, though.

Now she's already human as far as I know, say Grandmother Jaboti. Just having a horn don't mean you ain't human. The unicorn is more mythical, though, than the turtle, which is more a ordinary type and common animal, so she were more attractive to the people, especially the mens, white and colored, and especially them idealistic and romantic-type men that likes to idealize and romanticize women, you know, like Mrs. Smoot, you know, the pharmacist's wife was saying about her husband, or that's just her conceit about herself or her conceit about him, than the Turtle Woman or them other confabulatory women that they had at that carnival, you know, 'cause the turtle is ordinary and a common animal, and people even makes soup out of turtle. I don't believe anyone would make soup out of a unicorn, even if it weren't a mythical beast. They might try to corrupt its purity, like in that movie we seen, you know, but ain't even a fool would try to make soup out of a unicorn. I wouldn't eat turtle soup myself, though. Or turtle pies neither. Although people who considers theyselves good people eats turtle soup and turtle pies too. But you don't make soup or pies outa unicorns. The Unicorn Woman. . . . more men would go to that Unicorn Woman's tent than to the Bearded Lady or the Turtle Woman, and there's even them that considered her the ideal of womanhood, like I said. And she told me that she received a note from one of them romantic gentlemen that came to see her and that kept following her from carnival to carnival and the note say that he think she the ideal of womanhood, and there ain't many colored women that they considered the ideal of womanhood in them days, just like Cornella said. Except the woman name Horne, that Lena Horne. They would consider her a beautiful woman by anybody's standards, I mean anybody that's got standards of what's beauty, and don't mean us all gots to look like other men's woman. Now ain't none of the mens told me that I'm the ideal of womanhood, though, or even that I'm especially beautiful. Being a beautician don't means you's got to be beautiful yourself, it just means you knows how to beautify. Now, the mens, though, they's told me I'm a genuine woman, that is since I've been transformed into a genuine human woman and ain't a turtle, genuine or ain't, but it takes a true mythical woman to be the ideal of true womanhood, colored or ain't. Why, even the proprietor of that first carnival she was at become obsessed with her, until he found him a woman that he thought the more ideal of womanhood than herself. Then he sold the Unicorn Woman to another carnival, 'cause he didn't want them competing ideals of womanhood.

Least I think that's why he sold her to another carnival. The Unicorn Woman, I mean. . . . He didn't sell me to no other carnival, on account of I ain't no everyman's ideal of womanhood, except my man's, but the Unicorn Woman. . . .

Unicorn Woman my hairbrush, said Mother. Unicorn Woman my straightening comb. Ideal of womanhood? Woman's gotta be her own ideal of womanhood. Can't depend on a man for it.

Grandmother did the little dance, and shook my braid in the air, and told me again the tale of the Unicorn Woman. There's plenty of mens crazy about her, like I said, crazy in love or in infatuation and even follow her from carnival to carnival, her being a mythical-type ideal woman, but she ain't follow none of them. And she is still a carnival woman, except she ain't with the same carnival, she's got her own troupe of confabulatory-type people. She's a free woman now, free and independent, and can't nobody sell her, or rather sell her contract, when they decide that another confabulatory woman is their new ideal of womanhood. Now she got her own carnival troupe. I know a few fools myself that usedta follow her from one carnival to another, even since the war years, and is still following her from carnival to carnival, though now it's her own carnival, 'cause some mens is like that, but she didn't follow none of them men. If it's possible for a woman to follow her own-self, it's her. Free and independent. And's still gots mens crazy about her. Course to be crazy about a woman don't mean you's in love. It can just mean you's in infatuation, like I said. I think she were in love herself with a man they advertised as the tallest man in the world. But they's always advertising men as the tallest man in the world, and there's always another tallest man. But a Bearded Lady's a Bearded Lady anywhere. And to my knowledge there's only one authentic Unicorn Woman. And got her own carnival now. If I could transform myself back into a turtle, I could join it. But once you's a human being, you hunger for being human. Them that don't hunger for being superior to humanity.

SIXTEEN

The groom held the reins of the mare, a blackish-brown beauty, graceful, delicate. A horse like that could only be a Thoroughbred. I wondered what sort of horse I'd be. I mean if people were classified like horses. Well, I guess some people do classify people like horses. When they talk about such things as breeding. Only certain kinds of people are said to have breeding. Usually rich. Usually not nonwhite. Still I often found it curious that in horses Thoroughbreds were mostly nonwhite. You didn't see white Thoroughbreds. In the movies, sometimes the good people rode the white horses, or the wannabe good people rode them. But in the real world, the world outside horse racing, the people with breeding were mostly not nonwhite. Except in Africa itself. But somebody said that the names they have for African people in the New World are actually names of different breeds of horses or donkeys. Mulatto, for example. Some type of mule. Or like that woman I heard lecture. Joan videotaped her and made me listen to her lecture. The University of Creation Spirituality. Her name? I just remember Joan said from the University of Creation Spirituality. And she said the word ass. Said she preferred the word ass to the word donkey, because ass was a good American word, a good Anglo-Saxon word. Did she say Anglo-Saxon or just American? And fool. Her other favorite word. And Joan said those were her own two favorite words. Except that woman said, or seemed to say, that the only acceptable fool was a fool for the Lord. I don't know if Joan considers any fool an acceptable fool. Something about native religions. Part Native American, but a Catholic nun. Mary Jose? Joan had to explain to me some of her vocabulary. "Your vocabulary's gotten better since you met me, you know," she says. Except ass and fool. I don't think there's anyone who knows the English language who don't know the meaning of ass and fool. Anyway, Josef and I stood behind the black fence scrutinizing her.

She looks like a winner, I said. I leaned across the fence. She gave me a fierce look, as if she were not yet broken in, but I knew she was. I'd seen her maiden race, and I had the autograph of the jockey who rode her.

She's top-class, said Josef. People at the Fasig-Tipton wanted me to sell her, but I won't. Said one of their clients saw her and wanted to buy her. For breeding purposes, though, not to run any races. At least I think they said for breeding purposes; the client who wanted to buy her was kinda ambiguous. She's a fine specimen. She's top-class. You don't sell a top-class horse.

The groom holding the reins glanced at me and Josef. When Josef didn't give the horse more praise, he praised her himself. Her maiden race she did six furloughs in one and ten. Now you know this is a good horse. Ain't nothing ambiguous about a good horse. Top-class like Mr. Fremd say. And you don't sell a horse like this just for breeding purposes or even ambiguous purposes. They think 'cause she's a filly she ain't meant to run races. They just wants her for breeding purposes or other ambiguous purposes. This horse is top-class, like Mr. Fremd say. Be a major challenger in the Derby is what I think. Did brilliant at Aqueduct and Seminole. Impressive in the Santa Anita. Anybody that anybody in the racing business say this a good horse. Ain't nothing ambiguous about a good horse. A good horse is a good horse. All the sportswriters say that. I mean, all the sportswriters say this a good horse. I ain't read a sportswriter that ain't say this a good horse. I read one sportswriter, though, to lie and say we had to put them green goggles on her to keep her from being skittish on the track, but this ain't a skittish horse. We ain't never had to put no green goggles on this horse. He was talking about some other horse and lied and said it was this one. I don't trust none of them media people. There was some media people going around talking to the grooms and the exercise boys, 'cause they wanted to get a view of horse racing that ain't just the muckamuck's view, the view of the racehorse owners and the trainers and the star jockeys, you know, the muckamuck's view, so they come to the grooms and the exercise boys to get our opinion of the horse racing industry, to hear the opinion of the ordinary workingman, and I wouldn't talk to them, 'cause I don't trust them media people. They ain't truthful, and especially now like the man say that they accepts hearsay and innuendo and gossip as the truth, they ain't to be trusted, them media people. I heard one of us poets on television—maybe you seen her on television talking about the arts? The same poet that reads to the people to say that facts about a people ain't always the same thing as the truth about them, so I guess you can say the same thing about horses. But when they say this a good horse, they's telling the truth. Ran a big race in the Santa Anita, ain't she, Mr. Fremd? A super race. And that was a gummy track. That was a muddy track. A good horse on a gummy track is a good horse anywhere. She got her early speed like it were her Independence Day and did near-record time. Ain't she, Mr. Fremd? That's when some of them Fasig-Tipton people seen her and wanted to buy her, or one of their clients wanted to buy her. Why, if I weren't an ordinary workingman and could afford a good horse like this, I'd buy her. And I wouldn't buy her for ambiguous purposes. But you don't sell a horse like this just for breeding purposes. This ain't just a top-class horse, this is a classy horse.

She looks like a winner, I said.

She's top-class, said Josef. Bred right here.

Well, she looks like a winner.

She is a winner, said the groom. He held out a sugar cube or some bit of sweet for the horse. A good horse on a gummy track is a good horse anywhere. And when it comes to a stretching duel, she's the best. When it's a fast track, the mature horses, though, have got more confidence than this one. She ain't a nervous filly, she just needs more confidence in herself when it's a fast track and she's amongst the mature horses. But when it comes to a stretching duel, she's the best. I ain't never put no green goggles on this filly. This filly knows who she is and knows who she wants to be. That's how you train a horse. If I was a trainer myself and ain't just a groom, that's how I'd train my horses. I wouldn't train them how I want 'em to be, I'd find out what they want to be, and that's how I'd train 'em. Course you gotta have a top-class horse for that. You gotta have a classy horse for that. Some horses the only way you can train 'em is how you want 'em to be. They make good horses, but the best horses is them that knows what they want to be. Then all you gotta do is find out what they wanna be and that's how you train 'em.

The Thoroughbred flicked her tail, turned a huge brown eye towards me. It wasn't a fierce eye now. It was more curious than fierce. She whinnied. I wondered if any of them horses ever thought of training and taming people.

I usually like them with more exotic background, though, I said.

This is exotic to me, said Josef, waving his hands at the rolling green of his four-hundred-acre farm. America is exotic to me. So you think she'll win?

Win easily, I said. She'll start good and slow, though, move gradually, then she'll rally. As long as the pressure's good.

Yeah, that's when she behaves her best, said the groom. Ain't nothing nervous about this filly. The media man that said that is a liar. And the sportswriting women is as good prevaricators as the men. Them sportswriting women thinks if they's as good prevaricators as the men then that's equality. Why, when Mr. Fremd bought this farm, there was someone come out here talking about urban development. Now, they weren't talking urban development until Mr. Fremd bought this farm. 'Cause they didn't want a man like Mr. Fremd to own a farm like this, so they started talking urban development. They's good prevaricators, ain't they, Mr. Fremd?

A light urging, I said.

A little light urging, not too much, said the groom.

The jockey should ride with her, let her pull, I said.

Yeah, the jockey should let her lead. Let her lead, said the groom. 'Cause she knows who she is and who she wants to be. You know your horses.

You sound like you know her, said Josef.

For sure. She's the best. I could be a sportswriting man myself, and

I know enough about horses not to prevaricate. I usedta wanna be a jockey myself, though, but then I started getting too tall for a jockey, you know, so I become a groom. But this filly, she's the best.

And those were the days when you never really expected a filly to win.

And that's exactly what the groom said. There's them that don't expect a filly to win, but I'll bet on a filly any day.

On the shelves are books for horsemen: *The Illustrated Veterinary Encyclopedia, Breeding Management and Foal Development, Treatments and Medications, Feeding to Win, Equine Genetics and Selection Procedures*. I read somewhere once that Lexington had been a breeder's town in slavery days. Lexington at Cheapside had been the principal marketplace: horses, cows, Negroes. *Negro Genetics and Selection Procedures*. I wondered if they'd had such books. *The Illustrated Negro Encyclopedia, Breeding Management* and *Pickaninny Development*. I wondered whether people who used to breed slaves, when slavery was abolished, started breeding horses, transferred their knowledge of breeding slaves to breeding horses. I thumbed through the volume on *Breeding Management* while waiting for Josef to come back from the yard. The book was a gift to Josef. It said To Josef with Love, from Stellina. Mrs. Fremd? Or another Stellina?

Here you are, he said coming in, holding two glasses of white wine. He wore a blue-and-white-striped silk robe and a white cloth wrapped around his head. He looked like a Moroccan nobleman. Maybe he'd got that robe when he was in Alexandria, which he said ain't in Morocco, but Egypt. Morocco a land without rivers, but that Egypt got the Nile. Ain't that Nile supposed to be the oldest river in the world? The river of civilization. He was wearing sandals. The straps on them were made of a rope-looking fiber, probably sisal.

I like her, I said, meaning the horse.

He handed me one of the glasses. Cheers, he said. And then he said the same thing in German. I said *kampai*, a Japanese word I'd learned from Joan. I tried to think of a drinking song I'd once heard. Seem like that drinking song had something about rivers in it.

He stood sipping his. I pushed my legs up in the leather chair and sat on my feet. The farmhouse was colonial, almost a mansion, built in the 1850s with high ceilings and long windows. The attic was shaped like a castle turret. I think they're turrets, though they look sorta like dunce caps. The base of them is stovepipe-shaped and then at the top they's what looks like a dunce cap. And he got one of his security people sitting inside that dunce cap. And I think Nicholas' room somewhere up in that turret. It was like the builder of the farmhouse was trying to suggest something of the Old World in the New, and since there weren't true castles in America, to claim something of royalty. This supposed to be a democracy, somebody said, but throughout its history you still have people wishing they's kings, or wishing for kings and other royalty, and if they ain't trying to transform theyselves into kings and other royalty, then they's trying to transform other people into kings and other royalty. That's why they always likes to refer to other Americans as the king and other names of royalty. The real kings in Europe and America's kings fiction. They's even got a few true castles in America, because they's always them that think that a nation ain't a true civilized nation unless it's got castles. Seem like one of them early American writers said something about that, that America weren't a cultured and civilized nation 'cause it didn't have no castles in it. But they's always looking at the people's architecture to decide whether they's civilized or not. If they architecture look different from they own architecture, or if they civilization ain't in they architecture, then they ain't civilized. This mansion ain't a true castle, it just got a little turret on it, like it a wannabe castle. There are former slave quarters, but they'd been converted into bunkhouses where some of the hired men stayed. His top security people, though, like Nicholas and the former Vietnamese soldier who'd fought in the tunnels of Cu Chi, had rooms in the farmhouse. I stared out the window at a man sitting in a walnut tree. I think he one of the former CIA people, or one of them men claim to be former CIA or other government security people. He wearing braids, though, and I don't think when he worked for the CIA they would have allowed him to wear braids unless they'd wanted him to infiltrate some group of Rastafarians in Jamaica or something, but I don't believe the U.S. considers them Rastafarians a threat to their national security, so he must've started wearing braids after he left the CIA and started working for Josef. Maybe even that groom might be a security person disguised as a groom. I thought of a book of Joan's called *The Tree of Culture*. It had a Rastafarian-looking man sitting in a tree like that. The first chapter was about the pygmies of the Ituri Forest. Different people sat in trees indigenous to their cultures. An African sat in a baobab tree. Them Japanese sat in them banyan trees. I think they's banyan trees. Then them Japanese have got them miniature trees; they cultivate them miniature trees. I remember when Joan was in Japan, the Japanese announcer had introduced her as a "musical giant" from America. She'd mumbled before going onstage, "Musical pygmy." I didn't understand Japanese, so I didn't know he'd introduced her as a musical giant, but when I'd asked her why she'd mumbled "musical pygmy," she explained that it was because he'd referred to her as a musical giant, and she herself didn't think she was worthy of that title. "At least in America I'm a musical pygmy," she'd said. "But I heard someone say even Americans like to make people superstars before they're deserving of that title." Josef, beside me, held his glass in one hand and stroked my shoulder with another.

Kampai, I said again.

I like you, he said.

There's a man in the tree, I said. How come you got so many security people?

Josef looked toward the window. When people wanna play dirty tricks on you, you gotta be a prudent man. Do you want me to close the curtains? he asked.

Unless you want him to take pictures, I said.

I noticed he was sounding more like me, and I was sounding more like him.

At the corner of the stable, I watched the young groom rub Absorbine Hooflex on the hooves of a yearling. The young man sniffed some as he worked. A lean young man with the physique of a young Kenyan I'd once seen win the marathon.

Is that a good high? I joked.

He handed the bottle over to me, I sniffed some, felt my forehead ready for takeoff, passed it back. Too strong for me, I said. What does it do for the horse?

It's supposed to keep the hooves flexible. You know your horses on a racetrack, but you don't know your horses, do you? Horses are intelligent. They know you if you don't know them.

I watched him clean and brush the yearling, using a tiny vacuum cleaner to clean the hair on the flanks and remove dirt from the hooves. I watched him brush the horse's head and mane, apply medication to the bottom of one of the hooves. He had a handsome, clean, dark oval face, a tiny mustache and intelligent but unsettled eyes.

I think she's got a little infection on the hoof here, he said. She had a splinter fracture in the cannon, but that's all healed.

Will it mean a problem? I asked. I mean the infection.

Should clear up in a day or two. Get her ready for her first set of shoes, ain't that right, darling?

He rubbed her silken mane. You want to get out there and graze, don't you girl? You know I can't let you out there till tonight. Sun's too hot now. Bleach your hair. You don't want the sun to bleach your hair, now do you girl? You won't be as pretty with your hair all bleached out. He patted her. She's a good girl.

Someone came up behind me. Thinking it was Josef and without turning around, I grabbed at his hands and caressed them. Then I turned to stare up into Nicholas' face. I felt like a fool.

Why didn't you tell me it was you? I asked.

You already had hold of me, he said.

I moved away from him and walked back to the house.

She's a good girl, I heard the groom say again. You can't fool a horse. A good horse knows you better than you know yourself.

Nicholas said something that I couldn't hear. I don't know whether he was talking about the horse, though, or me.

SEVENTEEN

And now Ladies and Gentlemen, our star, the fabulous Joan Savage, or as she prefers to be called, Savage Joan the Darling Bitch! Ain't that a contradiction in terms? A Savage Darling? A Darling Bitch? I like a good bitch, even a darling bitch, who allows you to call her a bitch, though, 'cause some bitches even the nicest darling bitches, when you calls 'em bitches, even the bitches that they are, even the bitches that they know they are, even wonderful bitches, like this wonderful bitch, or my wife who's a sometimes bitch, 'cause she ain't a bitch with everybody, bitches at you for calling 'em a bitch, and you better not call certain bitches bitches, even the bitches that they are, even bitches who are bitches and knows that they's bitches, even knows that they's wonderful bitches, even bitches as wonderful as this wonderful bitch, or my wife, who's sometimes a wonderful bitch herself, and even knows she's a wonderful bitch and knows how to bitch wonderfully, 'cause if you call certain bitches a bitch even when they call themselves a bitch like my sometimes bitch of a wife sometimes calls herself a bitch even if you calls 'em a wonderful bitch even a nice bitch then you learn the true meaning of bitch. This routine comes to you with apologies to you know who, who should never apologize for calling a mean bitch a mean bitch even when he calls the wrong mean bitch even a nice mean bitch a mean bitch. I heard somebody refer to comedians like us as comedians to the niggerphobics, but as a young comedian to the niggerphobic myself, with apologies to the author of *Negrophobia*, I could tell you the truth about some of the meanest bitches, and I ain't just talking about bitches of color neither, 'cause everybody likes to call bitches of color bitches but that ain't every bitch, except you know who, who should never apologize for calling a mean bitch a mean bitch even when he calls the wrong mean bitch even a nice mean bitch a mean bitch. . . . Anybody who watches the politically incorrect Comedy Channel knows who I'm talking about, but you better not call 'em a bitch, even every bitch. . . . My wife ain't no mean bitch, though, she's a sweet bitch, I mean a nice bitch, when she's a bitch sometimes, but suppose every woman's a bitch, suppose every bitch's a bitch, the mean bitches and the sweet bitches, the nice bitches, the wonderful bitches, the darling bitches, and the good bitches, if bitch was as common as woman or lady or girl, then you'd have *A Portrait of a Bitch, Maggie: A Bitch of the Streets, Fanfare for a Common Bitch*—there's a fanfare for a common bitch the same as a fanfare for a common bastard—I better say bastard or some of you bitches'll, especially my wife, start bitching at me for not being a egalitarian, *Don't Let Cowbitches Fool Ya*, you gotta be literate to understand my allusions, *Fanfare for a Common Bitch* is a piece of music, though, but I usedta be a professor of English before I became a comedian, but being a professor of English was a bitch, so I became a comedian, 'cause as a comedian I get to call a bitch a bitch, but suppose every noun was a bitch, then you'd have *A Bitch of a Bitch*, suppose every verb and verbal was a bitch, then you'd have *The Bitch of a Bitching Bitch*, but *Bitch and Bitchibility*. . . . and ain't none of y'all better call my little daughter no bitch.

Joan marched onstage to applause. The announcer, a local entertainer-comedian, a round-faced dark-complexioned man, who called himself Mr. Show Biz Hisself Though Not the King of the Comedians to the Niggerphobics with Apologies to the Author of *Negrophobia*, kissed her hand, referred to her as "our darling bitch" again, made a few gallant flourishes like the knights of old, or like the court jesters, and marched offstage. She was dressed in golden leotards with her hair in golden strings. She was wearing a sweatshirt that said SAVAGE JOAN THE BITCH DARLING rather than Darling Bitch as the announcer had said. She was wearing deep red lipstick and her cheeks were the color of Delicious apples. She was grinning. She was glowing. Then she just stared at the audience. Even from backstage, I could see that little wrinkle above her nose. A wrinkle or scar I'd noticed the first time I'd seen her. She said she didn't know what it was. She'd been born with it. A sort of birthmark. Anyway, she just stood and looked at her audience. Then she asked, Have you read the *Kama Sutra* today? then she started singing.

I watched from backstage. She was always good to hear. Always. A golden peacock. Like her other fans, I watched as she pranced across the stage. I remember when she first asked me to manage her. Do you like my singing? she'd ask. Yes, of course, I'd answered. She said that she knew of a certain singer whose manager didn't like her singing, but he managed her anyway. That seems sorta duplicitous, don't it? she'd asked. To be somebody's manager and don't like their singing your ownself. Not duplicitous. Duplicitous ain't the word I mean for it. I mean, you don't know when they're managing you and when they're managing you. She was drunk on gin and tonic and kept talking about this singer she knew, managed by someone who didn't like her singing. So she had to be sure I liked her singing, at least liked most of her songs, before she let me manage her. She sang mostly in English, but when she spotted a Japanese woman in the audience, she said something in Japanese and then sang a snippet of a song she'd sung in Japan. Then she sang in English again.

Onstage she was wonderful, but after each performance she'd shake her head and wring her hands in the dressing room. She craved but never trusted the applause. Sometimes she rushed backstage almost before the applause had happened. She reminded me of a young French woman violinist in a movie that we'd seen, a young woman who always needed assurances that she was good.

That's me, that's how I am, she'd said after the movie. I can't understand artists who are so sure of their goodness.

Why would someone want to be an artist who didn't think themselves good? I'd ask, for I thought that every artist had the conceit that they were good, or they wouldn't be artists, and then I wasn't sure what sort of goodness she meant.

When I sing, I can't hear how I sound to others, and when I listen to myself I'm too judgmental.

You were great, I'd say. She'd sit in her dressing room, silent. You were great, I'd say again. Don't toady me. I really fucked up tonight. I'd poured myself a glass of bourbon and her a glass of a weird favorite, a combination of tomato and pineapple juice. They love you out there, Joan. They love you. Don't you know it? And that bit of Japanese you sang, that sounded really good. It adds another dimension to you. You ain't just another girl singer, you know. She'd light a cigarette, gulp a bit of the tomato and pineapple juice, sip some of my bourbon, then jump up and hug her shoulders.

Do you know Jamey never saw me perform, she said. He doesn't approve of me being a singer, you know. I don't even keep any of my albums up at the farm, because I know he won't listen to them. I'd be embarrassed for him to listen to me anyway, I mean, knowing he doesn't approve. If someone doesn't approve of you anyway, how do they know if you're good? And if he came to one of my performances at one of the clubs or even a concert, how'd I know it's really me he's hearing singing, or if he's just hearing the kinda singer he thinks I am? I don't think the others' applause would change his opinion, like that guy in that movie. He heard the others applaud the person he didn't think any good, so that changed his opinion. He didn't think the person a good singer himself, but he figured that so many people were applauding this person at this rock concert, that they must be good. Jamey would hear the others applaud at my concerts and be even more convinced I ain't any good. He'd hear the applause at my concerts and it would even more convince him that his opinion that I'm not a good singer is right. Or maybe I'd start singing like the singer he thinks I am and not the singer I know I am, just knowing he's in the audience. Like that time you told me you thought you saw Jamey in the club, and then I started singing like crap, like the singer he thinks I am, and then I realized it wasn't Jamey in the club and then I sang pretty good, at least like the idea I have of myself. He thinks enough of us jigs are singers and dancers anyway. That I'm just another stereotype. Playing the Nigger Entertainer. Like that magazine I subscribe to, for African-American entertainers, he doesn't think we need a magazine like that. How does he know I ain't playing myself? Maybe that's who some of us are. Maybe I'm the Archetypal Nigger Entertainer and not the Stereotypical Nigger Entertainer. Should I run from who I am? I remember we were watching this show and they had these so-called high achievers and when they got to the colored girl, they asked her what were her high achievements in and she said proudly, Singing, Dancing, Acting. . . . I think Jamey was expecting her to say something like Mathematics, Chemistry, or some of the other sciences, you know. Or even the languages, being some sorta linguistic prodigy. Russian, Chinese, Japanese. But she says Singing, Dancing, Acting. . . . one of the high schools of the performing arts, you know. Jamey just changed the channel. Nonsense. To tell the truth, I was kinda embarrassed myself, her considering those high achievements. Talents, maybe, but should they have included her among the high achievers? I mean, maybe I coulda understood her naiveté, to think those high achievements, but I know the folks who included her among the true high achievers weren't that naive. I mean, when the whites and the Asian Americans were saying such things like Mathematics, Chemistry, Physics and then she says Singing, Dancing, Acting. They coulda brought a black girl or boy out there who said Mathematics, Chemistry, Physics, you know, or some of Jamey's students, like one of his former students's a oceanographer in South Florida, and a colored girl, they shoulda had someone on like that, the real achievements, but instead they get someone who says Singing, Dancing, Acting, the stereotypes. . . . I was kinda embarrassed myself. So he's never watched me perform. Never. Never listened to any of my recordings. Never wanted to encourage me in that shit. The only colored girls he'll listen to are the divas, the opera singers. And only the best of the best divas. Jessie, Leontyne, Kathleen—is it Kathleen? All their different classical training, and the different languages they've got to learn. They're like Renaissance women. They're like Rembrandts. But me? Another Nigger Girl Entertainer. I was good, though, wasn't I, girl?

Yeah, but how come you asked them about that *Kama Sutra*?

Ain't you read the *Kama Sutra*?

Naw.

I'll have to buy you a copy. James has a copy. When I was up at the

farm I saw it. A present from one of his little infatuations. Maybe she's
a great infatuation. I don't know. A woman who works with him at his
think tank, I know that much. An Indian woman, I mean, an Indian
from India. I'd forgotten all about the *Kama Sutra*. I'd read it once when
I was in college. Well, I didn't read it. I saw it once when I was in college.
You know, the translation by Sir Richard Burton. Well, you don't know,
because you don't know what the *Kama Sutra* is.

Richard Burton, the actor?

Naw, Sir Richard Burton. Supposed to know twenty-some languages
and even more dialects. An explorer of sorts, a translator, and a lord in
Queen Victoria's England who usedta travel around Africa and India,
you know, the old British Empire. Anyway, he usedta translate what the
Victorians considered nasty little books, you know. *The Amorous Man
and the Sensuous Woman*, you know. But not just men and women, even
the gods can be amorous and sensuous. The West can't imagine gods
who are sensual, you know. Because spirituality is supposed to tran-
scend the sensuous, you know, because all the Western gods and holy
men are supposed to be virgins. Or celibates. You can't be holy and
sexual. Anyway, the Victorians could only see the sensuality, you know,
not the spirituality, or they couldn't understand a spirituality where
there's. . . . to tell the truth I don't understand it myself, spiritualized
sensuality or sensualized spirituality. I'm too corrupted by Western
thought, I suppose. Whenever I look at the *Kama Sutra* it just makes me
horny. Did I tell you when we first met, Jamey thought I was an Indian
from India? The way I wore my hair, and the sorta clothes I wore then,
those madras blouses, you know, and long skirts, and when Cathy told
him I was in the sciences, for some reason, he thought I was Indian.
Then, of course, he found out I wasn't. The accent he thought he heard
was in his own mind. I told Jamey he forgot his *Kama Sutra*, that I didn't
want it at my farm or in my possession. How could someone have a
book like that in their possession and not just stay horny. . . .

EIGHTEEN

Back in the hotel room she sat with her legs thrown over a crimson chair. She was looking through an order form of paperback books she'd been working on: *100 Best Songs of the 20's and 30's*, *Test Your Own IQ: How Smart Are You?* (she wanted me to take the test, but I refused), several Dorothy Sayers detective novels featuring Sir Peter Wimsey, *Caligula: Emperor of Rome*, another Jim Thorpe biography, *Mao Tse-tung and His China*, *Brontë Country*, *Jack's Life: A Biography of Jack Nicholson*, *The Adventures and Misadventures of Peter Beard in Africa*, *Lupe Velez and Her Lovers*, *D. H. Lawrence: The Story of Marriage*, *Il Duce's Other Woman*, *The History of "The Gingerbread Man."* She tossed me *The Jockey Club's Illustrated History of Thoroughbred Racing in America* and kept looking through the other books: *O'Keeffe*, *Iva Toguri*, *Dictionary of the American Indian*, *The Cherokee Nation*, *The Counterculture*, *Concise Encyclopedia of the American Indian*, *Vamps and Tramps*, *Kingdoms of Gold, Kingdoms of Jade: The Americas Before Columbus*, *Anansi the Spider*, *Frederick Douglass*, *Black Americans: The FBI Files*, *Malcolm X: The Speeches*, *Island Encounters: Black and White Memories of the Pacific War*, *Ultra Intelligence: How to Make Fake Identification Papers and Become Any Nationality You Want to Be*, *Resistance in Hitler's Germany*, *The New Superpowers: Germany, Japan, the U.S., and the New World Order*, *International Politics*, *The Amanda Wordlaw Reader*, *The Wish for Kings: Democracy at Bay*, an anthology of African-American literature edited by Clarence Major, *The Moby Dick Project*, *Private Security Systems*, *Smalltown Girl Big City Notions*.

You don't have the name of the anthology edited by Clarence Major, I said. I can't order books without the name.

I don't know what the name of it is. I just know it's edited by Clarence Major. Not *The New Black Poetry*. I got that one when I was in grad school. I mean, one of his recent anthologies. You know, I'd like to record one of his poems. Maybe I could get Jimmy Cuervo to do the music. You know, one of his early poems, or one of the jazz-type poems. Do you think any of his poems have been put to music? Can you imagine making a musical out of one of his novels? Avant-garde, you know.

Then she told me to call him.

Call who? I asked. Clarence Major? I don't think he'd want you singing one of his poems. Who's his agent?

Call him, she said. I don't mean Clarence Major, fool.

Call who? I asked. Norvelle?

I still can't believe that you've been to Africa. I can usually tell people who've been to Africa. I don't mean they get Africanized, I mean I can just usually tell people who've been to Africa. I almost been to Africa. My friend Cathy Shuger, the sculptor and her husband Ernest were going to the Sudan, and they invited me after I got my divorce from Jamey, you know. But they're weirdos. Ern's okay. He's the one wrote a nice article about Jamey for one of those popular science magazines. But Cathy's a real weirdo. But they been to Africa, though. Cathy heard about that so-called new slavery in the Sudan and wanted to go over there. I think there was some sort of advisory for American tourists not to go over there to the Sudan, though, so Cathy says, I ain't an American tourist, I'm an American artist. So I think they went to Canada first and then went to the Sudan from Canada. I think they got as far as the Ivory Coast, though. Is it still called the Ivory Coast? I'm sure Jamey's told you about Cathy and her husband? She sometimes tries to kill him. Now she's seeing this Chinese allergist, I think he's Chinese, who thinks she's got an allergy to wheat. And's put her on some kinda allergy medication. Jamey's interested in that himself. You know, if her so-called lunacy might just be biochemical. You know, Jamey's interested in shit like that. I hadn't seen Cathy for years and then she writes me telling me

she heard about my divorce and wants me to go to the Sudan with her
and Ern, and telling me about how they think that her insanity might be
an allergy to wheat. Her and that Amanda Wordlaw are friends, you
know. That novelist I read. I haven't met her myself, though. She usedta
run around the globe with Cathy and Ern, you know. A lot of rumors
that they were some kinda ménage à trois, you know. I don't believe that
shit myself, 'cause I know Cathy and Ern. I think Amanda got fed up
with their bullshit, I mean Cathy's bullshit, so Cathy hears about my divorce, you know, and wanted me to go to the Sudan on some expedition
to find out whether it's true that there are still slaves in the Sudan, so
Cathy's on the freedom trail thinking she can buy some of their freedom,
you know. I mighta been interested in going with them to the Sudan, you
know, but not with Cathy over there singing another one of her freedom
songs, or her equivalent to freedom songs, you know. Another freedom
song, you know. She don't like my music either. I mean, she likes my
voice, unlike Jamey, but she thinks I oughta just be singing freedom
songs, you know. Just music with meaning, you know, the music of
ideas, the music of revolution, the music of revolutionary ideas. Then I
saw her again in New York, that's where I met you, and she told me that
this Chinese allergist they met in the Ivory Coast, I think, says he thinks
she might have an allergy to wheat. They were sitting in this café and he
noticed how she started behaving when she started eating this wheat
loaf. You know, he's sort of an expert witness, you know, as well as an
allergist, whenever allergies cause criminal behavior, you know, and so
he saw the way she was behaving after eating this wheat loaf, and how
when the waiter put knives and forks on the table, Ern returned them,
and put out plastic knives for Cathy, you know, and then after she ate
this wheat loaf Cathy reached toward Ern with one of those plastic
knives. Every woman's fantasy.

Not mine.

I think it's a game with Cathy, though. People say she's a lunatic, but
I just think it's a game myself. Of course, if they prove it's an allergy, then
it ain't exactly a game. But I think it's still a game with Cathy, though,
allergy or not. 'Cause I remember in New York, Cathy was telling me

about this woman she went to art school with, some bitch, who said that she wouldn't let anyone kill her art, that she'd kill them first, some shit like that, so I think it got in Cathy's imagination, you know. Whether a lunatic's imagination or pure imagination, I don't know. They were talking about women and art, you know, this friend of hers and Cathy, and about the relationship between men and art, and how most women don't usually behave like Gauguin, you know, that women artists don't pull a Gauguin, you know, not most of them, like if Cathy had to choose between Ern and her art, her sculpture, you know, she'd choose Ern, you know, so maybe she imagines that Ern does things, you know, to kill her art, to sabotage it anyway. That he's always doing these things to make her choose between her art and him, and she's always choosing him, but then what this bitch told her kinda got into her imagination anyway. So she doesn't like the fact that she can't pull a Gauguin, you know, that she can't devote herself to Art the way that male artists do, and people still consider them good people, you know, or good artists, if they're good artists. That how they treat their women doesn't mean anything usually. They're still great artists. I mean, if they're great artists. But women can't be good women and good artists. Something like that. That's why she admires Amanda Wordlaw, sorta in a perverse way, 'cause she abandoned her husband Lantis and her daughter Panda—Panda usedta be one of Jamey's students when he taught at the university, so he knows all the dirt about Amanda Wordlaw, you know. I mean she abandoned her husband Lantis and her daughter Panda for Art and her Art ain't shit. I mean, if you're a woman and you're gonna pull a Gauguin seems like to me you gotta be pretty sure your Art is Art. Well, some of her stories in *The Amanda Wordlaw Reader* are pretty good, almost Art, but seems like to me if you're gonna be a fool for Art, you gotta be pretty sure your Art is Art. I read Amanda Wordlaw 'cause she's entertaining, but the shit is still shit. I don't know. Some women are fools. I've met Ern, and he seems like a nice guy to me. Sorta like Jamey. But Jamey ain't that nice. Maybe Ern ain't that nice. I think he just takes that shit from Cathy, though. He ain't the sorta man just to take anyone's shit, you know. Jamey neither. But Jamey don't even take shit from me, though.

Jamey don't take shit from nobody, least the Jamey I know. That's why I call him sweet. He knows what I mean. Why, if I behaved like Cathy, least as rumor has it, Jamey and I'd've been divorced even before we even got married. I mean, I didn't even pull a Cathy and we're divorced. Well, I can tell who's been to Africa, though. And you don't look like you been to Africa or even almost Africa. You don't even look like you been to Detroit. Call him.

Sometimes when I'm with Joan I gotta look around to remember where we are. The generic hotel room. Oriental carpet, though—plush, silky, flowered.

Norvelle? You said you didn't get the number or the name of his hotel. I can't call all the hotels in Zanzibar. Plus, he's probably not in Zanzibar now, knowing Norvelle. He could be in some little African village that don't even have a telephone. I think he's still with that Masai woman I told you about anyway. He's writing this big book about her healing. He wants it to be a big book as comparable to the books on Western medicine, you know. They ain't lovers or nothing, at least I don't think so, 'cause I think they got a tradition that the healing women are celibate or something, I think it's their tradition, I know it's one of the traditions among some of the healing women that he's written about among the shaman women and healing women, you know, but he wants to write this big book about her healing. I got a note from his editor who wanted permission to use some of my photographs. You know I been to Africa, 'cause how could I take photographs of Africa, but ain't been to Africa.

You ain't been to Africa.

I couldn't take photographs of Africa and ain't been to Africa. I got photographs I took in Africa. I mean, they're in Norvelle's possession, but the credits is still me. He can't use any of those photographs without crediting them to me and paying me for them. I tried to get his address from that editor, but he claim he don't know it, that Norvelle secretive about his address. Seem like if Norvelle really wanted me, he could just give that editor his address and telephone number. I don't know, he musta called you when he was drunk or something. Too much palm wine. 'Cause, if he wanted me, he knows where I am. It's me who don't know where he is. Well, I know he's in Africa, but Africa's a bigger continent. You know, Africa's a bigger continent than's on the map. When you see a map of the world, they got it so that Europe and America is the center of the world and the biggest continent, but Africa's a bigger continent than it is on the maps. They just do the maps like that, 'cause they want you to believe in Europe and America, and we's supposed to consider them more important, you know, in the history of the world. But none of the maps you look at is the true maps of the world. Norvelle he got him a true map of the world, that shows Africa as big as it is and it dwarfs them other continents. That's the true Africa. And I been there.

Naw, you ain't. I look like I been to Africa and I ain't even been there. Call him.

Call who?

Call Jamey, you fool, she said. Naughty Jamey. His real name's Naughton James, you know. If I didn't call him Jamey, I could call him Naughty. He just calls himself James, though. He prefers James to Naughton. He prefers James to Jim. Sometimes I call him Naughton. I ain't never call him Jim. Naughty Jim Savage. That sounds like one of them gamblers, don't it? You know them gamblers on those riverboats. You know those movies about the gamblers on the riverboats. Naughty Jim Savage. Probably the sorta role Clark Gable might play, one of those riverboat gamblers, you know. Who else could Jim Savage be? A riverboat gambler. Call him. We can tell him to give up smoking. We can tell him that smoking ain't a habit worth having. Maybe we can convince him to give up smoking.

Don't be an ass, I said.

Call him, she said.

What do you want for breakfast? I asked.

Let's fly to the farm, she said, and have breakfast with him. Surprise him. See who he's with. What new little infatuation. How'd you like to see our Jamey screwing some new little infatuation? Or maybe the *Kama Sutra* woman, you know, the one who gave him that copy of the *Kama Sutra*. I mean when I caught him with you that was nothing to catch him with you. . . . And you're still chewing on that old chestnut. I mean, you're a girl scout you're a schoolgirl compared to what's in that book, the *Kama Sutra*, I mean. You're still in grammar school, girl-friend. You're still in elementary school when it comes to sex. Maybe you're in junior high school when it comes to love. I bet the only position you know is the missionary position. Do you know how the missionary position got its name? You been to Africa. Or do you just think Jamey's up at the farm peering into his primitive little microscope or working on some new chemical formula? Do you know something? I think Jamey's too good for the both of us. I think Jamey's too good for the likes of us. Sweet Jamey. I'm glad he's got a great infatuation. A woman worthy of him. Maybe he's got a great infatuation now, do you think? A woman worthy of him. Maybe he's in love again. Do you think he's in love again? He's some man, ain't he?

You're an ass, I said.

Don't you care who he's with? You're at least in junior high school when it comes to love. Maybe it's not just some little infatuation now, maybe it's some great infatuation, a woman who shares his ideals. A woman worthy of him. Jamey's great love. A woman who shares his ide-als. I don't mean just the *Kama Sutra*, I mean she works with him at the think tank, you know. He's admitted her into his little circle of serious thinkers. I can imagine them, his group, and her the only woman in it. Scientists from around the non-Western world and her the only woman. She's supposed to be this great intellect, you know. In India, she couldn't use her great intellect, so she came to America. She's supposed to be the woman he imagined me to be when we first met. Can you imagine your Norvelle meeting the woman he imagined you to be? she asked. If I'm an ass, you're an ass's ass. An ass's ass's ass. An ass's ass's ass's ass. Don't you care who he's with? What little infatuation. Maybe she's just a little infatuation and he imagines she's great. . . . I know one of the guys who works with Jamey at the think tank and asked about her. He looked at me like he thought I was some kinda subversive. You know, the think tank people aren't supposed to tell anyone their little think tank secrets. But then when he knew that I knew about the *Kama Sutra* he started tell-ing me about her. Not the sort of woman who's a little infatuation for any man. He said all the guys at the think tank are a little in love with her, you know. Then she gave Jamey that book. I suppose it woulda been sexual harassment, you know, if he'd given a similar book to her, I mean, if he'd given her a copy of the *Kama Sutra*. But the *Kama Sutra* is a classic of Indian literature. . . . I mean, it's not like some crude flirtation. . . . It ain't like giving someone a copy of *Penthouse*. She coulda given him a collection of Kalidasa's plays, though, or *The Indian Art of Spiritual Harmony*. . . . Ain't like your crude flirtation. . . .

No. I mean, you're an ass.

That's bullshit, she said. You know, girl, I saw the way you were look-ing at him when I first introduced y'all. Aren't you at least jealous that he's met a woman who's sensual, spiritualized sensuality, or sensualized spirituality, not the vulgar sensuality of the West, or whatever. I'm too corrupted by the Western idea myself, all sensuality is erotic, a beauty anyway, and a great intellect. Jamey's ideal woman. I guess I can respect Jamey that his ideal woman is intelligent, but this male pursuit of beauty I've always been ambivalent about.

You're beautiful.

Yeah, when I wanna be. But that ain't the point. And I ain't all that. Who is? All that, I mean.

She's supposed to be all that, you know, Jamey's ideal.

She probably ain't all that. You're beautiful.

But why women gotta be all that? Why we gotta be flawless? It's just control. It's just power. You know, Jamey pointed out the first line in my forehead. He has lines in his forehead plenty, from thinking, you know, but he points out the first line in my forehead. I'm just sitting there read-ing, maybe listening to Miles and he points out this line in my forehead. You know, you got a line in your forehead. I remember when I had my first date, this guy says, You know, your complexion isn't so flawless up close. So what did that have to do with anything? You know. And then Jamey. My first line in my forehead he notices. I guess he didn't mean anything by it. It's just the nature of a man, you know. Pointing out a woman's flaws. Or the nature of anybody in power. Pointing out the flaws of them that ain't. Not that some fools don't need their flaws pointed out. You know what's funny. I don't mind him pointing out my flaws of character—all virtues to me. That line in my forehead, though. I'm thinking, what's this, so he's supposed to be pointing out every line I get in my forehead? Every wrinkle I get he's supposed to be telling me about it. But I ain't no fool.

I hope that ain't why y'all divorced, 'cause he pointed out the first line in your forehead.

Naw, I'm just telling you about the beauty thing. You know.

I think the beauty thing's your hang-up. So some guy noticed your complexion ain't flawless, so what? Guys always telling me about my flaws. I remember the first man that called me outa my name called me Possum, on account of I usedta didn't say nothing to nobody about nothing, and especially men. You couldn't get me to say a word to especially a man. In fact, Norvelle the first man I said more than a few words to. The psychologists would probably say it's because my daddy stayed in Korea with some woman, you know, some Korean woman rather than returning to America, or if he thought Korea the promised land coulda sent for us to come to Korea with him. We couldn't compete with that promised land or that ideal of a woman. I don't know. But I think a man like Jamey could love a woman just the way she is. Or how it pleases herself to be. That's what my friend Nadine says, that most men wants you to love them like they's a tree, you know, like they are, but they ain't supposed to love you like no tree. I love Norvelle, and even love him like a tree, but I just don't want to stay in Africa and follow no man around, you know, not even Norvelle. 'Cause that ain't my idea of a woman. Maybe if that was my idea of a woman, I'd still be in Africa, whether you think I ever been there or not. I know Jamey don't like your music, but he loves you like a tree. And I don't think there's many women that can say that. Loving somebody like a tree don't mean you gotta take they shit, though. What do you want for breakfast?

Bullshit, she said.

On toast? I asked. I phoned in an order. Ham and cheese omelet for her, Western omelet for me. I imagined eating my Western omelet on one of those riverboats with the gambler known as Naughty Jim Savage.

Like Joan say, the sort of role a Clark Gable type might play, or somebody resemble the Clark Gable type. Except I couldn't imagine me as my real self. Probably some blonde. I always wonder, though, why the ideal for a man tall dark and handsome, while the ideal for a woman always some blonde. 'Cept in them countries where everybody blond. Nadine say in them countries where everybody blond, blond ain't the ideal. 'Cept amongst the nationalistic types and their ideal of Nordic womanhood. If people is blond seem like it okay for blond to be they ideal, but not amongst people that ain't blond and try to imitate the blond ideal, or think they ain't beautiful cause they ain't blond. Joan say, though, when she put on her blond wig, it to satirize that ideal.

Did I do good? she asked.

You're an ass, but you're good, I said. You're a good ass.

I'd rather be a good ass than just a good piece of one, even a good piece of intelligent ass.

CHAPTER NINETEEN

When I grew older, I didn't believe the Turtle Woman stories, not the magical ones. Not the tales of how when she was a turtle she'd had to play all kinds of tricks to keep from getting caught by humans and put into a pepper pot floating with wild onions and garlic. I believed the one about the carnival, and even the tale of the confabulatory Unicorn Woman, but not that one. Not the tale of metamorphosis, of how when human beings chased her, like every turtle, she ran so slowly that in order to avoid getting caught she had to transform. Once they chased her into grass and she became grass. Another time they chased her into a valley, and she became a running stream, but all the time afraid that one of them would stoop and cup his hands and drink, so that when she willed herself back into a turtle again she wouldn't be whole. She'd have to look for the part that was missing. Even when I went to Africa with Norvelle and heard African transformation tales which sounded very much like that one, I still didn't believe it, or I thought it was just folklore.

Once when my grandmother was telling me her turtle stories, my mother came up on the porch with a bag of groceries, stopped and listened, shaking her head at the nonsense. The celery stalks at the top of the bag shook their green heads at the nonsense too. As soon as my grandmother finished her tale, my mother explained, Maybe you was a magic turtle in th'old days and maybe you changed yourself into grass and a stream, maybe that tale is true and not the carnival one, but you borned an ordinary human woman now. And an ordinary daughter's daughter. The celery stalks raised their green heads and nodded.

CHAPTER TWENTY

I'm going up to the mansion now, said his sister. Norvelle and I had just married and were visiting his parents' home in Memphis, Tennessee. Their house usedta be a boardinghouse; they'd purchased it and renovated it. Norvelle's father who do some freelance contracting, has his own freelance contracting company, had renovated it hisself, and they rented a few of the upstairs apartments. Norvelle's father look like a older version of Norvelle, but a more rugged-type man being a contractor, while his mother a petite little woman kinda remind me of that woman played Tina Turner in one of them movie and Malcolm X's wife in another of them movie and also played in one of them futuristic action movies, you know, them new feminist-type movies where they got the woman to play the action hero. Usually it a white woman to play the action hero, but in this movie they got the African-American woman to play the action hero. Angela Bassett. That her name. She look like a petite little woman onscreen and up beside Denzel who play Malcolm X in that movie, though I don't know if she truly a petite little woman. She might just look petite in the movies. His sister, I mean Norvelle's sister Cayenne, was dressed in an old man's blue felt hat and a white organdy dress, her cheeks thickly rouged. She'd have been a beautiful girl if she weren't "off." No one had told me she was "off" at first, not even Norvelle. He'd just waited until I saw her and discovered for myself. It amazed me that neither Norvelle nor his parents behaved as if the girl were in any way an embarrassment to them. Ain't like one of them stories I read by LeRoi Jones before he become Imamu Amiri Baraka— ain't that his new name?—about people hiding crazy peoples like that in they attic. I ain't remember the exact lines of that story, but it say something about certain middle-class African Americans or colored people keeping crazy peoples like that in they attic. And ain't just colored people, but peoples in general 'cause seem like in one of them Brontë novels that man hide his crazy wife in the attic. Anyway, they took her as she was, I mean Cayenne, and expected others to accept her, as if her madness had its own logic. Even them that rented them apartments upstairs didn't treat Cayenne like she a crazy woman, and it even Cayenne who would collect they rents from them, and keep them rent books.

What mansion? I asked.

The King's, said Norvelle's father.

We were sitting on the long porch of the boardinghouse, or the renovated boardinghouse. Norvelle's father and mother was sitting in one of the swings. Cayenne was sitting on the porch steps and I was sitting in one of them lounge chairs. Norvelle across the street talking to a man who reminded me kinda of a brown bear. The man pruning one of them trees look kinda like a monkey puzzle tree, and Norvelle standing talking to him. I think he say the man's name Mr. Melville, the man who originally sold them the boardinghouse. Mr. Melville said the boardinghouse originally belonged to a woman named Wooley Boatman, but Wooley Boatman moved up to Alaska, at least she said she was moving up to Alaska, boarded up the boardinghouse and went North. Then he got a letter from her saying that she was in Toronto not Alaska, and sending him the ownership papers to the boardinghouse. Since he didn't know nothing about running a boardinghouse he sold the house to Norvelle's daddy.

What king? I asked.

The only king of Memphis. Elvis Presley, said Norvelle's mother.

Whenever his name was mentioned, Cayenne's face lit up. She'd go to the Presley mansion and stand outside the gates with his other fans, even when there was no longer any King to get a glimpse of. After a while, one of her family would walk up there and get her. She could be trusted to go there by herself, but she couldn't be trusted to come back. If no one went and got her, she'd stand out there all night.

They'll tell you the lie that he said that the only thing black people can do for him is shine his shoes, but that's just a lie, said Cayenne. That's just a true lie. Even Mr. Melville knows that that's a lie, and he usedta work up there at the mansion before he bought hisself this boardinghouse, or claims he usedta work up there, if that's the truth, but he knows things about Elvis that ain't in none of the fan magazines so he musta worked up there and say he even knew Elvis before that when he were a little poor boy like any other poor boy here in Memphis. I seen all Mr. Presley's movies, every one of them, and he's a better actor than a lot of these actors that they says is actors even if he ain't got no colored people in his movies. I ain't read nobody to say what a good actor he is, and that they shoulda put him in better movies, why if they'da put him in better movies, or movies with colored people in them, but you know they wouldn't want him to be the king of acting and singing because that would be too much king, but he can sing any type of music, though, and not just colored people's music. I got all his music. They tells me I ain't supposed to like Elvis, not really like him, but I likes him anyway. They tells me I ain't supposed to like Elvis, not really like him, 'cause he ain't originate that style of music that his claim to fame, 'cause his claim to fame ain't nobody else's music, 'cause that country music ain't his claim to fame, but I likes him anyway. And I don't believe that lie that they say about him saying ain't nothing colored people can do for him but shine his shoes, 'cause the colored people's liked his music before even the Grand Ole Opry people, 'cause I seen that in a movie. Course even in that movie they just marginalized the colored people, like Norvelle says, and you'd think he invented the colored people's music hisself.

I'd heard the same tale myself, but a different version of it. Somebody said it was some African-American women in his audience, who were behaving just like the white women were behaving about him. The King, you know. So the King stops singing whatever song he's singing, looks at them colored women acting just like the white women in his audiences, and says, Ain't no use of y'all colored women behaving like that about me, 'cause cain't none of y'all do a thing for me but shine my shoes. But then in some of them documentaries you got the King saying that his style of singing was influenced by listening to black people's music. Of course they don't mention the colored people every time they mention Elvis.

That evening Norvelle and I walked up to get her. He couldn't understand why she was such a big fan of Elvis, cause Elvis ain't even her generation. She collected all of Elvis' albums, though, and Elvis posters and other Elvis novelty items and collectibles. Norvelle ain't say whether or not he hisself like Elvis. I know he likes the pure African music, the pure music of Africa itself, and even have that music from South Africa even before Paul Simon introduced it to the world. My favorite Paul Simon, though, is when he singing his own music, that song about meeting his woman again after all those years and still being crazy. Not Paul Simon himself, but the man singing in the song. When I first heard that song I think he mean crazy, then when I hear it again I think he mean crazy in love. 'Cept it a better song to say just still crazy. That's a first-rate songwriter when you just say still crazy. Another songwriter think he supposed to say everything he mean. If he mean crazy in love he think he supposed to say crazy in love. Or maybe he mean both kinds of crazy, maybe he mean crazy crazy and crazy in love crazy and them other type of crazy like when people say that crazy man or you crazy man.

I don't know what she thinks about when she stands out there, he said as we neared the mansion, and could see her peeking through the gate with a crowd of others. She's in her own world.

We came to her and Norvelle pulled her away from the crowd of tourists mostly and draped a sweater on her slender shoulders.

Did you hear him? He was singing, she said.

That was probably some tape being played, said Norvelle. Maybe one of his other fans was playing a tape of Elvis' music.

During my stay with them I was afraid to be left in a room alone with her. I didn't know what to expect. Once, though, I'd come into the kitchen to get a glass of water and she'd surprised me there. I'd put the glass in the sink and turned. Standing in the doorway, she looked at me like she was the normal woman and I was the one a bit "off."

Is you going to travel with him when he goes collecting his folklores in Africa?

Yes, I said. We plan to honeymoon there. In Kenya, then Tanzania. Norvelle has to go to Houston first, though. He's supposed to give a lecture at the university—there's a medical anthropology conference—and then there's some people there who run this refugee center, I think, who want him to do some interpreting. He's the only one who knows a certain African language. . . . Some sorta refugees, I think. I think there's some sorta refugee center there. Maybe they're some illegal refugees or some shit, the way Norvelle explains it.

I hope you's a nice girl. I hope you's a nicer girl than you looks like you is.

It depends on what you mean by a nice girl, I said.

I hope you's a nicer girl than you looks is what I mean. 'Cause you don't look like you's a wifeable woman at all to me.

B O O K

T H R E E

I told the gum-chewing secretary who look like a Scandinavian, you know, one of those Viking types, one of them blond types, kinda look like a movie star herself, seem like I seen her in one of them movies, that we were there to see Mr. Schacter. I gave her Joan Savage's name, then my name. She said, You're early and told us to be seated, that he hadn't arrived yet. I stood looking at his wall of stars—that is the people that his company had made stars. And then there was another wall of them that he referred to as "emerging talents" because they weren't yet stars, but the Schacter people were promoting them and had faith that they'd become stars. In fact, the Schacter people referred to themselves as starmakers, although their wall of stars in the larger world of show business superstars might still be referred to as "emerging talents"—there weren't any Madonnas or Michael Jacksons or the Artist Formerly Known as Princes or Queen Latifahs or Whitney Houstons among them—but if Joan were so insistent on wanting to make it in America, her own country, I figured the Schacter people were good people for an emerging "emerging talent."

Joan was dressed in a feathered headdress and a feathered boa, pink toreador trousers, banana yellow stockings, one high-heeled boot and one high-heeled shoe, wearing some kind of makeup that looked like neon, and looking like the very stereotype of a fool. The secretary looked at her matter-of-factly, like it was normal dress for the sorta entertainers that Mr. Schacter was usedta seeing. Rock star wannabes. Mr. Schacter didn't represent many rap singers, except for the mainstream-type rap, the "bubblegum rap," but none of the gangsta-type rap singers. She turned back to her computer. She herself was wearing one of those pink linen or linen-look suits, a white sweatshirt—not blouse—with blue necktie scarf, and on her feet were white running shoes. Except for the chewing gum, she fit the stereotype of the high-class broad, the modern high-class broad who wears running shoes. A Joan Fontaine type, though.

Weren't you in *Chinatown*? Joan asked, signifying. I mean, the movie, with Jack Nicholson.

I know who she signifying about, 'cause she do look kinda like that woman in *Chinatown*. But look kinda like all them blond women in the movies, like she could be all them blond women in the movies.

Mr. Schacter came in in a rush, took one look at Joan and knew who we were. Over the telephone I'd imagined an older man, but he looked like a youngster. I first met him through reading some of his Rock Journalism, though, and shoulda figured him for a youngster, since some of his comments on classic rock seemed from the perspective of a younger generation, not the Woodstock Generation. A tall, thin man, dark-haired, shaggy aggressive eyebrows, maybe like a young Jack Nicholson's, though taller than Jack Nicholson, and what Joan calls Steppenwolf eyes. Reminds me, though, a little of that James Woods, that other movie star. A young James Woods. And maybe even a little of Robert DeNiro, though they ain't the same type. A mixture of Jack Nicholson the Steppenwolf James Woods Robert DeNiro and a Wall Street banker type, the stereotype of a Wall Street banker type, like in that movie *Wall Street*. Before even taking us into his office he started talking fast. It was only until someone else came into the outer office, a demure-looking young woman, that he rushed us into his.

Have a seat, gals, he said. He rushed out the terms of the contract. So what do you think, Harlie?

Now I don't like nobody to call me Harlie, or any diminutive of my name, especially nobody I don't know. I coulda told the fool a thing or two, but I didn't want to screw up things for Joan. I didn't wanna sabotage her career, you know. I wanted to separate my manager's ego or rather my Harlan ego from my manager's ego and Joan's entertainment possibilities and entertainer's ego, so I just let him call me what he wanted, Harlie me, though I wanted to say, That's Mizz Eagleton to you, boy, sorta like that song Billie Holiday sing. Billie Holiday ain't her true name, but she wouldn't let nobody call her outa her name. Course her name already Billie so anybody calling her Billie would call her Billie, but that song she sing ain't nobody call her Billie. That's Mizz Eagleton to you, boy. Now, if he had called Joan Joanie I mighta said something. Or she herself mighta said something to the fool.

You don't talk to her, you talk to me, said Joan.

Ain't Harlie your manager? You're Harlie, ain't ya?

I'm Harlan, yes. Mizz Eagleton.

Well? From what I hear you're a real hot shot of a business manager, one of the best new managers in the business actually. Somebody called here asking about you, Nance said, probably read somewhere in some entertainment tabloid—what's that new magazine, the *African-American Entertainer?*—about your negotiations with us, trying to get you to manage them, I suspect, but we didn't give out your number, no I think Nance did give 'em your number, then she realized it's your private number ain't to be given out, I apologize for Nance she's got show business dreams herself, you know, and likes to be nice to these bums 'cause don't know who'll be a big star, you know, so treats every show business bum like they's a big star, you know, but told them as far as we knew you only manage Joanie here. To tell the truth, before our Joan got you for her manager, I hadn't even heard of this girl myself. I know Mizz Cavada—that's Nance my secretary—hadn't heard of her and she knows every bum in the business. She knows more bums in the business than I do and I'm in the business. But when you got show business dreams you think the more bums you know in the business, you know. To tell the truth I only keep up with the stars I make myself. I'm the power behind the stars, at least the stars I make myself, so I don't have to know every bum in show business, and I sure don't treat every bum in the business like a big star. I don't even treat big stars like big stars. The bigger the star the more you treat 'em like ordinary people. They ain't royalty. Course there's royalty that flirt with show business, but they don't want you to treat 'em like royalty. That's true royalty. But even true royalty can't buy stardom. They might can buy fame, but they can't buy stardom. Of course, stars gotta make themselves, but I'm one of the men who gives them the opportunity to make themselves. And most people haven't even heard of me. They've heard of the stars I make, those who've done the best at making themselves, but not of the man who makes the stars. Some starmakers advertise themselves, but not the Schacter people. She'd heard of Harlie, Nance I mean, but she hadn't heard of you.

Toot her horn for her, said Joanie. Maybe you should hire Harlan to manage you the tales I hear about you, boy. I'm my own manager now, Schacter. She cain't do a thing for me but my makeup, and the way I tell her to. Me myself and I. That's who you talk to. Me myself and I, International. I'm my own manager now. I'm my own starmaker, but I hear you're pretty good, though. Harlan says you write pretty good Rock Journalism. *The Village Voice*, ain't it? I ain't read any of it myself.

I sat down in one of the vinyl chairs and looked at them. I'd been her manager on the way to the Schacter office. I'd been her manager when we first started negotiating with the Schacter people. I just figured she was trying to embarrass me in front of one of the top booking agents, so I refused to be embarrassed. I sat down in one of the vinyl chairs. It was real leather, but it had one of those modern looks, you know in the old days they made vinyl that tried to look like real leather, now the modern designers are trying to make leather to look like real vinyl. Mr. Schacter even had one of those little stereotyped miniature practice golf sets, so's he could practice his golf swing. Joan looked at the miniature golf set like she wanted to practice her golf swing, though she don't even play golf, then she looked at the posters on Mr. Schacter's wall. He collected the posters advertising his talent's first concerts, at least the first concerts they'd had after signing with his company. Most looked like carnival acts, but a multicultural carnival, even a Native American among them—I didn't know any Native American pop singers—who the poster said combined traditional Native American music with contemporary rock. The poster also said he was collaborating with several contemporary Native American poets on a Native American rock opera.

Then one of Mr. Schacter's coffee table books caught my attention: *Spite, Malice & Revenge: The Complete Guide to Getting Even: Three Diabolical Volumes in One*: An A–Z collection of every dirty trick in the book. Warning: This volume contains some techniques which may be illegal; therefore it is offered for entertainment purposes only. The original publisher's price was over fifty dollars but Mr. Schacter had paid only nine ninety-five for it. Or maybe someone had sent it to him as a complimentary copy. Schacter didn't look like the type to need a catalogue of dirty tricks. I went over to one of the shelves that had a collection of Rock Journalism, including his famous essay on Madonna.

Well, from what I know, she's done more for you than that, said Mr. Schacter. Your makeup I mean. And if she did that makeup you're wearing, I'd get me a new girl to do my makeup and keep her for my manager. Makes you look like you're advertising yourself. Why, you look like a Las Vegas casino, or maybe one of them cheap Atlantic City casinos where you figure all the roulette tables gotta be rigged. With our label and connections you won't have to try so hard to sell yourself. You can be yourself. I like my stars to be themselves. I know you're more intelligent than you look.

And less intelligent than I wanna be, said Joan, then she started mimicking and improvising off of something we heard on the Comedy Channel, something that one of the politicians said, or someone satirizing one of the politicians said. Ah got more intelligence than Ah need, and more intelligence than you think Ah got, but less intelligence than Ah want. I manage my own career now, boy, she added, strutting about the room. Peacocking. She picked up the revenge book, looked at it with amusement, and probably made a mental note to add it to her collection—though she mostly liked to collect the obscure sorts of paperback books, fiction and nonfiction, that didn't make the best-seller lists—but didn't open it. She put it down.

I like my makeup and I like who I am, said Joan. Every dirty trick in the book.

. . .

That's all right by me, said Schacter, handed her the contract, and winked at me.

I glanced back into the Rock Journalism book, at the various photographs of Madonna. Tina Turner the only rock star of color in the book, though someone had written an article about the Japanese and rock, this place in Japan where the Japanese youth imitate their favorite American rock stars.

And those freaks you got on your walls don't look like they're striving to be themselves or anybody else, added Joan, then she looked at the contract casually and signed. I shrugged my shoulders, put the Rock Journalism book back on the shelf, then sat back down. Joan paraded over to the desk and handed Mr. Schacter the contract. Mr. Schacter smiled, winked at me again, and looked like the proverbial catbird.

Coming? said Joan imperiously.

I stood.

Good day, ladies, said Mr. Schacter.

He got you for a song, I muttered outside. He screwed you royally. You didn't even read that contract. I faxed him my corrections but he gave you the contract I originally bitched about. He screwed you royally.

I expected her to come back with something witty, one of her own metaphors for a royal screwing, or to tell me who screwed her royally before she even met Mr. Schacter or the Mr. Schacters of the show business world, but she didn't. At least, not until we got into the lobby, then she whispered, Who screwed whom before who caught whom screwing whom before who screwed whom?

This is marvelous, Joan, I said, peering into the microscope. I hadn't peered into a microscope since high school. I'd audited a course in research cosmetology at beauty school—not research cosmology, as I once read in one of those entertainment tabloids that profiled new managers in the business; they'd interviewed me and I'd said something about an early interest in research cosmetology but the media woman had written it up as research cosmology—I don't know a beauty school that teaches research cosmology, but you know how that is. We didn't even peer into microscopes in the research cosmetology class. They just told you about the chemistry of different cosmetics. And we learned how to make cosmetics using different foods: cucumbers, avocado, mayonnaise. Anyway, so I turned and it wasn't Joan standing in the bedroom door but her ex-husband, James.

I thought you were Joan, I said. This is nice. Is this yours? Well, I guess it must be yours. Joan don't use no microscopes in her act.

Yes.

It's like a whole little world.

He came and stood next to me. He smelled of tobacco and lavender.

That's my first microscope, he explained. My father gave it to me when I was seven. I was hooked. They make more powerful microscopes than that nowadays, though. Computer imaging and all of that. That's really primitive compared to the new electronic microscopics nowadays. I'm designing one myself. Looking into a microscope is rather like discovering new worlds, new galaxies.

He pulled out the slide I'd been looking at and put in another one.

This is wonderful. This is a whole little world, though, ain't it, primitive or not? . . . That's how my husband got interested in what he does. My ex-husband, I mean. His father gave him a record of African folk songs when he was little. And that's when he first started learning different African languages. He taught himself most of those languages just listening to them singing, and then he went to the local library to try to get African-language books, but then the only language they had was Swahili. So he wrote to the Library of Congress and got some books from them on the different languages. They sent him some of those books that the military use to teach their people different languages. He learned a coupla those languages when he was a little boy and just kept learning different ones. They're African Methodists or something, you know, so he's always been more romantic about Africa than I am. He's always thought of Africa as his land of origins, whereas for me my land of origins is New Orleans, you know. America. I don't think I should call it romanticism about Africa, though, because he ain't a fool. He knows who he is and he knows what Africa could be. I don't think he ever saw himself as colored, though, like most of us. You remember when we usedta be colored? Like that movie. You know, that Tim Reid movie. I know I usedta be colored. I paused. He goes around collecting medical folklore, though. I mean, my ex-husband Norvelle. He's an anthropologist. He was interested in being a naturalist for a while, though. But he's always been interested in things African, you know. And it ain't like a fad like with a lot of people. When Africa's in vogue, they's African. You know how a lot of us colored people are. When Africa ain't in vogue or Africa's just a land of embarrassments, we's multiracial or some shit. Or we's just Americans and don't wanna be no hyphenated Americans. Or they don't want you to be no hyphenated American when you's proud of being African. When they can shame you about Africa, then they tell you you ain't no true American. Norvelle, though, he's got all these African sculptures by people I'd never even heard of, you know. The traditional African tribal sculptures, anonymous, you know, 'cause them traditional tribal sculptors didn't put they names to they sculptures, like them European sculptors, but also he probably owns the largest collection outside a museum or even inside a museum of sculptures by named Africans. He's really cultured, I mean in our culture, in African and neo-African culture.

You needn't qualify it, just say he's cultured.

I know, but when people talk about culture, you know, when they say people are cultured—well, you know what they mean. They always just mean European culture. They don't even mean Chinese culture and they say Chinese culture is a more ancient culture than European culture, that them Asian cultures is more ancient than them European cultures. I remember when I was in high school, though, we had this teacher who was talking about culture, and you know, she kept talking about culture how people gotta have culture and treating us like none of us had any culture, mostly African Americans and poor whites, you know. That was when the schools first got integrated or desegregated and all the rich whites and numerous middle-class whites went to private schools, so in the city public schools you had mostly the African Americans and the poor whites or the lower-middle-class whites. So I guess she'd applied to teach in one of them private schools, but maybe she wasn't cultured enough herself, so there she was teaching in the public schools where ain't nobody got no culture, so she was talking about culture, like I said, and I thought she was cultured, you know, 'cause I only thought culture meant their culture. But Norvelle, that's my ex-husband—I said that, did I say that?—he sorta reminds me of them African noblemen. Why, a lot of us men remind me of African noblemen when you look at them as African men and not as colored people. So when I met Norvelle and went to Africa I learned that you could be cultured and not be European, you know. Like those Masai we met, they all act like noblemen, like men of culture, though they ain't all noblemen. But they's all men of they own culture. And the womens all women of they own culture, though the Masai men seem more cultured to me than the women.

He removed that slide and placed in another one.

Where's Joan? I asked.

She's out riding.

You got horses?

Just two. Both named after herself—Joan and Savage.

Your name's Savage too, I said. Savage ain't Joan's original name. Them horses is named after you and her.

He said nothing. I finished looking at the slides and sat down on the edge of the bed. He leaned against the counter where the microscope and slides were kept. His forehead was shining. On the shelves were a few chemistry books.

Where did you and Joan meet? I asked.

Harlem. We have a mutual friend who's a sculptor. Catherine Shuger. Joan calls her the Renegade. Do you know her work?

Sounds familiar.

A real nutcase, actually. A real strange woman. You've probably heard tales about her. From Atlanta, originally. In and out of asylums, not just asylums in America, but asylums all over the world—I remember somebody said she probably needed a good witch doctor—but she's a fine artist, though, I think. In some ways, she reminds me of Joan. I don't mean that Joan's a nutcase, I mean something in the personality. Anyway, she was having a showing there in Harlem. Does that kinda scavenger-type collage sculpture and that puzzle sculpture. Sorta introduced us. She's a bit of a matchmaker. Catherine Shuger, I mean. Has a husband who just puts up with her. Writes articles on pop science. The husband, I mean. Did a profile on me for an article on African Americans in the sciences.

Yeah, Joan showed me that article. That photograph they got of you don't do you justice. I take better photographs than that. You a more handsome man than that photograph.

They refused to print it anywhere but the *African American Journal*, the article I mean. Writes science fiction under a pseudonym. Well, he doesn't see himself that way. I mean, as a fool. He's in love, you know. Name's Ernest. Fine name. They say she's even tried to kill him several times—not the artist Catherine, but the other self.

Joan told me about her. I think. Or I read about her somewhere, in one of Joan's books. You know, she's always reading books, when she ain't doing her music. Seems like I read about her in this book of Joan's on sculpture.

Now she only makes what she calls Sculpture You Can Eat. Catherine Shuger. I don't mean to say that Joan's anything like that, it's just in the essential personality. You know, like sometimes when you read novels by the same writer, and it's like they're always inventing and reinventing the same character, the same essential character. That's Joan and Catherine.

People say I'm kinda like this friend of mine Nadine. We ain't nothing alike to me, don't even look alike, but a lot of people say we kinda alike, you know. We kinda talk alike, but we ain't nothing alike. People say I'm a big woman, but Nadine's sorta a giant compared to me. She's sorta like some of them African women I met while I was in Africa. From Kenya or Tanzania. Or like some African Amazon you might read about, you know. I guess they's got African Amazons. We's both from Kentucky, though. I didn't meet her in Kentucky, though, I met her in Texas. Then when my ex-husband introduced us, I discovered we's both from Kentucky. Now she's in New Mexico, though.

She's working with an allergist now that has this theory that it's biochemical. I mean, Catherine Shuger's aggression. It just might be. Some people believe that personality itself is merely biochemical. I'm a scientist, but I don't believe that science explains who we are.

Are you from Harlem yourself? I heard you say something about meeting Joan in Harlem.

Naw, I'm from Maine.

Maine? You mean they's got nigs up in Maine? Excuse my French. I guess you do kinda sound like Maine. Kinda high-toned. I was thinking you got a high-toned kinda voice when Joan first introduced us. I was thinking you kinda sound Canadian, but I know if you's Canadian Joan woulda told me you's Canadian. I know there's nigs up there in Canada, so they must got nigs in Maine. I know some nigs from Virginia that sound kinda high-toned like that, though, almost like them nigs from England, you know. You don't exactly sound like you's from England, though, but you's got one of them high-toned accents. We was watching this thing on television about the Maine fishermen. It was after one of Joan's gigs, and I kept wondering why she so interested in them Maine

fishermen, and must be 'cause they kinda sound like you, and I don't
know no other reason she be interested in watching no Maine fishermen. I mean, I found it interesting them talking about the different fish
they's catching and how mens farms the ocean, but that ain't the sorta
thing that interest Joan. I mean, if it ain't politics or the Comedy Channel or politics on the Comedy Channel, it's romance. You kinda sound
like them, though. Them Maine fishermen. Except more classy. Now
that's the true North. Up there in Maine. I mean, beside Canada itself
that's the true North. I guess the slaves that made it up there to Maine
didn't escape all the way up there to Canada.

I'm descended from free blacks actually, not slaves.

Oh, yeah? I heard about them. You think it makes a difference?

What?

I mean, you think it makes a difference whether you's descended from
free blacks or slaves? I mean, they's the same people, ain't they? Or you
think they's got a different mentality? Somebody say a slave can have
just as much respect for theyself as a free man. I don't know if that true,
though, 'cause seem like they's always telling you that if a slave got any
respect for theyself, then they try to escape, so I don't see how no slave
can have as much respect for theyself as a free man, 'cause then they be
a fugitive. But then every free man ain't no fugitive. I mean, the free men
that blames the slaves for being slaves and not free men, a lot of them
ain't no fugitive.

He lift a eyebrow but don't say nothing.

In the stories set in Maine, there's never any nigs in 'em, though, fugi-
tives or free men. I remember when I was in high school, we was assigned
to read these stories set in Maine, and wasn't a nig in them. Sorta like
those dialect stories but the dialect Maine dialect, you know. I know in
that television show they didn't show any nigs fishing. 'Scuse me. Joan
says I shouldn't refer to us as nigs. But she's got a book where they refer
to theyselves as nig, I mean the narrator of the book refer to herself as a
nig, not only her own nig but other people's nig.

Our Nig?

Yeah, I think that the name of that book. *Our Nig.* Then when I say nig she tell me I ain't supposed to say nig, and she got a book that say nig.

So how did you and Joanie meet? he asked.

At a party in New York. Not Harlem. Manhattan. To tell the truth, I sorta sneaked in. I saw these African-American musicians, one of them carrying a French horn, and sorta followed them, you know. I guess somebody musta thought I was one of them musicians' girlfriend. It coulda been a party for that Catherine Shuger you're talking about, 'cause it seem like somebody kept saying Sugar, and I know it was a party for some artist or one of those artist types and some of that food they had for you to eat looked like sculpture, like sculpture you could eat, and I thought they was just calling somebody Honey, you know, or had a sweet tooth. Seem like Joan introduced me to a woman named Sugar or I thought she was just calling her Sugar, you know, though it surprised me to hear a northern woman call somebody Sugar, even though they say a lot of northern people's got they roots in the South on account of that Great Migration. Anyway, I met Joan and we started talking and she asked me what I did. I said I was a beautician. She laughed. I guess because I was the only beautician at the party. Not even a makeup artist. Anyway, so she asked me to make her up and I did, right there where they were all partying around us, and she liked it. After a while, some of the party stood and watched, and maybe even the woman named Sugar amongst them, and after I finished, they applauded. Seem like I heard her say, Sugar, you think you a artist, this is a true artist. Or maybe I'm just thinking I remember that 'cause you telling me there's a real woman name Sugar. Or Shuger. So she hired me on the spot for her makeup artist, Joan I mean. She said she'd have hired me, though, even if the others hadn't approved.

And the managing? How did that come about? From beautician to business manager, that's a big leap. I mean, someone who doesn't know anything about the music business, who doesn't have any degrees in business or anything. It's rather incredible, to tell the truth. You're rather incredible, to tell the truth. Joan said that I'd think you a rather incredible woman.

It just evolved. I started doing the books, you know, making calls and stuff. She noticed it and said I might as well be her business manager. She'd been handling all that herself, you know, but she was getting more known, and she wanted. . . . I don't have no business training or background or degrees in business like you said and no I didn't know anything about the music business, just beauty school. And she uses it too, you know.

How do you mean? He was still standing near the microscope, but I had moved to the bed. You know. How do you call it? For pointers, for scores. She likes telling people I usedta be her makeup artist, a beautician. That the only degree I've got is a degree from beauty school and she ain't even sure about that. You know how Joan is. Like when we're at a party with some other entertainers and entertainer's expensive-ass high-powered Hollywood-type business managers and entourage and shit, and there's just me and Joan, and like her career's blossomed since I started managing her. . . . at least in Europe and Japan. . . . But I'm good. You can ask anybody in the business.

I have.

Hire a detective?

No, just casual conversation, you know.

Joan says you don't care shit about her career.

Oh, yeah? I don't. I care about her, though.

I said nothing. I crossed my legs and leaned back. His shirt was open at the collar. Tufts of curly hair peeked out from his broad chest. His skin was a wine-colored brown and he wore a mustache, like I told you, and had the look of a man I can only describe as being of another generation, though he's Joan's and my generation. Looking at him made me feel as if a old photograph from the 1930s or 1940s was staring back. Some portrait photograph by James Van DerZee or some of those African-American actors in those old Oscar Michaux movies, only darker complexioned than his leads.

He looked at me with a intensity. They tell me you're smart and you're tough, and Joanie's in good hands. I didn't hire a detective, but I know a few music people. Mostly people in advertising, publicity people, though, not musicians.

I said nothing. I got up and looked back into the microscope. I could feel him peering at me. I imagined him and Joan together, not making love, but maybe rubbing noses like the Inuits. "Give me an Eskimo kiss," some woman said to her lover in a French movie, a video Joan had rented once after one of her gigs, when we were back at the hotel. She listened, so that she could keep up with her French, while I tried to read the captions. I hugged my arms and thought of one of Camille Billop's sculptures with a woman hugging her arms. A ceramic. And then I thought of another sculpture, one of Norvelle's. The one where one sculptured figure—of a man?—held another—of a woman?—aloft. And they both seemed as if they'd taken wing, as if they were flying. Was that a Catherine Shuger sculpture? Maybe that was where I first had heard her name. He said it was by some African-American woman sculptor, but I couldn't remember her name. Maybe Catherine Shuger?

You don't like her singing, though, do you? I asked.

No. I think it's trash. I really think it's trash. Everybody doesn't need to sing. Especially us. The Houston woman, now there's a voice. If you wanna think of pop modern music. You know, the Houston woman. I'd say she's got the best modern voice. Bobby Brown's wife.

He'd love that. Bobby Brown, I mean. She treats him like he her Majestic Prince. You know, I bet on that horse. I don't think I won anything. She's very talented, you know. Joan. I mean modern singing is modern singing. It's not all about the great voice, though I admire great voices. Like Joan, she hardly ever reads the great writers, the great books. I mean, she reads the Great Books, she's got shelves of the Great Books. She reads them, but she also reads the trash, not just the trash, but she likes to read a lot of that obscure nonfiction, but she says the trash, the tabloid journalism, the tabloid novels, have more to do with the modern world, the trashy nonfiction, the trashy novels, the tabloids. Like she says those people who think the modern writers should write like the Great Novels, that that's not modernity. That the techniques of the trashy novels and even the comic books, the new type of comic books, describe modernity better than the Great Novels. Some people say it's supposed to be trash. Modern music. Like the new photography, you know. Like modern art. You can't have a renaissance unless you've got decadence, someone says.

He said nothing.

She's really better than you know. I don't think she's trash myself. I mean, I don't think her music is trash. It ain't trash trash. If anything, she kinda satirizes the modern, trashy culture.

That's not all of American culture. It's American pop culture. I've heard that description of American culture myself, but it's just the pop culture people are describing, the media culture. Some of the technological culture, perhaps, but mostly the media culture.

But Joan would say that the pop culture's the only true American culture, that the other so-called culture is just wannabe Europeans. Like in architecture, McDonald's and Taco Bell–type pop architecture, that's more true American culture than the cathedrals. I ain't a culture nut myself, but I think she's got the right idea about modernity. The Madonna culture. I like Madonna, though. Like somebody said, she's a tramp, but I like her. I don't think she's a tramp, though. Maybe she satirizes the tramp ideal or the ideal tramp. I think she just, you know, satirizes pop American culture, and people think that's her. Like maybe Joan satirizes pop African-American culture. Like a lot of people think pop African-American culture, media culture is us. But that's sorta what you're saying, ain't it? And I guess we got our African wannabes like they got their European wannabes. I ain't a culture nut myself, though. Unless it's New Orleans culture, which is everybody's culture. She's really better than you know, our Joan.

I want her to be better than she knows. You know, she was a chemistry major when I met her. Our sculptor friend was sort of a prodigy, you know. Having her first shows when she was still an undergraduate. I was in New York for the first time. When I met Joan, when Shuger introduced us, she just started talking to me like she'd always known me and not talking the typical woman talk, and I asked myself, Who's this brilliant young woman? She was the first truly brilliant woman I'd met. I don't wanna qualify it and say African-American woman, because I think her intelligence is world class, or could be. Our mutual sculptor friend's a prodigy, but that's art. Intelligence in art ain't the same. Who are the lights of our century? I mean, in the areas of science and art. At least that the world knows about. Picasso and Einstein. But Picasso's not Einstein. That's not the same sort of brilliance, you know. People don't think of intelligence as synonymous with Picasso, but Einstein, yes.

I left the microscope and returned to the bed.

When we were in New York, Joan took me to a play about Picasso meeting Einstein. Joan thought it was good, but it wasn't as good as *Cats*. But I guess you gotta know more about Picasso and Einstein to appreciate a play about 'em, but everybody knows about cats. I played with the geometries of their crazy quilt.

Though when you look at those Einstein formulas, the formulas in his notebooks, someone said that kind of looks like art. And when you look at some of those Picasso's most abstract paintings it's kind of like science. Like a scientist's journals. Anyway, Joan and I, we went back to our mutual colleges, her in Connecticut and I at Fisk, but we kept corresponding and even made plans to do research projects together. We went to the same graduate school in Rhode Island, though. She was pursuing her intellectual theories, then she needed money to help pay her way through school, you know. She was a scholarship student, but it was just enough to pay tuition. She could've gotten in the Work-Study Program as a research assistant, any of the professors would've hired her, but she didn't want that. I think someone harassed her, you know, but I'm not sure, because in those days, you know, it wasn't a big notion, sexual harassment, though I remember there was a big ballyhoo about an article one of the professors wrote. "Up the Down Coed," I think. Someone from the English Department. I spent most of my time in the chem and biology labs, though. Only a few African-American professors in the sciences. Our advisor was one of them, but he was a physicist not a chemist. I remember Joan used to spend a lot of time talking with him about some of her theories. He indulged her, but his own interests weren't in chemistry. And there was another professor, a German, a chemist. Joan was doing something with spectroscopy, and he was one of the leading experts in that field. I think he was an old Nazi myself. I had only one course with him. Or rather I started to take a course with him, but the first day he wouldn't even acknowledge my presence in his class, my African presence, so I walked out. Joan stayed in that class and took courses with him, though. I guess she sort of forced him to acknowledge her African presence, or maybe just the fact that she's a female. Even our writers don't write tales of invisible women, at least none I've read. Anyway, Joan started singing at a local nightclub rather than be anyone's work-study assistant. I don't think it was harassment, though. If anyone harassed, it was probably Joan. I remember she used to develop these intense relationships with people. Not lovers, you know what I mean. And she's not like the other girls in the sciences, most other women who take up the sciences. Most people who take up sciences, for that matter. Not just the idea people have of them in the popular imagination. The nerds. Of course, we scientists have a range of personality types like anyone else. But Joan's more spontaneous and witty than most of the so-called rational types. Maybe it's just her ego. Or I guess she prefers the limelight. There's not much limelight in being a research chemist. Unless you're one of the celebrity-type scientists. A pop scientist. When Ernie Shuger wrote that article on me and I got a couple of fan letters, Joan kidded me about becoming a pop scientist, a celebrity scientist. I think not.

She's brilliant onstage, I said. Don't you think? She's spontaneous and witty there.

I've never watched her perform. I don't like her singing.

I took my shoes off and put my feet up on the bed. Maybe I was trying to behave spontaneous and witty, if that was the sorta woman he liked. The odor-eaters in them were worn. I shoved them under the bed.

I bet you like her singing, I said. I bet you're a closet fan. I bet it ain't true that you don't listen to her, at least her recordings. I bet you're a closet Joan Savage fan. I love your crazy quilt.

Let's go downstairs, he said.

I'd rather stay up here.

After her recording session Joan wanted to come back and have dinner in the room, so I ordered up. She sat on the corner of the bed, brooded and ate a ham and cheese croissant. I sat in a chair, a bowl of chef's salad on my lap, and turned on the television. The Comedy Club. Then on another channel they were talking about a bidding duel at a yearling sale, a bidding duel between a Saratoga breeder and another man, a foreigner. Then they referred to the other man as a German, but when they showed a closeup of the man's face, I almost dropped my salad.

That's the guy, I said, pointing.

What guy?

The guy I spent my summer vacation with. Up in Saratoga. Didn't I tell you about that guy? He's from Germany. You know I told you I met this colored guy from Germany. Did I tell you about this colored guy from Germany? African German.

I asked you who'd you win in Saratoga, but you didn't tell me. African German?

I don't know if that's what he calls himself, though. Like those Portuguese friends of yours from Rhode Island, they don't call themselves African Portuguese, they just call themselves Portuguese. You know, those Portuguese friends of yours, you said when you first met them in Rhode Island, you thought they were jigs, but they're Portuguese.

I didn't tell you that. Jamey musta told you that. They're his friends, not mine. I did sing in a club owned by one of them. I think Jamey got me a gig in that club. He didn't want me to sing in just anybody's club, you know. He won't admit it, and he never came to that club to hear me sing. 'Cause that friend of his said, How come Jaime never comes to my club anymore—I think he calls him Jaime. He had this club fixed up to look like a little fishing village in Portugal. Well, upstairs looked like a little fishing village in Portugal, but the downstairs part of the club looked like a regular Lisbon nightclub, which really looks like a nightclub anywhere. Anyway, so it was because I was singing there. I mean, that Jamey wouldn't come to the nightclub anymore. So this friend of Jamey's just thought it was because Jamey thought I'd be nervous, you know, with him being my lover in my audience, but I knew the true reason, that he didn't want me to be a singer anyway, he just got me the gig there so's he'd have some control, you know. I did think they were jigs, though, then found out they're Portuguese. A lot of them my own complexion, you know, but calling themselves Portuguese. Like the people from Cape Verde, you know. But you know, the Portuguese all over Africa and the New World, and the Portuguese the first colonists, and wanting to hold on to their colonies longer than anybody else, except maybe the English in Ireland. I learned to sing a few songs in Portuguese. That's when I first got interested in singing in other languages. . . . He's from Germany?

Yeah. They been in Germany since the seventeenth or eighteenth century or some shit. I thought maybe he was the son of one of those African or African-American soldiers that stayed in Germany after the war, you know, like you know after the war a lot of African-American soldiers, well some of them, stayed in Europe and the Pacific and married foreign women, you know, after the different foreign wars, rather than just be second-class citizens in America, you know, but he says they've been in Germany since the seventeenth or eighteenth century, not just since the war. That they're as German as the Germans. In fact, during the war they fled Germany, he says, and went to Switzerland, but then they returned to Germany after the war. But he says they're as German as the Germans.

I don't think anyone's as German as the Germans. I usedta have this German professor for chemistry. He's one of the leading chemists in the world. I think he's a former Nazi or some shit, Jamey thinks he's a former Nazi, but they still consider him one of the world-class chemists. He said he spent some time in Argentina after the war, but that don't mean he's a former Nazi. There were Germans who were in the Resistance, the Germans had a Resistance just like the French, but you just hear about the Nazis, and Jamey thinks every German of that generation was a Nazi. I don't think he's a Fascist son of a bitch or anything like that, though Jamey thinks he's a Fascist if not a Nazi and wouldn't take any classes with him. I think he started to take one class with him and then walked out. I remember he gave me this reading list. I thought it was going to be chemistry, but it wasn't chemistry, it was German philosophy. He said it would help me to develop my rational mind. And he usedta listen to Wagner all the time. You know what listening to Wagner means. That's probably why a lot of people rumored him to be a former Nazi, because the Nazis usedta love Wagner. But then when he'd listen to Wagner, he'd look all romantic, you know. I remember I saw him in the pub—the Graduate Center had a pub—in the pub listening to Wagner, earphones in his ears, but I knew he was listening to Wagner. He curved his little finger for me to come over, and when I came over he bought me a beer and asked me whether I thought in pictures, whether when I thought I thought in pictures, or whether I thought in words or in numbers or in abstractions. That was all he asked. I didn't answer, of course, because I thought everybody thought in pictures and words and numbers and abstractions, and that a scientist, even a true scientist didn't just have to think in abstractions. But I knew what he was trying to suggest, that if I thought only in pictures, that I must truly be a primitive. And I knew he was listening to Wagner because of that romantic look. . . . and he never called me by my first name, like the other professors. He called me Miss, well my name wasn't Savage then, but it might as well have been, the way he said it. But I liked the way he said it. And he asked me once why I hadn't chosen him for my advisor. Because I had this African-American professor for my advisor, you know, even though he wasn't a chemist, but a physicist, and he, the German professor, he was the most renowned of the professors in our department, more renowned than the advisor I'd chosen, and's got chemistry textbooks used in all the major universities and could've done more for me. I remember his study was some type of fish that was supposed to have healing powers or healing substances. I keep thinking the remora, but it was another fish, some type of tropical fish. I remember his colleagues thought he was a lunatic or something, thought he'd already made his reputation, so he could pretty much do any type of research he wanted. I remember I envied his freedom, though. A free man among free men. He worked with only a few graduate students, and only those he wanted to work with, and he was free to pursue his research. A free man among free men. He helped me decide what I wanted to be.

What do you mean? Free? A free woman among free women? I joked.

By helping me to decide what I didn't want to be. He said I could come and work with him and just pursue my own research. That was what I wanted. That was my ideal. I was developing this spectroscopic theory that I thought had real potential. I don't remember anything of it now. He knew I was having financial worries. He knew I didn't have enough financing for the sort of research I wanted to do. My scholarship barely paid my tuition. I could have gotten more money if I'd agreed to teach after college, but I didn't want to be a teacher, I wanted to do research. He said I wouldn't have any financial worries. He offered me money. He asked me whether I needed money. He asked me how much money I needed. He'd won prizes, he said, and so he didn't have any financial worries himself. And the university was quite generous, and he was always receiving grants to pursue his own research. He simply asked me how much money I needed for my research. He had a wife, he said, but he wasn't making any proposals to me that she wouldn't consent to. He had helped other students who needed money. And then he asked me whether I thought in pictures. . . . African German. I didn't know they had slaves in Germany. But I guess they've had slaves everywhere in Europe, made slaves out of Africans as well as each other.

I think they just came over to Germany, not as slaves. I don't know their history. I think he said he's part Hottentot or something. I found that interesting, that he actually knows his African tribe, that he could say, I'm part Hottentot. He said they weren't slaves when they came to

Germany, they came as free men. Hottentot, I think. I think he said
Hottentot.

I read about that somewhere. That they usedta bring these Hottentots into Germany and put them on exhibit. One of those countries. I
took an anthropology course once and they were talking about the relationship between the Hottentots and the Germans, but I don't remember exactly what they said about the relationship between the Hottentots and the Germans. I know they used to bring Africans into Europe
and put them on exhibit, you know, when they weren't making slaves of
them. Like the Hottentot Venus. I read somewhere about the Hottentot
Venus. Somebody wrote a poem about her, but I read it somewhere else,
in one of my nonfiction books, so I know it's real. But I think that was
France. I know, they used to put Africans on exhibit in France. You
know, in those intellectual saloons. I like to call them intellectual saloons. Zooing them, you know. That's what I call it, zooing people,
when you don't treat them like human beings. I think that professor
would've zooed me if I'd let him. If I must be zooed, then I'll zoo myself.
There's a famous African man they put on exhibit like that too. I forgot
the name of that man. A pygmy, I think. Somebody wrote a book about
him, though.

Anyway, he's got all these bodyguards. I don't know if he's paranoid
or what. Real wealthy, you wouldn't believe. That African German.

Yeah, I'd believe, she said. When I was playing that club in Paris, you
remember that group of wealthy freaks we met. From New Orleans, I
think. I read about them too. The free coloreds who used to go to school
in Paris.

They weren't freaks.

You mean he didn't give you the bum's rush?

No. Maybe he thought I had money myself. At first anyway. He was
treating me like he thought I had money. You know how people treat you
when they think you've got money, and then how they treat you when
they find out you ain't got shit. Or when they think you ain't got shit,
and then they find out you got money, or they think you got money. Like
this woman working in this company was talking about how her bosses

were treating her like shit, but then when she moved up in the company, the people started treating her like sugar, and the same people used to treat her like shit, and then she became their boss. They were like bossing her around and then she became their boss. I read that in one of those books of yours on management styles and techniques. That's why, they say, you're supposed to treat everybody like sugar.

I treat everybody the same, she said. She straightened and watched the screen. The announcer was talking about the German buyer, how the German buyer had driven the bidding up to the largest it had ever been. The yearling he'd purchased had sold for five million dollars.

This is the largest that's ever been paid for a yearling, said the announcer.

Ain't he cute? I asked.

Naw, he ain't cute.

I mean Josef, not the yearling.

He ain't cute. He's beautiful. She sulked and bit into her croissant. How'd you meet him anyway?

I told you.

Tell me again.

I told her again.

Maybe he ain't paranoid. You know what they say about paranoia? How'd he get to be so rich anyway?

I don't know. I never asked him.

You wouldn't. Maybe he's a gangster.

I don't think so. He just breeds horses is all I know. Breeds and races horses. Gotta farm in Kentucky. Thought I was spying on him. I told him about you.

You told him about me?

Yeah. We listened to some of your music. He likes Wagner, though. You know, Mozart. That sorta music. I don't know what sorta business he was in over in Germany, though. He was telling me about some sort of business negotiations, but I wasn't sure what he was talking about. I didn't want him to explain what he was talking about because I didn't wanna sound ignorant, you know. I think he said something about arbi-

trage. That's when he thought I had money, and there ain't too many
people who's rich and stupid, and least whilst people thinks they's rich
they usually don't believe 'em to be stupid. But poor people can be as
stupid as they wanna be, I mean even when they ain't stupid people
thinks they's stupid, 'cause they's poor, you know. Like when people say,
If you're so smart, how come you ain't rich? He says he's in arbitrage.
What's that?

That's some kinda mediator. Arbitrage, you know. Maybe he's a mediator in different business disputes, you know, disputes between different businesses. Somebody Jamey went to school with does that shit. But
he's a lawyer, though. I guess you don't have to be a lawyer, though, to
do that. You can be a regular businessman and do arbitrage for other
businesses. I know there are businesses that are just in the business of
doing arbitrage for other businesses, contract negotiation and that
kinda thing. Or maybe he's just a gangster and telling you that shit.

Just because somebody tell you a incredible story don't mean it ain't
the truth. Like I remember when Norvelle and I went to this cocktail
party at his university. He don't like to go to them university cocktail
parties, but he went to this one, 'cause some famous African anthropologist or anthropologist of Africa supposed to be at the cocktail party. I
thought it was gonna be a man, but turned out to be this woman feminist anthropologist. He thinks she has a lot of interesting things to say
about Africa from the feminist perspective. There's another feminist
anthropologist he thinks is bullshit, but this one he seems to sorta respect. She's sorta a Afrocentric feminist, though. I don't think that's the
same as a feminist feminist. Or maybe she don't even call herself a feminist. She just look like a regular woman to me, though. So somebody
asked me what did I do, 'cause people always wants to know what it is
you do as if that tells 'em who you are, and I said I'm a beautician. And
they thought I was lying or joking, you know, 'cause they didn't believe
that Norvelle would marry a beautician, him being a university professor, that he would have hisself a professional woman, you know, maybe
like that Afrocentric feminist anthropologist woman, you know, being
a university professor and publishing in the scholarly journals puts him

in the middle class, you know. Now you know you're not a beautician, this woman says. The provost's wife, I think. And somebody else told her, She's a photojournalist. Because Norvelle had used some of the photographs that I took when we were over there in Africa in some of the articles that he'd published about medical anthropology, you know, and got them published in a more popular magazine than his usual little articles that he publishes in the little professional journals 'cause most of them don't use photographs, you know. Norvelle says the more popular the magazine the more photographs they use, that's why the most scholarly magazines don't got no photographs in them, and that's even anthropology, 'cause the scholarly magazines don't want you to confuse them with *National Geographic*, though he uses some of my photographs in some of the books he writes, but they usually print all the photographs together in one section so that the books still look scholarly. So anyway they preferred to believe that I'm a photojournalist 'cause that's a more credible story, you know. Even though Norvelle's origins is supposed to be inner city in Memphis, you know, he's supposed to be middle class. They do own this renovated boardinghouse now, though, then that sorta makes them the landlord class, though he grew up in the inner city of Memphis, the Memphis ghetto, you know. But being a university professor that's the only type of woman that they could imagine that Norvelle could love, a photojournalist, you know. And I guess you prefer to believe that he's a gangster, that African German, 'cause I suppose for you that's a more credible story of how a African, even a German African or a African German, that ain't no gangster or entertainer could get to be a rich man. Like that friend of yours from Chinatown, that girl you said you went to school with in that private school in Connecticut, you know, when you were in undergraduate school, who you said everybody thinks is a gangster 'cause she owns all those restaurants and shit.

You mean Isabel Kong?

Yeah.

Isabel Kong and Little Lady Kong. That's her daughter. I think she is some kinda gangster, to tell the truth. Some kinda bandit, but very urbane, the urbane type of bandit. She was an art student when I knew her at school, and had all these ambitions of becoming a great artist, you know. I thought she was really good myself. They'd have these student exhibitions, you know, exhibitions of the student artist, her painting and sculpture. She thought I was an artist, when we first met, because it was at a student art exhibition, and she asked me which of the paintings and sculptures were mine, and couldn't believe it when I told her I was studying chemistry. We had only one African-American artist there, or who had aspirations for being an artist. And at first she thought I was her. And she comes over and says, Are you so-'n'-so? Because she was going to tell me she liked one of my sculptures, but I said that I'm not an artist, you know. Anyway, I saw her again when you got me that gig in Amsterdam. She said she was opening a new restaurant there, and she also wanted to open a new restaurant in Hong Kong. I think she makes false passports now, though, for illegal Chinese. I hear all sorts of stories about her, but it's not the Isabel Kong I knew at school. When I started singing, she thought I was being truer to myself, though, than when I wanted to become a research chemist. I remember when I started singing in the clubs around school, she'd always come to hear me. Then she had Little Lady—she's one of those little girls that you want to say your ladyship when you see her, not that she's conceited or anything; her real first name's Javana—out of wedlock and left school and opened her first restaurant. She still paints, but she just puts her paintings on the walls of her own restaurants, you know. Sometimes people'll see a painting of hers on the wall and want to buy it, but she says she doesn't know whether they want to buy it because they think it's good, or just because she's the notorious Isabel Kong.

Well, I never heard of Isabel Kong till I met you, but then I ain't into gangster lore. Anyway, all I know is he breeds racehorses now, and that's the truth, 'cause I seen his farm. And he ain't a gangster. And he's got all these security guards. He's a paranoid fool, but he's a likable man.

When the television camera panned the Fasig-Tipton sales arena, you know the tent where they have the sales, in the background, near a post, stood Nicholas. I started to point him out too, but I didn't. I finished the salad and put the bowl back on the tray.

When do you plan to see him again? she asked.

I don't.

She chewed.

TWENTY-FOUR

Who finished seventh in the 1971 Derby? he asked. Tribal Line, I answered, offering him some mixed nuts. You do know your horseflesh, he said smiling, taking some of the nuts and nibbling. I know I do, I said. He counted out ten fives, handed them to me, all the while looking like he'd won. Make her go another round, said his buddy, frowning. He shook his head when I offered him some nuts. I've got to catch my train, fellows, I said, putting the bills in my purse. This is the second call. Fifth in 1969, he called as I hurried toward the doors. Top Knight, I called back. Fifth in 1972. Sensitive Music, I called back and waved. He was smiling. His buddy was shaking his head. I settled on the train and took out the new lead sheets Joan had sent. I glanced back out the window and the fellow I had won the fifty dollars from was waving and looking like he was in love, while his buddy stood nearby looking disgusted. I blew them both a kiss, shook some more mixed nuts into my palm, and settled down to go over the leads.

CHAPTER TWENTY-FIVE

They were crowding outside the door, there for their daily handout, but Grandmother Jaboti wouldn't let them in. If they were mine, she said, I'd put them to work sweeping the floor or cleaning my brushes, and then I'd give the bums something to eat after they'd done worked for it.

She shushed them away from the door, telling them to wait till Cornella came.

You would think with all Cornella's saints that she'd tell these bums that they's only to eat by the sweat of they brow.

They ain't called bums nowadays, Grandmother Jaboti, I said.

A bum's a bum, she said. I ain't a politician, but I know a bum.

After a while, we heard footsteps upon the porch, then a jiggle in the latch of the door. Here's Cornella now. Watch 'em come running back.

Harlan, darling, what a surprise, she said as she entered. We hugged and stood smiling at each other and then Grandmother's bums and Mother's little Christs came marching in. Now, there weren't just men among the "bums," though, but a few women and children.

TWENTY-SIX

Cornella, you want to take her or you want me to? Grandmother Jaboti asked.

Now I should explain here that Jaboti ain't my grandmother's real name. She say it her carnival name. That once when the carnival she was working for went to Brazil, to Rio, that one of them Brazilians named her Jaboti instead of Turtle Woman, and so she just kept that name. Jaboti, she said, was a turtle trickster in Brazilian folklore. Me I don't know whether that's one of them true lies or not. I just know that everybody call her Grandmother Jaboti like it her true name.

You take her, said my mother. Mrs. Smoot, the pharmacist's wife, is due in here in ten minutes. Little girl didn't make no appointment, did she?

Naw, just popped her head in the door. Well, I've told her she's come to the right beauty shop because we only use New York and imported beauty products in our shop. We might be local, but our beauty products come from all over the world.

I didn't know I had to make an appointment, the girl explained. This my first time in a beauty parlor. She looked about seventeen and timid. She said again this was her first time in a beauty shop, that she'd never had her hair professionally done before. Her timidity reminded me of me at her age, when they used to call me Possum.

This your first time in a beauty parlor? Grandmother Jaboti repeated, as the girl climbed into the high chair.

Yes ma'am.

Lay your head back.

The girl lay her head back so that it was over the sink. Her hair was carelessly straightened and tied back with a rubber band; it looked dull and damaged, its edges uneven. You could tell she'd never had a professional conditioning or trim.

When you pull your hair back tight like this it breaks the edges off, said my grandmother. See how bad your edges is. Girl, what is you doing to your head? White gals can wear their hair like this. Colored hair is fragile. You wants a permanent?

Yes ma'am. I'm going away to college.

Well, I can't give you a permanent until I get your hair in some condition. It's too brittle now. Colored people's hair is fragile, so you gots to treat it delicate. I gots to get it strong or else it'll fall all out if I try to put this permanent in it. 'Less you wants to wear it natural. Them Afros is back in style. They ain't never gone out of style with me, but you know how some folks is.

No, ma'am, I want a permanent.

How long you got before you go off to school?

About two weeks.

What school is you going to? Kentucky State?

No ma'am. Bennington.

Been what? Don't believe I heard o' that one.

It's in Vermont. I got a scholarship to go there.

Grandmother took the rubber band off her hair, spread the girl's hair in her fingers and looked at it. Well, child, I do my best. I wash and condition it this week and straighten it regular, with the straightening comb, and then you put this cream conditioner on it every night and every morning and then you come back next week. Honey, how'd you get your hair in this mess?

The girl said nothing. I lit a cigarette and watched while Grandmother Jaboti washed her hair with castile soap. While the girl sat under the hair dryer, Grandmother asked, You want me to do you next, stranger?

No ma'am, I said. I might start braiding my hair.

She told me my hair looked like it had after the African sun had got hold of it years back, then she gave me a little jar of cream conditioner, and started telling me about some cream that she was importing from Brazil that was supposed to be better than them permanents 'cause it ain't supposed to damage your hair, it supposed to use some kinda natural relaxer made from some Brazilian plants and herbs. And they say you can even eat it, that it so natural that you can even eat it, that it's made of natural and edible ingredients. And then she said something again about colored people's fragile hair. I guess it take them Brazilians to discover something like that for us hair.

You come and help me wash out my brushes, she said, when I stayed seated at the counter. Acting like these bums that come in here.

She winked at my mother who was putting a bib around Mrs. Smoot's neck.

Got to put this bum to work, even if Cornella's bums don't work.

Where'd you say you going to school, honey? Mrs. Smoot asked the girl, as my mother greased her scalp with Vaseline, preparing it for a touch-up.

Vermont.

Mrs. Rampart's daughter went up there up North up there to all that cajolery up there. A lot of folks thinks the North is the promised land. I been North. Well, went in that direction anyhow, and ain't no more promise up there than any other land. My husband started him one of the first colored pharmacies around here. If you's a colored person in this country you's got to make your own promise. That's what other people's do when they come to this country, they makes they promise. Course, it's more difficult for the colored man to make his promise than them that can claim white.

Y'all keep calling us colored. We ain't colored, they don't say colored now, said my mother.

Well, when my husband started that pharmacy we was colored. And some of us is still colored, and we ain't all black, so how come they wants to call us all black. And white people ain't all white neither but they calls theyselves white. And I know I ain't African, I'm American. I've been to Africa, and when I was there, ain't none of them Africans thought I was African. When I first went over there to Africa, though, I thought they would consider me a African from the New World, but they consider me the American that I am. And I'm talking about the true African people themselves. We usedta call usselves race men and women, though. Anyway, that gal I'm talking about, that Mrs. Rampart's daughter went up there up North and went wild. A sweet girl before she went up there. Them northern gals I don't think they's as sweet as southern gals. When I'm up North up there when my husband goes to them pharmacy conventions in New York they refer to me as a southern belle, and me a colored woman, but that's just 'cause I'm naturally sweet. Well, I hope you stay sweet, little girl. Some little girls go up there up North and don't stay sweet.

I lit another cigarette and said nothing. I know she signifying about me.

When Grandmother Jaboti finished straightening the young woman's hair, she looked like a photograph out of the 1940s, the war years, rather than a modern young woman. She looked at herself in the mirror.

It looks nice, she said.

Well, you put this conditioner on it and get it conditioned and tamed before I can put that permanent on it. And talking about New York, this conditioner is from New York. It ain't none of this local conditioner, it's the best conditioner on the market. Course if they send me that Brazilian stuff, I can put that straight in your hair, without even this New York conditioner, 'cause that ain't supposed to damage it. Them colored people in Brazil supposed to have invented it from the herbs in they rain forest. Supposed to be so sweet that you can eat it. I been to Brazil, and if colored people anywhere can invent condiments for the hair, it's them Brazilians.

Ever been to Vermont? I asked the girl.

No ma'am.

It's nice country. The grass is so green. You wouldn't believe. They say Kentucky bluegrass is green, but that Vermont grass is greener. Only African grass is greener than that.

And the green in them Brazilian rain forest. At least they say the green in them Brazilian rain forest is green. I just been to Rio myself.

TWENTY-SEVEN

I bet you she gives a good show, said my grandmother. I don't understand what she singing about, though, but I bet she a real good entertainer. She sounds like she's a real good entertainer, I mean for that rock 'n' roll–type music. They've got this new music rap, you know, and I still don't understand what these rock-'n'-rollers is singing. They think I'm supposed to understand this rap music and I don't even understand rock 'n' roll yet. I bet she's a real good entertainer, though.

She is, I said.

I know what she's singing, said my mother. I don't know what all them rappers is singing, 'cept for Jazzy Jeff and the Fresh Prince, but I know what she's singing. That Jazzy Jeff and the Fresh Prince seem like nice boys. They're not gangsters.

We listened to another song. It was a ballad, but it had a wild and raunchy edge to it, almost like gangsta rap. I saw my mother in the corner looking disgusted. They make a song out of almost anything these days, don't they? And that language they use in that music, it ain't nothing but obscene. Except for Jazzy Jeff and the Fresh Prince. And a lot of the good and nice girls get in that show business and even they start singing that obscene-type music and glamorizing gangsterhood and themselves and getting freakish.

Now what you know about freakish? asked Grandmother Jaboti. What do you know about gangsterhood?

She sounds like a nice girl, though, what you tell me about her, but you would think she would sing more high-minded and intelligent-type music than that. Even them high-minded girls when they get into show business. I guess intelligence don't sell. At least Jazzy Jeff and the Fresh Prince seem like nice boys.

They make songs out of any nonsense, though, and somebody said Jazzy Jeff and the Fresh Prince is just bubblegum music. I like them myself, but that's just bumblegum music, Grandmother Jaboti said. Public Enemy is supposed to be the princes of rap, but I don't understand nothing of what they're singing about. I mean, I understand what they're singing about, but I don't exactly understand their words. When finally understanding some of Joan's words, though, she laughed and shook her gray head.

Yes they do, I agreed. She's trying to experiment in that song, combining a rock ballad and rap. A lot of the male rappers refer to women as bitches, excuse my French, so she's sorta signifying on a bitch's, excuse my French, version of that type of music. It's supposed to be a satire, you know. On account of so many of the gangsta rap singers referring to women as bitches, you know. So she refers to herself as a bitch, you know, excuse my French. Except, she refers to herself as a darling bitch.

I like it better when she sings plain, though. She got a voice as sweet as candy when she wants to have one. She sounds like a darling. I don't like all that embellished fanfare, though, said Grandmother, then she looked at my mother. Reminds you of Jack, don't it?

Certain things don't belong in no song, my mother said. There's certain things that just don't belong in songs, whether it's rap or rock 'n' roll. Where is all the intelligent music that people usedta sing?

Grandmother Jaboti popped her fingers. She started to dance. Do she write her own songs? she asked, pausing in the midst of the tune.

Sometimes.

Them's obscure words all right. She continued dancing.

I hope you ain't cheating that girl, my mother said as I put on another tape. I hope you's doing right by her. I hope you ain't cheating her like I hear some of those stars' unethical managers do. They tell you all about that in the *Enquirer*. You's got to learn how to manage yourself before you can manage other people anyhow. And I ain't sure you should ever try to manage other people. Don't manage other people and don't have them to manage you neither. Of course, when they gets to be a big star, peoples have got to have some kinda manager, but they should still know how to manage theirselves. Some people think freedom is managing other people, but it ain't. It's managing yourself. Learn to manage yourself. If you're a big enough star, you might have to have a manager, but when you've got these unethical managers, you've got to manage your manager. But you've always got to manage yourself even when you've got you a manager. So I hope you ain't cheating her, whether she's a darling or a bitch, excuse my French, and spending all her money on caviar and champagne. She probably needs one of them entertainment lawyers anyhow. And they say even they cheats people.

Mama, now you know I wouldn't cheat nobody. Since when have you started reading the *Enquirer*?

Well, I don't read it, but you can't help but to read it sometimes peeking out at you in the supermarket. Why, them managers and entertainment lawyers is always cheating people. And it ain't just the little stars, like the star you manage, but the big stars too. Some people think that freedom is to manage everybody but theyself. Learn to manage yourself. That is the key to freedom.

After the concert we went back to the hotel and ordered a late-night snack of Swiss cheese sandwiches and grape soda. Joan stood in the middle of the room grinning, purple stains on her front teeth. Then she grabbed her Swiss cheese sandwich and nibbled.

They forgot to put mustard on my Swiss cheese.

'Cause you're the only fool puts mustard on cheese. Most people put mayonnaise on it.

Jamey likes mustard on his cheese. I know a lot of people like mustard on cheese. I don't think we're all fools.

I said nothing. I ate a bit of my sandwich. It was the one with mustard. I handed it to Joan. She nibbled some of it, then put it back on the plate. Then she grabbed her liter of grape soda.

Do you remember that gig we did in Paris in the old days? she asked. When she talked about her performances she'd say we as if I were up on the stage cutting capers with her. You know like you see them stars giving interviews and they's always saying "we." You ask them about theyselves and they says "we." I don't think they mean it as the royal we, though. Most of them work with a lot of other musicians and stage managers and shit. And maybe they think that "I" sounds too egotistical, so they say "we." Joan, though, says it like she mean the royal we.

Yeah, sure.

We went to this Moroccan restaurant and I tricked you into eating camel sausage? she asked.

It tasted good till you told me what it was.

And you thought the couscous was grits.

She laughed and sat down, scooting to the edge of the chair. Sometimes she sat the way girls and women are admonished not to sit: with her knees apart, so you could see her panties. I bet you you wouldn't eat it after I told you what it was, but you ate some more, she said.

Yeah, I remember.

You've dragged me all over the fucking globe, she said. All over the fucking globe.

What do you mean I've dragged you all over the fucking globe? I've got you some good gigs, girl.

Why can't a recording artist just record music? How come we got to go all over the fucking globe entertaining people? That would be my ideal, just to record music. Why do I have to go all over the fucking globe entertaining people?

That makes you a star. And it allows you to be able to record music. Anyway, people who like your music don't just want to listen to a recording. They want to hear you sing in person. And you give a good performance. Some people sound better on their records. But you, you're good on your records. But I think people have to actually hear you to really appreciate you.

Show business. I've worked hard, and you've just enjoyed yourself.

I've worked hard to get you gigs. There's more people who know who Joan Savage is now than when I met you.

Just 'cause you'd never heard of me don't mean other people ain't. I've worked my butt off.

But you've had fun too. You've had fun.

Me, I've worked hard. I worked my butt off. I hardly knew what fucking country I was in most of the fucking time. It was all for you, not me. Places you never would have got to go in a million fucking years, if it wasn't for me. Your husband took you over there to Africa, but you got to travel all over the world because of me. That's the only reason you stay with me, 'cause you know on your own you—

You've enjoyed yourself too. You enjoyed yourself in Amsterdam. When I got you that gig in Amsterdam, you said Amsterdam? Amsterdam? You couldn't imagine going over there to Amsterdam to give a performance. But then when we got there, you enjoyed Amsterdam. I don't think you coulda gotten yourself a gig in Amsterdam. You couldn't even imagine Amsterdam. The fucking people didn't even fucking know you when you first sang in that little club in Amsterdam, but they know you now. Some of your best music was recorded in Amsterdam. And you've got your own promotion over there. That little promotion company.

Little promotion company is right. In somebody's basement. I thought it was a fan club. Promotion company? And I lost my fucking voice in Amsterdam. How could I have enjoyed myself in a place where I lost my fucking voice? I lost my fucking voice in Amsterdam.

That sounds like one of your songs. Well, you did record that album there, and you got yourself that little promotion company. Then you lost your voice. But then you got it back in Brazil.

Because you always wanted to go to Brazil. That's the only reason you got me a gig there. Then whenever we go anywhere you're always seeking out the lowlifes.

What lowlifes?

In Brazil, the slums. What do you call those slums? What did they have crab races there or some shit that you went to. Or is that St. Croix that has the crab races? I know somewhere in one of those countries they have crab races. I don't know whether they always had crab races or you started that shit so's you have something to bet on.

I didn't start it. It's an old tradition there. I don't know who started it. I was surprised myself when somebody asked me if I wanted to go to a crab race. So the crabs had little numbers on 'em, you know. So you picked out the crab that you thought would win. But they weren't all lowlifes. You had some European royalty staying at that hotel betting on those crabs. At least somebody said they was European royalty. Well, you had all kinds and classes of people staying there. That's what I like about a little island like that.

And in Port-au-Prince, for instance. Those lowlifes.

Oh, yeah. I'd wanted to bet on the cockfights, but they didn't allow women in. He wasn't a lowlife. He just helped me get into the cockfights. He escorted me into the cockfights.

You were hanging all over him, a married man.

Just a gambling buddy.

I'd heard that women weren't allowed at the cockfights, but I'd gone anyway. No women, the man had said, when I'd got to the hut where someone said there were cockfights. I didn't understand Creole, so he told me in French and then English.

I stood outside the tin-roofed hut and waited for the proper fellow. When he came, I asked him to place the bet and promised that we'd divide the winnings. He rattled off the names of the cocks that were fighting, and I chose one.

You ain't seen the cocks.

I don't need to see 'em.

I handed him the money. He looked as if he'd never seen such a wad of bills before.

How do you know I won't run away with it?

I don't.

He shrugged and went inside.

I stood outside, listening to feathers fly. The man who guarded the hut gave me evil stares, like being a woman I wasn't only not allowed in the cockfight, but I shouldn't even be allowed near it. I lit a cigarette and moved away from the hut and waited near a palm tree.

Some time later the fellow came out waving money in his fists. He paraded in front of me like a bandy rooster himself, and then kissed my jaw, and would have lifted me skyward if he could have. We divided the winnings.

When Joan saw me "hanging on to him" in the Iron Market it was because we'd won. Joan and I'd been shopping in the Iron Market, and I'd spotted the man who'd bet on the cock for me.

Sandovar! I yelled.

We hugged and hugged. Now, he said, with his winnings, he could take his wife and children to another country. He said he didn't like his country and wanted to emigrate to another one. I asked him if he might come to the States. He said he didn't like the States much either. He said he might try to emigrate to the Bahamas. I hung on to him. He hugged me too, and tried to lift me skyward again, but like I said I'm a big woman. Joan, standing nearby, just looked at us. She wouldn't even come near enough to be introduced.

Am I embarrassing you in front of your friend? he asked.

No, of course not.

That's why I pretended not to know you, he said, glancing toward her.

You needn't pretend, I said.

Anyway, I don't give a good fuck what you do, Joan's saying. I don't know why I put up with you. I mean, a woman so starved to gamble on something that she'll bet on a fucking crab. A cock. I might bet on a cock myself. I work my fucking butt off, though, and you have a good time. Did you at least bet on the right cock? Did you win?

Sure.

I wouldn't set foot in Port-au-Prince today, even if you could get me a gig there. Talking about getting me gigs. I wanted that gig in New York, and you come talking about Port-au-Prince. Jamaica maybe, or some of them other little Caribbean islands. I liked St. Croix, though. Then when I did get that gig, I come in and the people don't even know who I am, giving me the bum's rush, and you're supposed to promote me.

Well, when they found out it was you, they treated you like royalty. You should be with me when I'm talking to some of the promoters and agents and club owners on your behalf. Talk about the bum's rush. Joan Savage, who's Joan Savage? If you were more famous, it might be easier to represent you. I think you're ambivalent about fame. You want to be a rock star.

A rock singer. Stardom is your game.

Well, whatever you want to be you always sabotage yourself.

When you and Jamey don't sabotage me.

How do I sabotage you? How has Jamey sabotaged you?

You only get me third-rate gigs, and Jamey. . . . he don't believe in me.

He don't owe you his belief. And I have gotten you some first-rate gigs, they just ain't in the States, and you think only the States is first-rate.

A first-rate gig in a fourth-rate little country is a third-rate gig.

She kicked the bottle of grape soda over, staining the thick beige carpet.

I got up and went into the bathroom and came back with paper towels. I dabbed up the grape soda, but there was still a stain. I mentioned the damage to the carpet and said her tantrums always made us have to pay extra.

What? Pay extra? You don't pay. You never pay. You play but you never pay. I'm the one who pays. Anyway, who's the man who's been following us? Another one of your lovers?

What man? What are you talking about?

The one who's been following us. One of your lovers?

CHAPTER TWENTY-NINE

I tissue makeup from Joan's round face, then rub in aloe cream. Let's go to a bar, I say.

I'm bushed, she says, slouching and hugging her robe. It's white with large, clownish dots. You think after a show I'm as gamely as you are.

No. I just want to catch a glimpse of that man. The one you said is supposed to be following us. Else you're as paranoid as Josef.

She perked up. Then she looked lazy, but she was game. Okay. Just put me on a little mascara and do something about these lines. She pointed to her forehead. You know that new cream you got that's supposed to erase wrinkles. Dr. Leonard's Facelift at your fingertips. And this stuff for my nails is great. You know, that hoof cream you said they use on horses but that's supposed to strengthen human nails?

Where is he? I asked, as we sat at a corner table.

I don't see him, she said, looking around. Don't you know your own lover?

She wore a dress that was the twin of the robe she'd been wearing. Oh, yeah, there he is. Over there at the bar now.

He's looking at you through the mirror. There's the bogger.

I stared at the mirror.

You mean you don't know your own lover? she repeated.

No, I don't know who he is.

Are you kidding?

I'd expected Nicholas, Josef's bodyguard, if anybody, though if he'd been following me I was sure he'd have been as visible as the lines in

Joan's forehead. The man at the bar was nondescript, ginger-colored, in a tweed jacket. He wore his hair longish, more the style of the 1960s or 1970s than the current style. I'd never seen him before. When he caught me looking at him, the man gave me one of those fish-eyed stares. I stood up.

Where're you going? Joan ask.

To find out who the bogger is.

Naw, girl, that man might be dangerous. I just thought y'all was play-acting, like some lovers do. I thought you knew him. He might be some crazy man. Look at that hairdo. He must think it's still disco. Speaking of disco, you were supposed to order that print of one of Donna Summer's paintings, the one I told you looks sorta like German expressionism. You know there are a lot of crazies these days.

There's always been crazies, I said.

Yeah, but not like these crazies.

Up at the bar, I didn't say anything to the man. I merely stood next to him.

I'd like a Josef, I said to the bartender.

What are you talking about, Lady? he asked, toweling off the counter with the end of his apron. What d'you want?

A drink. It's called a Josef.

I never heard of no Josef, ma'am. Must be a local drink. How d'you make it?

It's a German drink, actually. And you don't make it, it makes you.

Come on, Lady, gimme a break, will ya? What do you want?

I watched the man's expression through the mirror. It didn't change, still that fish-eyed look, but he swallowed his drink, set his money down, and left.

Well, give me a tequila then, I said. No, a sloe gin fizz. And a bowl of pretzels.

Lady. . . . He handed me my drink and a bowl of pretzels and I went back to the table.

So who was he? Joan asked when I sat down, saying nothing.

I don't know, I said, nibbling a pretzel. I think that fool I met in Saratoga, that Josef, the African German I told you about, hired somebody to follow me around. He thought I was some sorta spy or something. He kept asking me whether I was some kinda spy. I don't know what the fool thought. Maybe he is a gangster like you said. Or maybe he's just some wealthy fool who likes to have his women followed. Or thinks I'm his woman. I don't know. He thought I was a spy or some shit. He kept saying I was a spy. Then he caught me trying to find some scratch paper —I, er, you know, was having some ideas for some possible gigs and wanted to write 'em down—and he thought I was spying on him. He thought I was sneaking around spying on him. And he's the one invited me out to his farm. If the fool thought I was a spy, why'd he invite me out to his farm? Can you believe that? Now I think he's got some detective or some shit checking up on me. I remember joking with him about that. That he oughta hire some detective if he thought I was a spy or some shit. Maybe the fool did that. Seems like I'd've noticed him, though. You always notice them detectives in the movies. I think some of those neo-Fascists over there in Germany turned him into a paranoid or some shit. But why'd he think I'm a fucking spy?

Maybe he just wanted to know if you were telling him the truth about who you are. Or maybe Josef didn't hire him at all. Maybe your ex-husband hired that detective.

Naw, Norvelle wouldn't do some shit like that. I don't even think it would enter his imagination to hire a detective. Wealthy people hire detectives anyway. People who got something to protect.

Well, they have detectives now that you can hire to hunt up people, ex-husbands and shit, just dial an 800 number. If Norvelle is still in love with you, he could hire a detective.

Naw, Norvelle wouldn't do some shit like that. He wouldn't have to hire somebody to find out where I am. He knows where I am.

Maybe he hired somebody to find out how you are.

Naw, that ain't Norvelle. He wouldn't be hiring no detective. It wouldn't even enter his imagination to hire no detective. If he wanted to know how I am, he could just come and ask me. He knows where I am. I don't know where he is. I know he's in Africa, but Africa's a big continent. His editors don't even know where he is. I called one of his editors and asked how I could get in touch with him. I didn't want to actually get in touch with him, I just wanted to know where he was, and they said they didn't actually have an address for him, they just had a post office box, and they weren't even allowed to give out that information. Sometimes I'll read an article of his in one of the journals, you know. Sometimes I'll get a little money for some of the photographs I took while we were in Africa. Mostly photographs of that Masai woman and some Sonjo spearmaker. I took some photographs of the Moran and some baobab trees. Sometimes the journals and magazines like to use those photographs to accompany his articles, and I get a little money for those. I forgot to order for you. What do you want?

Nothing. She yawned.

I drank my sloe gin fizz, nibbled a pretzel and offered Joan one. She shook her head, then called over a waiter, who obediently brought her more pretzels and a beer.

Suppose he's dangerous? she asked, dipping a pretzel in her beer.

Who, Norvelle?

Naw, fool, the man following us. She sucked on her pretzel, and looked more nonchalant than she sounded.

Naw, it's just some fool. I had some fool like that following me when I was in beauty school. This guy came up to me and told me he was following me. They didn't have any stalking laws and shit in those days. And this some fool that I knew. He worked for this company that made these cosmetics that we used in our classes, this wholesale cosmetics company, and he usedta deliver the cosmetics and was always hanging around the beauty school, and he said he'd see me on the streets of Cincinnati sometimes and would follow me. He didn't pursue me or anything. He just told me that shit.

You don't know. Don't look like a fool to me. How do you know he ain't after me? Maybe I should hire a bodyguard.

You can't afford no bodyguard. And ain't enough people that know you around here for you to need none. Maybe it's Jamey. Maybe Jamey's checking on you.

Now I know Jamey ain't going to hire no detective for nobody. Jamey's the kind be his own detective if he need to do some detecting.

But then we'd know who he is.

We'd think we know who he is. She chewed at her bottom lip. Well, we can at least start packing those stunguns. Order me a stungun.

You with a stungun? Around me? Are you kidding? Yeah, I'll order you one. And maybe some of that pepper spray. And one of those little Swiss Army knives, if that'll make you feel safer. I don't think I'd trust you with anything else. It'd just be your motivation.

Back in the hotel room, she sat down on the couch breathing hard. She kept looking out the window to see if the man had followed us, but he hadn't. I turned on the TV. Mae West and Cary Grant. Maybe I ain't got no soul, Mae West was saying. Sure you have, said Cary, but you keep it hidden under a mask. Haven't you ever met a man who can make you happy? Sure, lots of times, said Mae.

CHAPTER
T H I R T Y

You're like your wandering grandfather, my Grandmother Jaboti said, when I came back from one of the tours with Joan. Before going to Saratoga to bet on the horses, I came back to Louisville.

As for my grandfather, since there were no photographs of him, it made him seem a legend too, like her Turtle Woman tales.

I followed him, she said, until I turned into a human being.

The beauty shop wasn't open yet, and she sat on a high stool, stretching and yawning while I dusted and polished the hair dryers. She was always telling me about my grandfather, always telling me the same story, but I'd listen to it again, as if it was the first time I'd heard the story. But then she never exactly told the story the same way each time. Sometimes she'd add new details, other times she'd tell the same details, but in a different order, in a different syntax.

He was a traveling salesman, your grandpap was. Sold farm implements mostly to colored farmers, you know, 'cause wouldn't none of the white farmers buy from him, so he sold mostly to the colored farmers. Some of the farmers would pay him in money, but a lot of them would pay him with the produce from their farms, and the different foodstuffs like honey and molasses and butter and cornpone and then he'd sell some of the produce and foodstuffs and make his other money that way. And a few of them Quakers, now a few of them Quakers would buy from him, because they have always been the true men of God. A lot of them Quakers could make their own farm implements, but they would also buy from him. Them Quakers have always been true men of God. Back in the seventeenth century, though, when they first come to this country, they usedta own slaves theyselves, but then they decided to abolish slavery amongst theyselves, because they believed that they couldn't be true men of God and own slaves, and after that there wasn't a Quaker to own slaves, and they would help the slaves to escape from slavery. I seen me some Quakers at the supermarket. I wanted to say something to them, but I didn't know what to say to no Quakers. A Quaker man and his wife. Cornella said they wasn't Quakers, that they's probably them Pennsylvania Dutch. Did itinerant repair work, stuff like that, your grandpap. Farms all through the Midwest and along the coast, even traveled up North. And plenty more colored farms then than nowadays. The colored people started leaving the farms and traveling to the city, or the white people drove them off of they land, or tricked them out of they land. You have a whole history of them tricking the colored people out of they land, or the colored people fool enough to sell 'em they land or leave the land for the city. Even them bad ole days of segregation everywhere you had more colored people to own and work their own land, though. Anyway, your grandpap, he said he loved me and 'ud marry me but he wouldn't settle down with me. I run off from that carnival with him, but he wouldn't settle down with me.

She turned toward the long mirror and looked into it.

He wanted me to have some kind of security, though, because I ain't by nature no wandering woman. I wandered with that carnival, but that were the carnival's wandering nature, not mine. And I did my share of wandering. I wandered plenty in my young days. When I was with the carnival, we wandered all through all the States and up in Canada too and in Mexico and I told you about Brazil where they renamed me after that trickster turtle. I think that Montreal the most perfect place we went to, though. But, really, I was not a wandering woman by nature and then you get to the point where you don't want to wander. Well, so he married me, brought me to Kentucky, bought me this beauty parlor, but he wouldn't settle down with me. 'Cause there is some mens that is just like that. Don't make them no less ideal of a man. I usedta wonder how come Mrs. Smoot's husband stayed with her and mine ain't stayed with me and is just a itinerant man. But mine ain't no less ideal of a man. Bought me this beauty parlor, so's I could always take care of myself.

Do you know where he is now? I ask.

Might be a ghost like your daddy now.

Grandmother Jaboti like to call my daddy a ghost, but he ain't. He fought in the Korean War and he stayed over there in that Korea with some Korean woman. Somewhere. After the war. Said there's a lot of colored men that found themselves more freedom over there in that Korea and stayed over there after the war. Like in them other wars, them wars in Europe, a lot of them men after them other wars stayed in them countries, even the enemy countries, 'cause they thought they had more freedom there. I don't know the whole story myself, though it seem like there would be more honor in it, in staying in that country he found more freedom in, if he were a single man.

B O O K

F O U R

Who was Aristides' jockey? O. Lewis. Vagrant? B. Swim. Baden-Baden? W. Walker. Day Star? J. Carter. Lord Murphy? C. Shaver. Fonso? G. Lewis. Hindoo? J. McLaughlin. Apollo? B. Hurd. Then she began to skip through pages. Plaudit? W. Simms. Manuel? F. Taral. Chant? F. Goodale. Exterminator? Knapp. What, No first initial? Just Knapp. Middleground? W. Boland. Count Turf. I like that. C. McCreary. Tom Tom? I. Valenzuela. Lucky Debonair? W. Shoemaker. Northern Dancer? W. Hortuck.

She tossed the racing book at me, then lay down on the couch and kicked her feet in the air.

Seattle Stew? Seattle Stew? Oh, I mean Seattle Slew. J. Cruquet. I'll take your word for it. I wish I had as good a memory as you, 'cept for Knapp. Tell me some more about that ex-husband of yours. Seem like you got a good memory for everything but that.

My husband, Norvelle, like I told you, is a medical anthropologist who collects medical folklore. After we married, I traveled with him to Kenya, to the Sudan, to Tanzania, to Zanzibar, to Pemba. We talked to blacksmiths, ironworkers, warriors. He'd have talked to lions, elephants, and gazelles if he'd known their language. He'd have talked to the mninga and camphor and mahogany trees. He'd have talked to the wild figs, if they'd spoken. He'd have talked to the oil palms. And surely the baobab if it talked back. He'd have spoken to the same dragonflies that I was trying to frighten away, if they'd spoken. He'd have spoken to all those mosquitoes.

It was only that Masai medicine woman who disoriented me because he wanted to stay with her, because he wanted to keep following her from Korogwe to Morogoro, from the Rufiji River to the Great Ruaha, from the Uluguru Mountains to Meru, in the Eastern Rift Valley. And I guess I also envied her independent nomadic life, traveling about, curing folks. I guess the only way she could express her wanderlust even though the Masai traditionally nomadic people was by being a medicine woman. Of course I thought the Masai men were more beautiful than the women with their bald heads and stretched earlobes. The men had long tresses and an elegance. I could understand the men's aesthetic of beauty, but not the women's. When I saw the warriors, the Moran, I was fascinated. When my husband talked to them in their own language I stayed back, admiring their headdresses of lion's manes and ostrich's feathers. Suppose I had followed one of them about?

Why did she spit in your ear? I asked my husband when he returned where I was standing, under one of those legendary baobab trees.

A sign of goodwill and respect.

We followed her to Sonjo territory. The Sonjo used to be the Masai's enemies, but now she's curing them. Now she's spitting in their ears.

We stayed in a hut that looked like it was made out of rock. A Sonjo blacksmith and his family. We sat in a circle and watched the Sonjo shape spearheads which he would sell to the tourists. Chants accompanied the shaping of the spearheads. Norvelle said that no work was done without chanting, which he called that space between speaking and song. I could tell by his expression that he was memorizing what the man sang, or rather chanted, and that he'd record it in his notebook. He said that a medical anthropologist had to have a good auditory memory. I asked him whether the Sonjo spearmaker would allow me to take his photograph. I didn't know if he, like they say when some of the Native Americans were first photographed, or when the Europeans first tried to photograph them, if would he think that a photo might capture his spirit. Norvelle asked the Sonjo spearmaker in his own language if I might take his photograph, and he said yes, and so I took his photograph.

And then the four of us were standing in the hut of that man who they said could detect criminals by their smell. It was not like the old days, Norvelle said. Now such men had to be licensed by the state, had to be official. Not everyone could be a criminal detector.

Then the criminal detector was looking at me. He said something to the medicine woman, and the medicine woman talked back to him. The man started staring at me more intensely, the medicine woman shook with laughter and I brushed flies. But the medicine woman let the flies sit on her face. It was their custom or religion.

Later Norvelle translated for me. He'd asked her what kind of criminal I was, and whether I was in exile from my own country.

What did she tell him?

She said to stop sniffing you, that you were already married, and that you don't like men who raise goats.

That made me like her. We followed her to a place where she helped a newborn baby into the world. She chanted as she worked. Norvelle said she referred to the woman as someone carrying two souls—her own and the baby's. She coaxed the new soul into the world. When the baby came, everyone gathered and spit on it for luck.

I brushed flies from my face and ate zebra meat with my fingers, a gift from the other women who had gathered to salute the new child into the world.

How long are we going to follow her? I asked Norvelle, as we lay on mats in a curtained-off corner of the hut.

She's a treasure chest of medical folklore, he said. She's a treasure. Why, I could write a whole book about her.

In the morning, outside, the woman was telling him something. She was shaking her broad shoulders ho-ho-ho-ho and Norvelle was laughing. Her face was painted like a zebra's.

What did she tell you? I asked when Norvelle spotted me, came and kissed my jaw.

Good morning.

What did she tell you? Why don't you speak English?

He looked at me, and then he said it was a joke.

What joke?

The Masai once had herds and herds of cattle, he said. The Sonjo once raided the Masai for their cattle. But the Masai proved themselves superior to the Sonjo in battle, so now the Sonjo raise goats.

I saw no joke in it. The criminal detector brought me a bowl of zebra stew, but the Masai woman took it from me. They stood fussing.

What's going on? I asked Norvelle.

She claims that he put love magic in it. That he put some sort of love magic in it so that you'd love him more than anyone else in the world.

Did he put love magic in it?

I don't know, he said. But don't eat it.

Now what's going on?

She's telling him to sniff himself and stop sniffing you.

That joke I understood.

Joan lets the snow from her fur boots drip onto the carpet. After the concert we'd trudged through the snow to the hotel. You know the scenes in the rock star movies or after the rock star concerts, the scenes where the fans are crowding around to get photographs, the rock singer surrounded by her or his entourage, the rock star's managers and bodyguards and handlers hustling them into a waiting limousine. Maybe the rock star'll sign a few autographs. That ain't Joan. When we finished her concert, she just trudged through the snow back to the hotel. I think there mighta been a coupla fans standing there to get autographs, and couple to have CDs signed. Nerdy-looking types.

He's not following us anymore, Joan said when we were upstairs. What did you say to him at the bar?

Not a thing. I ordered a Josef, so he must've told Josef we were on to him.

I turned the light on and she gathered into a leather armchair. I took off my rubber boots and put them on newspaper, but she let hers drip.

Or maybe Josef's sent someone else more clever. Take your boots off.

She took them off and placed them on the newspaper.

Doesn't it scare you? she asked. Having some man hire a detective to follow you around. Even if the man thinks he loves you. It's still some possessive bullshit. To think you got mixed up with some joker like that. You shouldn't pick up strange men, you know. Not in today's world. Admit.

Yeah, a little.

Not enough to make you stop your alley ways? Control yourself, girl.

Manage myself?

Say what?

I stare at her silver stockings, her braided hair smeared with red ocher. I turn my back to her. I light a Lucky Strike and inhale it into the pit of my stomach. I don't like people telling me who they think I am.

So what happened between you and Norvelle? she asked. I mean what really happened? I don't just think it's on account of that Masai woman. And I don't even know if I believe that story. Girl, I think you're just jiving me. I think you're just a con artist or some shit. A con woman. I think you just conned me. When we first met, I think you just conned me. Telling me you're a beautician. You knew I'd be intrigued. I bet you've just been conning my ass. Telling me all of your tales. You're probably a pathological prevaricator or some shit. I don't even know if there really is a Norvelle, or even a what's-his-name. Josef Ehelich von Fremd. Sounds like some name you made up or some shit. Girl, you got a credibility problem. And all that shit you told me about some tales sounding incredible but really being true, that's just better to con me with. Well, I saw him on TV that Josef. But he could still just be anybody. They didn't say his name. Probably somebody you read about. You're just a con woman. Shit. What's it they usedta call women like you? A adventuress? A colored-girl adventuress. A, what's that Spanish word, a *pícara*. They call the men *pícaros* and the women *pícaras*. Like the *pícara* Justina. Or the daughter of the Celestina. *Pícaras*. Rogues. Except true *pícaros* are always hungry; they're motivated by hunger, that's the motif in every picaresque novel, and you always seem well fed to me. Me I'm motivated by hunger. Maybe I'm the true *pícara*. But it's a hunger of the spirit.

I turn one hand on my hip, the other on the cigarette. I blow rings of smoke toward her.

Why don't I fix you up like a Masai woman, shave your head, put brass hoops in your ears? I ask.

So what happened between you and Norvelle, your imaginary ex-husband? she asked.

He took up with someone better, someone better than me, I said.

You're just conning me. Maybe we should tour West Africa? she asked. Or is it East? Maybe you could get me some gigs in Africa? We can hunt up your imaginary ex-husband and this imaginary Masai medicine woman.

I could get you some gigs in Africa, I said. Except I don't think they truly like your kind of music.

Sure they do. All over the world it's American music. In Africa, they love American music. American music is us. But those Africans, you can't fool them with fake music. It's got to be authentic American music. They know the real thing.

She went into the bathroom, and when she finally came back out, her head was shaved and she was wearing a crimson scarf around her loins. She gave an Oriental bow and showed her head a palette of colors, like photographs of aboriginal sand paintings she'd once shown me. Dreamings, they were called. This is art, she'd said. You make it and then you destroy it. Aboriginal. Dreamings. Then she sat on a stool and tissued off her head. Then she started singing one of her songs, too low for me to hear.

When she stood up, she plunged her fist into my stomach. I doubled over. I tried to straighten up, but there were spikes in the pit of my stomach. I started toward the bathroom and held on to the door.

You fucked him, she said.

Joan has purchased a videotape player, and in the hotel rooms after her performances, instead of watching the networks, even the Comedy Channel, we put in the videotapes. They ain't the sorta videotapes you'd expect. Not entertainments. Not video shows of her favorite rock singers. Not Tina Turner, or Rod Stewart, or Mick Jagger. Or the contemporary rappers: Queen Latifah, Public Enemy, Jazzy Jeff and the Fresh Prince. Or even the Artist Formerly Known as Prince. Or some of them other videos. I remember she once rented one of them videos on Australia told from the Australian aborigines' point of view, I think the man's name that narrated that video Ernie Dingo. The narrator a aborigine filmmaker. Then she bought a video by some singing group just because she like their name: Primitive Radio Gods. Or some of them old movies or old television series put on video. Instead of them types of videos, they're documentary films of international atrocities, in Latin America, Africa, Eastern Europe, the Middle East, and Asia. The titles of the videos are such as the following: *General Chun, Butcher of Kwangju, Pata Island Massacre—the Philippines, The Desaparecidos—the Disappearing Ones of Argentina, Eyewitness Reports of Repression and Terror.*

No one could survive after that, someone is saying on one of those films. I don't know how I survived. It was a miracle. Those people, they only look like human beings. They're devils. They're devils who only resemble human beings. They show nothing, no mercy. You tell them what goes on in there and they don't believe you. They put some kind of toxic substance on my tongue. That's why I speak the way I do. The doctors say there's nothing physically wrong, but it's memory. When they brought me out I had mold growing behind my ears. It was some kind of apparatus, something that looked like an iron gate. They stood me on my head for the whole day. They put this contraption on my hands. What it does is it stretches your fingers till they pop out of their sockets. They gave me a hundred lashes. They cut off my ear. They put it in and when they pulled it out it pulled out some of the rectal tissue. All I do is make candles, no politics, I'm a candlemaker, I'm not a politician. I do not make politics. I told them, but they were still shaking those rifles at me. I had a twelve-pound iron weight on my leg for two months. They put us in the cage with lizards and dragonflies. They made me put my fingers through some holes and something began eating my fingers. I kept hearing my woman through the door. He threw the rifle against my jaw. He pushed a fork in my groin. I kept dreaming of fruit, just fruit, and sometimes chocolate. Monsters. They put a hook in my shoulder and then they dragged me. They lay you down and put the iron on your abdomen so it will crush the abdomen wall. They made me sit with my penis in her face. They are animals, they are not human beings. They are devils. It was wasn't physical torture they were after, but forms of humiliation. They put my nose to the hole and made me smell vomit. Nothing but stench all the time. I was afraid because my wife was carrying a six-month-old fetus. At first they were going to torture her, and then they tossed her in the lunatic asylum. She says that there there was another pregnant woman. She will tell you her story. I'm ashamed to speak. I'm ashamed to tell it.

First they used thick cables, then blocks of wood, then the ends of lighted cigarettes. I was raped first and then they used the end of a lighted cigarette. They didn't do anything else to me, they just kept whipping my feet.

They just kept pulling my testicles. They made me do sit-ups all day.

They just kept asking me questions. No physical torture. Nothing but questions and questions and questions and questions.

I sat as far back as possible from the screen, but Joan pulled her armchair up to the screen, as close as she could get while the eyewitnesses spoke of their terrors.

They crowded us into a room, and then tossed a canister of some contagion. Everyone's ears began to bleed.

This time, as she stared at the screen, I sat manicuring her fingernails. I soaked them and scraped them with the emery board. I removed the cuticles. I buffed.

How can you listen to that shit? I asked. I don't know about people like you, you know.

These are real people, said Joan. This is how the world really is. That Josef of yours he's a right to be paranoid. Those Fascists sons-of-bitches. This is the way the world really is.

I sighed and looked for more cuticles to remove.

While Joan showered and dressed, I went down into the lobby and played cards with the night watchman, who kept a flask of whiskey in his breast pocket, and talked about Lulabelle, the woman he'd been married to for forty years and whom he said I had ears like.

You got ears just like my Lulabelle. I tell her they look like seashells. Something precious.

How'd you stay married so long? I asked. Everybody I know is divorced.

'Cause they's fools, he said. You shouldn't leave somebody until you knows the logic of why you's together. I don't know why we's together, me and Lulabelle, but I know I loves my wife.

Jack of diamonds, two aces, and a queen of hearts, I said.

How are you in love? he asked.

I wasn't sure what he meant until I gathered my winnings.

Upstairs, Joan sat naked on the bed painted up to look like a zebra. Onstage she sang better than ever.

Do you remember Jean Claude Duvalier? she asked her audience. Do you remember Baby Doc?

They roared, Yes, and then they waited for her song.

Multa!

A Italian woman got up, least she looked Italian, climbed onstage and sang with her. And not one of those nerdy types. They were wild together. The Italian woman full of black hair and thunder. A windstorm.

You're good, Joan told her when the storm was over, and they were drenched, exhausted, sweat racing down their faces. They stood hugging. The audience cheered.

Are you a professional performer? Joan asked, backstage.

No, no, no, no, said the woman, delighted though that Joan would think her a professional, still shaking her narrow shoulders and broad hips.

Come to my dressing room, come with me, will you? asked Joan.

Is it okay if I bring my husband? asked the woman.

Sure.

She went to a tall, brown-skinned man standing near the edge of the stage, his arms folded, sullen. I'd noticed him when I'd been peeking through the curtain. He was sitting there watching Joan but looking like he felt himself superior to the music. How I imagined her husband Naughton James mighta been looking if he'd gone to one of her concerts. He wore beige corduroy pants and one of his eyebrows seemed a perpetual arch. The Italian woman bent to him; he shook his head and waved her away. She whirled around in a silk dress that looked like an Oriental tapestry. Returning to Joan, she mumbled something. I followed the two women into the dressing room. I went to the bathroom and came back as the Italian woman was telling her story.

. . . they each said they were protecting my how-do-you-say honor? and feuded with each other. Oh, I could tell you all sorts of terror stories about love feuds when these Sicilian men get their honor up, for it's their honor, their *onore*, not our. It's always a man's *onore*. I could tell you all kinds of terror stories. A game they enjoy to play, and we're the pawns. All women. *Onore*. You, though, you look like you're *fortunato* in *amore*. You look like you have a man who really loves you. But men, we're pawns to them. Only a few of us are queens. The rest of us are pawns in a man's game. I've been all over the world and it's like that. All women all over the world are just pawns in a man's game. Why, I was even in one of those little countries where the women have several husbands and even there they're pawns. It's not because the women are in control to have so many husbands. It's because the men are so poor that they have to pool their resources. One man can't afford to have one wife, so several men share a wife. When I first heard of polyandry, I thought it meant that women ruled, but it doesn't. The men share you. They'll sweet-talk you, but you're just a pawn to them.

Per amore o per forza, said Joan.

Oh, *parla italiano?*

Un poco. Molto poco. Non lo pronuncio molto bene.

Oh, yes you do, very well. You've got a very good Italian accent.

Che belleza! You're a great beauty, Joan commented. I can understand why the men fought over you. Why, you're a beautiful woman. Why, to tell you the truth, you're the most beautiful woman I've ever seen.

Ah, do you think so? In my own Sicilia, there are many like me. But you see it's only a game, only a *partita*. What are we?

Joan spotted me standing in the doorway.

Carolina Tola, this is my . . . *La presento alla mia* . . . business manager, Harlan. . . .

We nodded and smiled to each other. She turned back to Joan.

Abio—that's my husband—and I, we both love your music. We love it. Of course I love it more than he does, because. . . . Well, you know how men are. There are things that a woman sings, and only a woman knows the full meaning. You may sing for men as well as women, but only a woman knows your full meaning. I am not a *feminista*. I only think a woman should be true to who she believes herself to be. Or who she wants herself to be. Or who she imagines herself to be. I don't know what I mean, or whether I'm true myself to any of that. I don't think there are many of us who are true to our possibilities. I don't blame men for it, though. I am as much Sicilian as the men who fought love feuds for me. But we both love your music very much, Abio and I.

Thank you. You were good, you know. I thought you were a professional yourself. You should be onstage.

I'm very aggressive, no? But I've never had the desire for show business.

You stole the show.

Abio was embarrassed for me, you know. That's why he wouldn't come back. He said I embarrassed him getting up there acting like a fool. He likes your music as much as I do. Well, he doesn't like it as much as I do, but he likes it. But he wasn't expecting this. Eh, he's embarrassed for me. I didn't think you'd let me back to see you, so I thought well, I said I'd make you see me. And I like it that you don't have people keeping the audience away from you. . . .

That's because I don't have the audiences that try to get to you.

Well, you should. I think you're wonderful. This is not flattery.

Joan laughed and scratched her chin. She sat with her back to the mirror. I watched the zebra stripes.

Abio thinks that one should not let others see their—how does he say it?—that everyone should keep his little devils or his little gods inside. He thinks I'm always putting myself on too much display. Sometimes he thinks we were brought together so that I could wreak havoc on him. And he's had enough havoc. He thinks I display myself too much. I'm just being who I am. It's okay for you, he says, because it's your business, your profession, that rock singers are supposed to display themselves, but me, I'm the witch woman. I'm the *strega*.

And you're his *moglie*? asked Joan. She glanced at me. I love the Italian word for it. It sounds just like what we are. What they want us to be. It sounds more like that than the word wife, doesn't it? *Moglie*?

Ah, yes, yes, yes, said Carolina. I'm his wife, yes.

Where'd you meet him? I asked.

She snapped her eyes at me, but turned to tell Joan.

I was in London and disconnected. And he was there. His books had been proscribed by the South African government, you know, before Mandela, and he was in exile and he was getting them republished in London. Oh, we got along so. I'm not sure he knew what I was. My hair was short and then the sun had baked my skin almost as black as his. Oh, I was very dark, you know, and when those men had started playing those war games around me I had cut all my hair off. I told them to all bogger off and then I went globe-trotting. Abio didn't know what I was. He thought I was from some island. I was as dark as he was.

Oh, he had to know what you were, Joan said.

Carolina's eyes widened. She shook her shoulders. I'm not sure he did.

Oh, sure, he must have, Joan persisted.

You can't imagine how I looked! After I got away from that love terror. But I used to sit out in the sun all day. I was in the Kensington Gardens or the Kew Gardens. I was reading. I suppose that attracted him. I had a job working in a little foreign bookstore. A nice little man who owned the bookshop, well not so small a man but his shyness made him seem so. He let me dust the books, you know, because at first I didn't have the proper papers. And then I didn't need the papers, because new laws were being made, and so I got a full job there, because I knew the different languages, and they were mostly non-English titles. When the men would fight their love feuds over me, I'd study the different languages. I thought I might teach, but the only idea they had was to wife me. What did I need to know languages for? What did I need but to know how to please them in proper Sicilian? But in London I'd borrow some of the books sometimes and go reading in the gardens. The title impressed him, I think, and we got to talking of it. Something fashionable at the time. *Alla moda.* I don't remember what. Something German. A German modernist. I guess Abio was thinking what would a girl from the islands be doing reading something German. We found each other fascinating, from our different worlds. But we Italians, we are everyone's people.

She glanced at me, then spoke again to Joan, spoke almost in a whisper.

He thinks I fooled him into thinking I was a decent woman, though. And all the time he is discovering me. And now. And now what a savage I've become! Ha! When I first saw him, though, I thought he was the most beautiful man in the world. You wouldn't believe it to look at him what a political controversy he is, or used to be in the old South Africa. Why, you couldn't even quote from his books without its being a criminal act. I'd read him from smuggled books and those printed abroad. He says to be a controversy in his country all one has to do is tell honest stories . . . But we both managed to escape our terrors. I tell him it is not the old South Africa, and he should return there now, that many are returning there now. But he wants to stay in this country. I tell him that now he's a voluntary exile, because he could return to South Africa if he wanted to. I started to write Mr. Mandela a letter on his behalf, but he asked me not to. I tell him now he's a voluntary exile.

Good for him, said Joan. I've been to other countries and I'm not romantic about anywhere. Harlie still has illusions about Africa. I don't. I don't have any illusions about America either. I don't have any disillusions about it, because I've never had any illusions. Bastards everywhere.

He wanted to come here. *Mi sono uniformato ai suoi voleri. Ha un talento enorme.* He has an enormous talent, so I simply conformed to his will.

The heat in the dressing room made Joan's zebra stripes begin to look like zebra swirls. She played with them like fingerpaints, first her knee and then her elbow. Though she looked distracted, she was listening intently. I could always tell.

Il paese dell'abbondanza, Joan said wryly.

I don't know what she meant. Abandoned country?

We don't know how long we can stay here, though, said Carolina hastily. He's talking to the people at the university where he's teaching, you know, but we're both deportable, you see. Especially now, they don't think he has anything to fear if he returns to South Africa. We're both deportable. I thought we might go to Italy, but he doesn't want to go to Italy. He doesn't like Europeans, except for me. And London these days. Even the bookstore owner I worked for is a little Fascist. He made promises to me, and then when he saw me with Abio, I knew I'd made an enemy. He tried to win me for himself, he told me it was just calf love with Abio, but I knew I'd made an enemy. The little Fascist. But he had this idea of me, you know, the idea men have of we Italian women. And he too thought I'd befooled him. And then there's my love terror, and I don't want to return to Italy myself. We stayed in a little retreat with Carmelite nuns outside London, very noble women, the retreat full of

Florentine-style sculpture, imitation Cellini, one of the nuns a collector of medieval musical instruments, the celesta and glockenspiel, I think, and a maker of the best turtle soup—Abio wouldn't eat it though. We stayed in a cellar. Abio wrote and I read French literature. *Cent nouvelles nouvelles.* And some Boccaccio. What looked like the original manuscripts. Tales from the days when men spoke of true wifehood, as if there could be such a thing. There was a little Basque woman staying there, an exile too. She spoke only a little English, but said that outside of Spain she felt like a new creature. I don't know the basis of her exile, but she looked like the keeper of the conscience of her people, you know the type. Abio wrote a poem for her called "The Mythological Enchantress." I know it's for her, though he doesn't say so. It's more philosophical poetry and not like his political poems and satires. There was a spy for the Germans staying there, who'd been staying there since the war, but he never spoke to anyone. A slender man with small eyebrows. He must've taken a vow of silence. Sometimes I'd see him in the study. Once I saw him reading Capellanus, *De Arte Honeste Amandi. The Art of Loving Honestly.* He didn't say anything to me. When he saw me with Abio, I thought I'd made another enemy. When I saw him in the study again, he was reading *Trollope, the Autobiography.* He said nothing to me. I did not read in the study, but took the book I wanted into the courtyard among the monkey puzzle trees. When I returned the book to the study, the book he'd been reading was open on the table where he or someone had underlined the passage: "She is by no means a perfect lady: but if she be not all over a woman, then am I not able to describe a woman." A strange man. And then we came to America, Abio and I. Abio has a small teacher's salary and he's working on his magnum opus. I like his work, but I don't understand it. It's beyond the comprehension of an ordinary woman like me. I understand English, but I don't understand his. But he's like a weaver of perfect language. A British reviewer calls it Caliban style, Caliban language, but I think it's perfect language myself. I listen to cantatas while he writes, or my favorite Russian music, or Wagner, or the tenors. Sometimes your music. Abio hears it as pure rock, but for me it sounds like satire on the rock 'n' roll genre.

She was silent. Joan said nothing.

Abio is thought well of . . . internationally. The police in South Africa wouldn't be after him now, I don't think. . . . He wouldn't let me write to Mandela. . . . And we can't go to my country, like I said. The devil and the deep . . . So we said tonight we wouldn't think about it, we wouldn't decide what country we'd try to go to, we'd just come here and listen to you. I found I had to do more than listen. And he. He adores you. He doesn't adore you as much as I do, but he adores you.

She kissed Joan's fingers. He says that you're one of the best because you use terror and turn it into music. You do in your music what he tries to do in his writing. I don't think he'd know how to write about the new South Africa. He doesn't know why he's such a controversy, because he mostly writes about how the black South Africans treat each other, not so much about any regime. His books do not ignore the regime, but he's mostly interested in how the blacks are with each other. So he is ambivalent about the new South Africa. What if he returns there and the black powers themselves don't like his writings. Would they jail him too? Would they imprison him too?

Joan watched the woman.

But love terrors are such little terrors, aren't they? asked Carolina. We could return to Italy. What are love terrors?

But still they can kill you over love, Joan said. They can kill you over love as well as politics.

I slouched toward an empty chair and sat down.

But you made us happy. Even though Abio was embarrassed for me, you made us both very happy. We think that you're wonderful. He would have come back if I hadn't embarrassed him. He wanted to meet you himself, but I'd embarrassed him.

That's what you mean, said Joan. That's what you mean. That's what you mean. I thought you meant that.

What? I do not understand, said Carolina. What do I mean? Should I excuse myself?

What'll you do if your university can't help you? I asked.

She turned toward me, as if rescued. I don't know, she said, because you see, we are deportable. There is an immigration woman I spoke to who thinks I might be less deportable than Abio. Who wanted to play the color politics. But if Abio is deportable, then I am deportable. We have a great allegiance to each other.

Frowning, Joan tore a page out of a notebook, scribbled something, handing it to Carolina. Here's a place you can stay, she said. Deportable or not. We're all refugees anyway, aren't we? We're all from the same country anyway. I'll call my caretaker and tell him to expect you and to let you stay. Nobody'll bother you there. None of the bastards'll even know where you are. It's like a hidden world.

Quanto si paga?

Non ti dar pensiero.

Carolina looked at the piece of paper. Oh, thank you.

It's my farm, actually. They won't find you there. She wrote on another piece of paper. And this is my private number, if you. . . .

Oh, you are so kind.

No, I'm not, said Joan. Not at all. I'm a bitch.

No, you're wonderful. Who else would do this for us? Strangers.

I wish I was wonderful. I wish I was truly wonderful.

When Carolina left, I asked Joan why she'd called James her caretaker and not her ex-husband. She was silent, then she said, It's too much to explain. Anyway, he'll tell them who he is.

Are you going to tell him who they are? Are you going to tell him it might be a crime what you're doing? That you could get into trouble with the immigration people? Especially now, with this anti-immigration bullshit.

It ain't bullshit. You're bullshit, she said. I don't believe you should just open your borders to just anybody myself. I know I shouldn'ta let you in my house. If I took better care of my own border, I'd deport your ass. Naw, you can't just open your borders to anybody. You gotta discriminate. I don't like the color politics either, though. The Mexicans, the Cubans, the Haitians. Plenty of illegal Canadians over here.

I think it's legal for Canadians to be here, I said. I know I like going to Canada.

Well, I know there's some illegal Irish here and they ain't chasing them back to Ireland neither. I like the Irish, though. They usedta have signs that said no dogs or Irishmen allowed. I'm part Irish myself. Don't laugh. I am. I've got as much true Irish in me as I've got true African. I'm multiracial. I just don't play the multiracial game. It's all politics anyway. My culture is African American, so I'm African American. You look like you're multiracial too. You don't have to be light-skinned to be multiracial. You don't have to look like Vanessa Williams.

Which Vanessa Williams? I asked. I'm supposed to have Afro-Cuban in me. Us real name is supposed to be Aguila and not Eagleton, but some Afro-Cubans came to America and changed their names to Eagleton. I think *águila* in Spanish means eagle, don't it?

And I bet you got a little Indian in you too, ain't ya? You remember when colored people usedta always be telling people they got a little Indian in 'em? Ain't know which tribe, or even that Indians—Native Americans—got hundred of tribes, they just know they got a little Indian in 'em?

I know what tribes—Seminole and Cherokee. But I'm still an African in America.

Carolina and Abio suddenly appeared at the door of the dressing room. He smiled and thanked Joan for her generosity. He said he might not need to stay there at her farm, that his university might come to his assistance, or some of his fellow countrymen who were exiled in America, but he expressed his gratitude. He looked at me with curiosity, but said nothing. Then they excused themselves.

Joan sat shaking like she'd suddenly turned all nerves.

What is it? I asked. You afraid of the immigration police after all?

Naw, she said. She calmed herself, picked up the phone and called James. She told him to expect some guests at the farm. She told him their names, but not who they were, and that they were deportable. She put the phone down. She turned toward me.

Come and wipe this shit off my face, she said. Wipe this shit off me.

You are wonderful, I said. But I hope you don't get your fool self in trouble. I mean, legally, like I said, it might present a problem. I've got some friends in South Texas who work with illegals, some friends of Norvelle's actually, always getting their asses in trouble, working with the illegals, refugees from different part of the world and people who come here as illegal aliens, and especially now with all this anti-immigration bullshit. I forget what they call their organization. It ain't Amnesty International, but it's something like that. Norvelle calls it the New Underground Railroad. He says it's sorta like in the old days of slavery, when a fugitive slave was illegal. You know, the Fugitive Slave Act, when escaped slaves had to be returned to their owners and that the people really for human rights had to go against their government, you know, like the Quakers, you know. Like in Hitler's Germany, when there were these Germans who would give shelter to the Jews and even print up fake identification papers for some of them and print up fake food coupons. I read that in one of those books of yours, about some of the Germans who would hide people hunted by the Nazis. Those people have the idea that there's no such thing as an illegal human being, and they consider the immigration police just thugs, but government thugs. They ain't all thugs, though. I know this African-American guy who's an immigration policeman. I met him when we were in South Texas. Then I seen him on television when those Chinese illegal immigrants were captured, and he was leading one of these Chinese women into the detention camps. He wasn't treating her like an illegal, he was treating her like a human being. I don't know about those white immigration police, though. I don't know if they see human beings or just see illegals, you know. Somebody said that African-American guy married one of those Chinese women, though, and stopped being a immigration policeman. Like that story I heard about this buffalo soldier who was fighting the Indians and then he realized he shoulda been fighting with the Indians, you know like in the Seminole wars, so he started fighting with the Indians. They's always praising the buffalo soldiers for being Indian fighters, you know. Anyway, Norvelle he contributes monetarily to the cause, I mean those people who are helping the illegal aliens in South Texas, because Norvelle's that sort, but he doesn't go run around South Texas with those fools or fool with any of those illegals.

But I got me good hiding places, she said. Survivalists usedta own that farm before we bought it. You know what paranoids they are.

I seen you with one of those survivalist manuals in that collection of books you got. And you talking about them being clowns.

I didn't say clowns. I said fools. I didn't even say fools, you said fools. One of the survivalists had that book in the attic, so I just read it, you know. I got another list of books I want you to order for me though.

Encyclopedia of Saints   The Marathon Monks of Mount Hiei, or The Running Buddhas   All of the Women of the Bible   The Priestess Tradition of the Ancient World: Spritual Empowerment   The Ethiopian Jews   Beauty in History   The Politics of Beauty   Aristotle: On Man in the Universe   Prehistory and Protohistory   Archeology, Ideology, and Naturalism   L'Égypte   Images of Ireland   The Cambridge Encyclopedia of China   Ireland   Havana (for you since you claim to be Afro-Cuban)   *The Unofficial Guide to Disneyland   Emerson's Essays   The Wisdom of Confucius   Natural History of the Intellect* (for Jamey because of his "quest for ideas")   *The Rhetoric of Science: Inventing Scientific Discourse* (a copy for me and Jamey)   *Who Stole Feminism?   The Third World and the Quest for Political Ideas   Japan   The Myth of the Explorer   A Social History of Ireland   China, Korea and Japan: The Rise of Civilization in East Africa Castles   India: Land of Dreams and Fantasy   The Complete Guide to Growing Nuts   Impressionist Cats   The Beauty of Horses* (for you)   *The Turtle: A Natural History* (for you, on account of that confabulatory tale you told me about the turtle)   *The Elephants* (you should send this to Norvelle c/o his editor)   *Animal Minds   The Herb Garden   Cats, Cats, Cats   The Cats' History of Western Art   Japanese Gardens   Medicinal Plants   Chinese Cooking for Beginners* (for you, because you're getting fat, girl)   *North African Cooking   Cats: Arts, Legend, History   Fake, Fraud, or Genuine?   Comic Book Artists* (they've got a profile of one of Jamey's favorite comic book scenarists, Martin Tage, you know the inventor of Guadalcanal, you know the first African-American woman comic book heroine)   *How to Repair and Restore Dolls* (I need a hobby)   *Politics or Culture?   Rumor Has It: A Curio of Lies,*

Hoaxes, and Hearsay (do you think you'd like this book?)   *The Cre-ation of Feminist Consciousness   Sanctuaries of the Goddess   Da New Album* (this is a tape not a book; a new rap group)   *German Ar-chitecture* (the book which has the chapter on gables and metal-work)   *African Architecture* (for Norvelle c/o his editor? or maybe you should read this, that shit you told me about preferring the tourist hotels to the primitive huts in the bush)   *Slavery as Salvation: The Metaphor of Slavery in Pauline Christianity   Disney Animation Art   Mary Cas-satt   Leonardo da Vinci   Start Sculpting: A Step-by-Step Beginner's Guide to Working in Three Dimensions* (I think this is the title of Cath-erine Shuger's book; if not make sure you order the one by Catherine Shuger)   *The Painting of T'Ang Yin   Drawing and Painting Ani-mals   Court Arts of Indonesia   Mask Making* (remind me to tell you about Jamey's Korean maskmaker friend)   *The Encyclopedia of Origami and Papercraft   Yasuo Kuniyoshi's Women* (Jamey's Women?)   *Actors as Artists   African Art   Joan Miró   Music and Technology   The Irish: A Treasury of Art and Literature   Dalí Singer-Songwriters   Elvis* (for Cayenne? She doesn't sound crazy to me)   *Mozart   Classical Music   A Beginner's Guide to Opera* (for you)   *Sculpture You Can Eat* (I know this is Catherine Shuger's book) *Frida Kahlo*   And the book about that Cuban woman you know the one who was with Castro during the Revolution we saw her on televi-sion   And the new Amanda Wordlaw novel, the one I showed you in that book review I don't remember the title but the book reviewer describes it as a "picaresque-jazz-impressionist-neo-slave narrative novel." I told you about the *pícara* didn't I?

Anyway the women in the book are supposedly not pleased with oth-ers' ideas of who they are and are constantly redefining themselves their own ideals or possibilities of womanhood. Not *Don't Let Cowgirls Fool Ya* or her early novels this one ain't just an American book but the hero-ine travels not just among different classes but among people of different nationalities and political persuasions it suggests more improvisational techniques and has sort of a modified frame and an open-ended resolu-tion that's why she calls it picaresque, you know the techniques in those novels, like Lazarillo de Tormes, anyway all the men in it have the same name and the narrator sorta reminds me of you she calls it picaresque but it differs from the true picaresque because the true picaresque hero or heroine satirizes others while the heroine of this book satirizes herself more than others do you still think she's a confabulatory author even Jamey thinks so he saw me reading so many Amanda Wordlaw novels that he thought maybe I'm Amanda Wordlaw in disguise I think it's Catherine Shuger myself writing under a pseudonym. . . .

What did James say? I sponged her face with witch hazel, then rubbed in aloe cream. Then I put on some wrinkle cream. I just put the wrinkle cream on her forehead, though.

It's my farm and my notion, she said. What can he say but yes? What can Jamey say but yes? He's my Jamey and I'm his even though we're divorced. Like what Carolina said about having a great allegiance to each other. I thought she shoulda said love, but maybe what she says is good itself. I still have a great allegiance to my Jamey. But I ain't a pawn in no man's game. You others can be, but not this bogger.

CHAPTER THIRTY-FIVE

In the hotel room, while Joan is sleeping, I turn on the videotape. A Vietnamese woman is talking. She speaks with a deeper voice than most Asian women I've heard. Mostly the Asian women have high-pitched voices, while the men have low-pitched voices. But this woman has a low-pitched voice, almost like a man's.

I covered my mouth and my baby's mouth, she is saying, but those whose mouths weren't covered. . . .

I begin to think of another Asian woman, a Korean. My father, I told you, was in the Korean War and after the war he stayed in Korea and settled with a Korean woman. He wrote my mother a letter telling her simply what had happened. He did not give any philosophy behind what he did. He did not rationalize. He did say that Korea seemed a better world to him than America. I was just a small child, but I thought that if Korea was such a better world, he could have brought us all to Korea, that it seemed like a selfish thing for him to stay there with that other woman he spoke of. But still I loved him. And even though I was a small child, I thought I could understand what he meant when he said that for the first time he could feel some power and control over his life. He felt in charge. Perhaps I understand what he meant. Had she read the letter to me, because being a small child, she'd thought I wouldn't understand it?

And the Korean woman? She never spoke of her or of him after reading that first letter, but whenever she'd see an Asian woman on the street or on television, she'd stare like crazy, as if wondering if that was her. She wouldn't look at her with hatred, but fascination. Was she like this one? If he'd chosen her, could she be a bad woman?

. . . .but if our mouths hadn't been covered we would have suffered the same as the others.

THIRTY-SIX

I don't know if she spends her days waiting for him to come back like the women in the storybooks and songs do. I don't know, for it is never spoken of. He had fought in the Korean War and after the war was over, he stayed there. What else I know about him I guessed on my own, or learned somehow. By osmosis. Jack B. Eagleton his name, the B. standing for Booker. So my name's Harlan Eagleton. Harlan T. Eagleton, but I do not tell anyone what the T. stands for, because I don't think it's a name that anyone should be given. Well, I'll tell you. It's Harlan Truth Eagleton. Named for Sojourner Truth, not Truth itself. I know people named Sojourner but not Truth. I do not question. But when I dream, I dream of strangers coming to the door. I'd go to the door always expecting to be surprised by a stranger who'd turn out to be my father, returned from Korea. And when my mother started taking in those little Christs, whom my grandmother called bums, giving them soup and clothing and a warm gathering place, I used to stare at them all, thinking maybe one of them was actually Jack B. Eagleton in disguise.

Look at that little girl how she looks at everyone.

Can't take her eyes off you, man. She must think you her daddy.

Something must be wrong with that girl. Come here, Possum.

When my mother wasn't holding soup to them or goodwill clothing, she'd be silent, watching them as if they were the most interesting people in the world, or listening to their conversations. What they spoke of, their stories, I could never seem to remember, or didn't want to, stories about poor men, though one poor man always spoke of railroads.

My grandmother wouldn't listen to their stories at all. She'd put the bums to work. Here's a broom, John Henry, go out and sweep off the sidewalk. There ain't any trains around here.

Woman, you ain't got no fellow feeling. And my name ain't John Henry. I'm Mr. Hauberk. I might resemble John Henry, being a big robust man, but my name's Mr. Hauberk.

I'm a woman, but only one man can "woman" me, Mr. Hauberk, if that's your true name. I'll Mister you if you want to be a Mister. And a big robust man like you oughtn't to be no bum. And naw I don't got no fellow feeling if fellow feeling means that you's a fool.

She handed Mr. Hauberk the broom.

And who might that have been might I ask? The man to woman you. He held the broom like a staff and leaned toward her.

Say what?

The man to woman you. Who'd have the nerve to woman you? Who'd have the nerve to woman a woman like you?

She cracked a tiny smile at him, and then she shushed and shooed him.

THIRTY-SEVEN

When I return to the hotel, Joan's talking to Sandovar and two other Haitians. At least I figure they're Haitians, since they're with Sandovar. I halt in the door, then say hello to the men. Sandovar looks embarrassed, then he and the other two men stand up, their hats in their hands. They're wearing khaki pants and shirts and them sandals that look kinda like huaraches. You know them sandals that them Mexican peasants wear. Or them American tourists, a lot of them like to wear them huaraches in Mexico. Sandovar ain't in Haiti, but here in *il paese dell'abbondanza*. Nor had I remembered him as a small man. Here in America he looks like a smaller man. Or maybe here I just judge other men by Nicholas. One of the little saints?

What? I ask. What's going on?

Nothing, he mumbles. The other men shake hands with Joan, and say something in French to her, you know that Creole French, and nod toward me. They go out the door.

So what's this? I ask Joan. What's Sandovar doing here? What's all this? I didn't know you knew Sandovar. When we were in Haiti you wouldn't even come over and be introduced to him, when we won that cockfight in the Iron Market. When we saw you in the Iron Market, you were too hoity-toity even to be introduced to him. Some Haitian peasant. I ain't calling him a peasant, but that's how you's looking at him when we saw you in the Iron Market, like some Haitian peasant. So what's this?

Joan's silent. She reclines in her chair, looking imperial. Or impervious.

What are you up to now? I ask.

I'm just helping Sandovar, she said simply. I met him again. In fact, I didn't even know it was Sandovar until he showed up at the hotel. He knows Abio and Abio told me about him. They were at the farm and saw this group of Haitians being detained, and Abio said he knew one of them, that Sandovar is actually sorta a poet, you know, a poet of the people–type poet, you know, a peasant poet and told me about him, and this mutual friend went to the detention camps, and then managed to get Sandovar and the others released and when we met we realized we already knew each other. They're all exiles. I'm helping them.

You're sending them to your farm?

She nodded. The government wants to send them back to Haiti, but they don't want to return. Some American poets who know of Sandovar tried to get him out of detention, but some of his peasant poetry is considered anti-American, you know. I don't think they shoulda even told the people that he's a poet, you know, and that ain't his profession actually. We managed to get them out of detention, but. . . .

What are you doing? I mean, a university professor and his wife is one thing, Abio and Carolina, but they ain't going to let you get away with this. What are you trying to prove anyway? How are Carolina and Abio, by the way?

She picked up the phone and dialed. *Come l'hai trovato?* Tell him *meglio l'uovo oggi, che la gallina domani . . . Ti verro a trovare . . .* Ah, *non ha orecchio per la musica.*

Then she put the phone down and said, They're fine. The university is being a bastard with them, like I suspected. And they're still trying to sweet-talk Carolina, telling her that she shouldn't have any problem herself with immigration. But she won't abandon Abio. If he's deported, she'll be deported. Isn't that ideal? So they still need me.

You're crazy.

THIRTY-EIGHT

I'm in Memphis in a rented car parked across the street from the Presley mansion, Graceland, watching Norvelle's sister, Cayenne. I don't know if crazy women remember, but when I step out of the car and go to greet her she reaches out her hand to shake mine.

Harlan, she says. It's wonderful to see you. Harlan Truth.

I don't know how she know my middle name. I figure Norvelle musta told her, but I don't ever remember having told even Norvelle my middle name. I ain't told you Norvelle's own name, have I? Norvelle Goodling. Needless to say I don't use his name. Or rather, didn't use it when we were married. Harlan Truth Eagleton Goodling? Or even Harlan Goodling? Or even Mrs. Goodling? Even Norvelle, when he first started submitting his articles to journals, everyone thought his last name a typo.

Cayenne's hair's in spit curls; she wears a white sweater and a blue, flared skirt. On her feet are tennis shoes. Pink ones.

I can walk you home when you're ready, I say.

No, no, no, no. Not with you.

Why not?

Because he told us what you did. He told us how you left him. You stranded him in Africa, and they don't like you anymore. I like you. But I told you that you're not a wifeable woman, and I told him so, and he wanted to wife you anyway. I don't like you. I don't like what you did at all.

When was he here?

Yesterday.

Is he still here?

No, he left last night. Back to Africa, where you stranded him. They don't like you anymore. I like you. But I told you that you're not a wife-able woman. Neither am I.

I nod. I think of a witch doctor's wife I met when I was traveling with Norvelle in Kenya. She was afraid to leave her husband and she was afraid to stay with him, because of his magic. And she was afraid even to tell me of being afraid. Stupidly, I thought of her appearance on one of those talk shows, maybe the Oprah Winfrey show, with a string of modern women talking about their acts of marital defiance, and Oprah urging her on to independence. Imagine being a witch doctor's wife. Imagine the consequences of a simple no.

I don't know why I thought of that while talking to the crazy woman. But I remembered asking Norvelle about her. We were back in one of the tourist hotels, sipping palm wine and I told him about the witch doctor's wife.

Who?

The witch doctor's wife.

I don't call them witch doctors, I call them wizards. But their own name for themselves is. . . . He told me their own name for themselves, some African word I don't remember.

But what about his wife, she's afraid of him.

What about her? he asked, scratching in his notepad.

But one of her—Norvelle's sister's—curls dangles. She spits on it and rolls it back up. Still it dangles. She looks at me. He went back to Tansamania, she says. I don't correct her.

Have you stopped liking me too? I ask.

I like you. I don't like you. I always like you. I said I like you. But you'd better go. There's Daddy Pop.

I turn to see her father. When he gets to us, he treats me like I'm invisible.

Come to fetch you home, he says to Cayenne.

Maybe only witches should marry wizards, I said, as Norvelle kept writing in his notebook.

You mean wizards should marry witches? he asked. That way you think they'd be equal? Suppose a wizard has more power than a witch?

But they only want to marry harmless women, I said.

No woman is harmless, he said.

Then he started telling me about some feminist anthropologist, whose research was bent on proving, he supposed, that men and women were natural enemies. Man was like a tiger; you didn't hate a tiger, you just knew what it was, and you took precautions. You, being a woman, that is. He'd just read an article by her about the Lele of Zaire, of the Kasai region. Traditionally, there the women practiced polyandry. Say what? I asked. It meant they had more than one husband. In other parts of Africa polygamy was tradition, the men having more than one wife, but among the Lele of Zaire, of the Kasai region, the women had more than one husband.

I can't imagine polyandry.

You don't believe it?

I believe it, but I can't imagine polyandry. The witch doctor has one wife all right, and she has one husband, but she's terrorized.

Her research is shoddy, he said, talking about the feminist anthropologist again. But harmless women? None of you are harmless. And if there are any of you who are, or who think you are, well, I'd recommend a good shrink.

THIRTY-NINE

I can't remember my dreams anymore, says Joan, waking up, yawning and wiping sleep from her eyes. She'd been drowsing in a hotel room chair in downtown Atlanta while I watched television. A book was open in her lap, *The Dancing Wu-Li Masters*. I don't remember by whom. I'd glimpsed two of its chapters—one called General Nonsense, and other Special Nonsense. Joan likes to read shit like that. Me I'm watching the Comedy Channel. A show called *Politically Incorrect*.

Say what?

I said I can't remember my dreams anymore. When I was a little girl I used to remember my dreams all the time. They were always vivid and in color.

Mine are always in black-and-white. I can't imagine high-definition, color dreams.

Do you remember your dreams? she asks.

Yes. Always. Well, most of the time.

On television the *Politically Incorrect* audience applauds and guffaws.

CHAPTER FORTY

When I go into Joan's dressing room, there's James leaning against the wall. He's the last person I'd have expected to find there. He looks animated, in conversation, till he sees me; then his look is noncommittal.

Speak of the devil, says Joan, layers of teal blue mascara on her eyes.

How've you been? James asks, moving a bit away from the wall.

All right, how about you?

Pretty good.

Pretty good, Joan mimics. How about a hug, y'all?

We keep to our own spaces.

Did you come to see Joan's show? I ask.

Naw, he's here in Chicago for the ASS meeting—

AARS, says James.

AARS, that's what I said. . . . and just happened to see I was headlining this joint. Our paths just happened to intersect, so he stopped over to say hello. The polite thing to do, you know. But he didn't see the show, did you, darling?

No. I couldn't get tickets.

I say nothing. I think Joan'll say something about getting him tickets, but she don't.

Maybe the three of us could have lunch tomorrow? he asks. There's a nice little French restaurant I saw around the corner. I know you like French food, Joan.

I can't, says Joan. And I don't like French food. I like New Orleans food, that's a little different. But maybe you and the fat lady control freak can have lunch. See how fat she's gotten? That's all that camel sausage and couscous and shit. And those sloe gin fizzes. And that sweet

tooth of hers. Course she probably just looks pleasantly plump to you.
Or is that pleasingly plump? Like those girlies in those old Renaissance
paintings when it was in vogue for women to be full-figured, you know.
Well, in my business I gotta stay slim myself. Rock 'n' roll keeps a gal
slim.

James clears his throat, glancing sideways. Would you like to? he
asks.

Okay.

You can pick her up at the Hyatt Regency, says Joan. Our control
freak. What's a manager but a freak who likes to control other people.

Say around one? he asks.

Okay.

Swingmeakiss, says Joan.

He bends and kisses Joan's cheek, nods to me, and leaves. There is an
odor like lavender and brandy. Not a heavy odor, a light one. And a hint
of tobacco.

He still presents a fine figure, doesn't he? asks Joan, eyeing me. Real
classy. Classy 'n' bold. That's one thing you can say about Jamey is he's
got class. Not everybody changes. Some of us stay the same. Some of us
are concerned about our figures. Course they say men age better than
women. I don't think so myself. I just think it's a power game.

She mighta said he hadn't changed. But he'd seemed a new sort of
man to me. Or maybe I was a new sorta woman. Somehow I felt less
bold in his presence. Either he'd changed or I'd changed. And not just
fat. And it's Joan the control freak. I just manage her career, but it's her
in control.

Why'd you do that? I ask. Invite us to have lunch with each other.

Because I know you want to. I know Jamey wants to. You, I can't always figure you, but I know Jamey wants to. And you like French food.
I know you like French food. They're known for their pastries. Or you
might take Jamey to the Montego Bay. They've got some good Caribbean food. And then there's Shy Harry's. I think they just have ordinary
American cuisine. But I know you like French pastries. And anyway
you're a bore. That's my act when I'm offstage, not yours.

You're no bore, onstage or off. That's what James said first attracted him to you. I mean, besides your intelligence—your spontaneity and wit.

Did Jamey say that?

Yes. You're no bore.

You want to fucking bet? If you don't have lunch with him, our Jamey, I'll bore the shit out of you.

In a French restaurant, we eat Chateaubriand, *pommes de terre, haricots verts*. I'm looking at the *haricots verts* but he's looking at me.

What's AARP? I ask, looking up from the plate at him, then I take a forkful of the *haricots verts*.

AARS, he corrects. American Association of Research Scientists. I also belong to AAARPS. African-American Association of Research Scientists. Of course, there aren't as many of us. And fewer women than men.

I lift another green bean. I think he's going to say something about Joan wasting her talents, her intelligence. Just another stereotype nigger entertainer, all those things Joan's told me he thinks about her, but he don't.

It's been a long time, he says.

Yes. I wasn't sure if you wanted to do this. But you know Joan.

Yeah, tell me. I feel like I've known her for centuries.

How's things at the farm? The immigration police been after you? I know a immigration lawyer if you need assistance. Or rather I know of one. I usedta meet all sorts of people when I, I mean when I when Norvelle and I, my ex-husband, you know.

No. Things are okay. Abio and Carolina went back to Italy, to Rome, not to Sicily. Several East Africans are staying there now, and several Haitians. Joan's even got a linguist staying up there, 'cause they don't all speak English. But you know Joan, she's always inviting strangers up there, so there's no problem there. A lot of people in the area just think they're her musicians. Show business people, you know. Anyway, it's Joan's farm.

What about the Haitians?

What Haitians?

You said there were several Haitians up there.

Yeah, I think they're Haitians. I think that's what Joan said. I don't really communicate with them that much, because I'm not as garrulous as Joan, and we decided it's best I don't know too much about them anyway. I don't know what Joan's ambitions are. I just do my research. . . .

What university do you teach at?

I don't work for a university, actually. I do my own private research. I use the labs of the institute, that's sort of like a think tank, you know, I'm a co-partner.

Oh, yeah, Joan told me something about that. That you generate ideas.

Yeah, we generate ideas and then research them, or other people research them, do the practical research, you know. It's really ideal. And then I have my own research. It's what both Joan and I wanted to do when we were young graduate students, form our own research company, not work for some corporation, you know, not work for the man, or even some university. Joan's always had these ideas about good, you know. I guess as a people, we African Americans have our own ideas about good, you know, the sorts of people we allow to be good, to consider themselves good. That only those who devote their intellect to the race problem can consider themselves good, that solve the race problem. Joan said she dreamt once that she came up with a chemical formula that solved the race problem, and it freed African-American intellectuals to devote their intellects to whatever other people, free people, devote their intellects to. But then after you devote your intellect to the race problem others come asking you, whites and blacks, why haven't you invented any rocket ships, sent men to the moon and the other planets, developed any new theories of the universe, built great cities. You know, the game. You're expected to solve the race problem, devote all your energies to the race problem, and at the same time you're held accountable for not creating anything, for not being an intellect in everything else, making grand contributions beyond race. That's why I went to Fisk rather than to one of the white schools, although I got several scholarships to them. The beginnings of affirmative action, you know. But I'd scored high on all the tests, felt I'd met the standards anywhere. I went to Fisk. I felt I could be myself. Not be out for myself, but just be myself. And to tell the truth there were more blacks at Fisk with my interests, interests in the sciences, than at the elite white schools. Joanie went to an elite white school, a private college in Connecticut, and said that she was the only African-American chemist there. The others were sociologists or anthropologists or some shit. I think one African-American botanist. I mean undergraduate school. Like I said, we went to the same graduate school. A lot of problems with self-esteem, you know, when she was in undergraduate school. Should she just do her chemistry research or play at revolution? And if she devoted all her time to the revolution, then what about chemistry? You know. Well, I shouldn't say play at revolution. Some of her classmates from those days are still waiting for the revolution. And one of them, a girl from Colombia, I think, the country Colombia, was in a real revolution. Or maybe from Chiapas. I usedta teach at a university, though. I taught at Fisk for a while, then I taught at a private college in the Northeast. Then I and a colleague I met at the AAARS decided to start this think tank, you know. It's more ideal for me, it suits my character more.

What is your character?

You know me. And I'll go up to the farm to make sure there're enough supplies. I know enough to help keep Joan out of trouble, though.

You'd keep her out of trouble, wouldn't you?

Yes.

No wonder Joan loves you.

He says nothing. I roll the sleeves of my cotton blouse up to my elbows, all my muscles tense. I breathe in the air of almond croissants and *escargots* cooked in garlic butter that infiltrates the tiny dining room. I look at the fluted crystal ashtray near his elbow and wait for him to light up a cigarette, but he don't. There is still, though, the slight smell of tobacco. There're tiny beads of sweat like dew on his upper lip and his forehead's shiny, but he ain't nervous. He don't seem so. He came in in a rush while I was already seated at the table. I notice that his upper lip is thin while his bottom lip is full. I try to remember kissing them. Norvelle told me once that Africans don't kiss. The traditional Africans. The detribalized ones kiss. But in Kenya, he said, among the Kikuyu, it had once been taboo to even make love in the daytime. If one did, one had to go through a rite of purification. One had to go to a wizard, a mogo-whatever to be purified.

Why'd you just disappear? he asks. When I got back to the farm, you weren't there.

What did Joan tell you?

Not much of anything really.

She did admit seeing us, didn't she?

Yes, she said she saw us. Then she said all sorts of sinister things about you. That I shouldn't expect anything. That you're rather like an alley cat.

I make zigzags with my fork across my plate, plowing through mashed potatoes and green beans.

I started to write you a romantic letter, you know, but I never did. I started to call you, but I didn't do that either. Actually, I did write the letter, a rather passionate letter really, but I never sent it. Anyway, I wouldn't have known where to send it, except in care of Joan. And I wouldn't trust her to give it to you anyway.

So where are you staying? What hotel? I ask, cutting the Chateaubriand.

The Sheraton.

How long will you be in town?

Several more days. I'm glad you want to know.

Profiterolles au chocolat. Isles flottants. Tartes aux pommes.

I prefer Italian food, I comment. Joan says I like French food, but I prefer Italian food.

They say most Americans do.

I'd like to come and see you, I said. But Joan and I are flying to Amsterdam tonight.

He takes out a notepad and scribbles something.

Here's my permanent address, not Joan's farm. If you ever want to find me.

You know where I am, I said.

Yes.

Joan said your real name's Naughton. That it's Naughton James Savage.

Yeah. I've always sorta liked it. But Joan never has. The AARS has me as Naughton James Savage, though.

What about the AAARS? I ask, as the waiter brings our *isles flottants*.

Professor Doctor the Right Honorable Naughton James Savage, Esquire, he jokes. You know how we are about titles. Don't ask me about the ASS, though.

B O O K

F I V E

CHAPTER FORTY-ONE

What brings you here? She is sitting on a couch, her ankles crossed. Then she rests one ankle on the other knee and leans forward. Square yellow shoulders, square yellow eyebrows. Her eyebrows are shaped like the eyebrows of the Japanese courtesans—I think they're courtesans— in those imake paintings, those scroll-type paintings. I believe she's even wearing yellow contact lenses, but it's a long room and she's half in shadow, and I can't be sure.

Well, tell me what you're doing here? I've got all the help around here I can use, she says.

So you've finally decided to fire me?

Yeah, why not?

I stare at her yellow nails. Square. I turn and walk down the yellow-carpeted hall.

It is my first dream in color, not black-and-white.

F O R T Y - T W O

I throw a section of the *Times* at Joan. We're standing in the entrance of the recording studio, in New York, where I've waited for her. Did you know what you were doing?

What are you talking about?

I motion for her to read. It is only a short paragraph. I probably wouldn't have even noticed it if Joan had gotten to the recording studio earlier. After I'd read the sports section, the horseracing page, I'd thumbed through the entertainment section, and then through items of world news. That's when I saw the little paragraph, hardly a paragraph. She reads it in clumsy haste, then gives me a blank look.

Did you know what you were financing? I ask. Did you know they were using the money you got from the Schacter contract—I suppose that's the money you used—to buy weapons? So they could try to take back their country?

Joan says nothing.

I thought you were financing them so that they could stay over here in this country, maybe hire themselves a good immigration lawyer, not to try to mount some kinda idiotic little coup. I mean, I thought that you were just helping them to stay here. You coulda hired them that good immigration lawyer I told you about. That woulda made more sense.

Joan says nothing.

They were all killed. Except Sandovar. But he's been detained. And you know what that means.

Joan says nothing.

I didn't know it was that. If I'd known that you were such a fool as that. Why didn't you tell me it was that? Did Jamey know what you were doing?

No. Jamey would've talked me out of it. He's like you.

I thought it was like with Abio and Carolina, helping them get political asylum or some shit. That you were just helping the refugees. That sorta fool, but not this other sorta fool.

Maybe we could hire someone—you know those mercenaries we saw on television—who can go into the country and get him out. You know, like the ones we saw on television who were training those people how to defend themselves. You know, Nicodemus—

Nicodemus?

That's his name, Nicodemus Sandovar. He's your lover and you don't know his name.

Oh. But he's not my lover.

Anyway, his family's still at my farm, his wife, his boy and girl. We could hire someone to go into the country, you know. . . . find out where they're detaining him and—

Stupid. Stupid. This ain't the movies, girlfriend. This ain't the movies. You're just stupid. Putting on your Quixote act.

When Castro returned to Cuba, he only had a few men in a boat. When he marched into Havana, he only had a few men.

Sandovar ain't Castro.

There must be mercenaries who do things like that that we could hire to free Sandovar.

Yeah, you could just hire you your own fucking private army, huh? Well, that takes more bucks than you got, darling. You ain't a big enough star for that.

What about that man you were telling me about, that Josef, if he's so rich. What about some of his security people?

Naw, that's bullshit. I don't even see Josef, and if I did, I wouldn't tell him about some bullshit like that. I told you I know some fools in South Texas who are into some illegal shit with illegal aliens, helping illegal aliens. I can give you their names, but even they don't get into bullshit like that.

It's not bullshit. I thought of asking Isabel Kong for help, you know, but if she's the gangster that they say she is, I might get myself into more trouble. Or she might think she'd get herself into more trouble, you know, than just the rumors about her. And Little Lady's a musical prodigy, I call her Kongapoo, a magical prodigy, you know, at one of those ritzy musicians' academies, and. . . . Anyway, these people you know, are they mercenaries?

Naw, they ain't mercenaries. They're just regular people who believe in freedom, free borders, you know. A few rumheads among them, but otherwise they're regular people. They're mostly working in the border towns, you know, and it's not shit like that. They're not mercenaries, they're just ordinary people.

How'd you meet them?

They're more friends of Norvelle's actually. I met them through Norvelle. He met them, well, he usedta be a guide for different African groups, you know, when they'd come to this country. I first met him when he was escorting some group of African Baptists. I told you he's a medical anthropologist. Well, he speaks different African languages, so some of these sanctuary movement types when they had this group of African refugees from some little country got in touch with him once to do some interpreting, 'cause he was supposed to be the only one in this country who knows how to speak this certain African language, so he took me with him when he went down there to South Texas. Anyway, I don't much keep in touch with them myself, 'cause they're originally friends of Norvelle's, you know, except this one woman's got a little cantina-style restaurant in Cuba, New Mexico, usedta help transport some of them illegal aliens. When I first met her I thought she was an illegal alien herself, and then Norvelle said she was helping to transport them. Things got too hot for her in South Texas, I think, so she moved to New Mexico. It ain't that commando-type bullshit, though.

We don't know how many there were. That's just how many they reported there were. Maybe the others can get Sandovar free.

Just stupidity. Crazy fool. This ain't TV.

But they did something. They did something. They did something.

They tried to change the world and make it better. They didn't just whine like all you. . . . They acted. That's why I admire Isabel Kong, if all the tales about her are true. They try to make her into a gangster, but she helps the Chinese. She didn't become the great artist she imagined she'd be, and maybe she doesn't have her idealisms like when we were in school and is more cynical, but she's a better woman. They say all idealists become cynics. Anyway, she's a better woman than she might have become if she'd just become that great artist.

Stupidly. I don't mean Isabel Kong, I mean you fools.

Well, they're real people, real everyday folks, not pretenders, like us. And the best you could imagine for your Sandovar is a cockfight.

A good cockfight. And at least we won.

How we met. Joan and I. Birds glowing. On the wall, a tapestry of birds of paradise. I awoke, curled up on somebody's sofa. There were people in the room. Partying people, show business people, holding drinks and paper plates and some near the stereo dancing. A couple near the stereo dancing to Miles. Should you dance to Miles? Can you? Near me a couple was sitting. Man and woman talking. The man gets up to refresh the woman's drink. The woman says hi. Where am I? I ask. Where are you? But before she answers he's back with the refreshed drink and they're talking. I'm standing. Hangover.

Vaguely remember a bar. I'd just come back from Tanzania. On my way to Saratoga. Vaguely remember a bar. Where am I? Who brought me here?

Can I have a tequila, please?

Sure thing.

So whose party is this anyway?

Damn if I know. A party. I know a coupla the musicians. There's a famous fashion designer. A famous artist. But damn if I know. They just sent me over.

Who'd I come with?

I don't know. Scan the room. The man in the braids? Chinese? No, he's too dark for Chinese. But they have dark Chinese. In the mountains? Norvelle once showed me some.

Wait for someone to look at you with familiarity, like they know you. The stereo in the corner. All the other men could be my Norvelle. Shades and variations.

Who'd I come with?

Damn if I know.

How'd I find my way here?

Hello.

Did I come with you? Hi, I'm Joan Savage.

Savage or it was Eagleton. No, my own name Eagleton. I'm Harlan Eagleton. She has this full-lipped smile. I like her already. Scar near her nose, or a wrinkle.

Do you know whose party this is?

Some party, huh.

She hasn't the foggiest either. Her first New York party. Friends brought her. Friends of friends of friends of friends.

So you, are you an artist too? You look . . .

I told her.

Say what? Cosmetician? You mean makeup artist?

Naw, I work in a beauty parlor.

She laughed and then she cheered. It's about time I met somebody real for a change. Not these muckedymucks. A real gal.

But I. . . .

Come over here I want you to do my makeup. . . . I wanna see how good you are.

FORTY-FOUR

In Saratoga, in a hotel room, I sit with Nathaniel. The old jockey. Paradise. We're watching TV. We're sitting in his rocker/recliners, the kind that massage you. A Brazilian actress is talking about a new Brazilian film, called *Pixote*.

. . . because we have so many problems to solve before art, though art is my life . . . so many people living terrible lives . . . but art is my life . . . I wanted to go with them. It was a difficult choice. A difficult choice. But I come from an old artist family. I'm a dancer first and a singer and I make humor . . . *Ele esta louco por ela* . . . *Sim. Sim. Sim. Sim* . . . I don't want to make only one thing in my life . . . I want to know all the mystery, make all the mysteries that my art can do . . .

Suppose they'd allowed Joan to go with them? I ask. I think she'd've been that foolish. Playing revolutionary. Well, she could play revolutionary, but for Nicodemus Sandovar and the others it wasn't play.

So where's she now?

Back in the studio, recording her new CD. Something to do with refugees or some shit.

And what about you? Where are you?

I don't answer.

Paradise pours me another glass of champagne, bought with our winnings, then he pours himself a new glass. We all meet as strangers, and mostly stay strangers, even when we think we know each other. It's funny, I was thinking of you, though, and then you appeared.

Speak of the devil, huh?

Or think of her. But I know better than that. All I know is it's better to love, it's better to love. . . . What do you think?

Norvelle once told me that there were certain African folk tales that never gave you an answer; they only left you with a dilemma. Dilemma tales, he called them. What else had he said about them? They were a way of learning. They were another way of learning. What had I learned? I'd just grown fatter, as Joan had said. But Joan. What had she learned? She'd started singing more revolutionary songs. But I don't think she'd really learned anything. Maybe she thought if she got really good, got famous enough, she could hire her private army—free Sandovar or some others. I don't know what the fool imagined.

More champagne, please. Tell me your whole story.

No one ever tells their whole story. What's the name of Joan's new CD?

Siamo del medesimo paese. I told the fool don't everybody know Italian.

What does it mean?

Siamo del medesimo paese. We're all from the same country. *Siamo del medesimo paese.* We're all from the same country.

In the storage room, Mother and I open boxes of new supplies. Grand-mother Jaboti has ordered a whole box of Royal Crown and Mother complains that only the old-time women still use Royal Crown, that modern women put on light conditioners and texturizing creams.

Did you ever believe her turtle stories? I ask. I mean when you were a little girl and she first told you.

She puts several jars of hair dressing on the shelf before she answers. Yeah, I suppose I did. I suppose when I was a little girl I did. Little girls like to believe fantasies like that. I even imagined that I was a Turtle Woman transforming myself to free myself from the tyranny of others.

She puts several more jars on the shelf. But I'm a grown woman now and not so foolish. I'm a grown woman now and got my own grown girl.

CHAPTER FORTY-SIX

Harlan, Harlan, exclaims Josef, giving me both his hands and ushering me into his house. I thought I'd see you in Saratoga, he's saying, still holding both my hands.

I tell him that I didn't go this year, that I don't gamble anymore, that there are no longer any horses that I want to bet on.

Not even mine? he asks.

No, not even yours.

Come on. I want you to see someone.

I expect to meet his wife, but when I walk into the living room, there's Joan curled up on the sofa.

Your Joanie, says Josef. You made me a fan of hers, and so I invited the two of you. I thought it would be a pleasure. Joan's not dressed in her stage clothes, but looks like any ordinary woman in ruffled blouse and straight skirt. Except the edges of her hair are lavender.

Well, what's it to be? Joan asks, rising. Champagne, Manhattan, Screwdriver?

I've got to go check on one of my Thoroughbreds, but you girls can catch up on old times. And to Joan, he said something about some proposal she'd made to him. I'll consider your proposal, he said. At least, I might know some other people you can submit it to. Had he invited her here or had she invited herself? Was she still on that old chestnut about trying to free Sandovar?

Did you know he was married? Joan asks, handing me a Screwdriver.

Yes, I knew. I told you I knew. I told you about his wife, and how he hadn't sent for her because of the dangers.

No, you didn't tell me.

Yes, I did. Why didn't you tell me he'd invited you here? When I spoke to you about that new contract. They sent it to me and I told you I'd be forwarding it to you. You could have told me he'd invited you here.

Then you'd not have come.

No, because I'd figure you'd got someone new to play games with.

I used to admire you. I mean in the beginning. Poor girl makes good and all that. I admired you so much, your will, your determination to better yourself, and still keep some integrity, a little integrity. And I liked the way you ran things, the way you seemed to belong anywhere you decided. Like when I first met you at that party. If you'd told me you were an artist I'd have thought so. You could have told me you were anyone and I'd have believed you. I used to think you were real, not an imposter like everyone else. Not a pretender like those other jokers.

You've always thought me a rogue.

No, not in the beginning. And even if you are sort of a rogue, you never really pretended to be anything else. I forgave you my ex-husband. After all, he's my ex, and I believed you. I believed in you.

I sip the Screwdriver. And now I will tell you the truth of it. Josef has gone out to check on one of his Thoroughbreds, like I told you, and left us alone together with drinks. But it is not intoxication. It is not insanity. It is Joan holding the knife. She has come up to the chair, in the living room, looking as if she is bathed in light, and there is something sparkling. Suddenly the knife is here and casually she drives it in. This is the truth of the story. Not Nicholas' tale, but this one. The knife bends even before Nicholas gets to the chair to grab her arm, and save me. I think it has struck bone and bent. But it's struck not where any bone would be.

I thought you were a real person, she says. But you're not even a human woman, you're not even a real human woman.

This is the truth of it. The knife fell out. I put my hand to the wound and it healed. Nicholas came to save me, and Joan stood there raising her arms to the ceiling in disbelief.

And when you discover you can heal yourself, that you simply put your hand to a wound and it heals, you soon discover you can heal others. First a horse suffering from a fractured phalange, and then a Turtle Woman.

But Joan, though she witnessed the first healing, didn't believe it then and claims not to believe it now, no matter how many wounds I cure or bones I straighten.

I still listen to Joan's music, though. Joan's new music, the music of revolution, the music of refugees. And if I happen to be healing folks in a town she's playing in, I'll go sit in her audience and applaud. I still believe in her.

But me? She thinks I've set myself up as a healing woman just so that perhaps my husband Norvelle will leave the Masai woman and start following me around. But that's baloney. That's pure baloney. Let Norvelle follow that Masai woman to Kingdom Come for all I care.

Is it her? Yeah, that's her. She don't look like no healing woman to me.
You sure she can heal? She healed herself first, then a horse and then a
woman who looked like a turtle and I have read testimonies of peoples
that say she done healed them. Don't look to me like she could heal a
flea. What's that she wearing? Aw, girl, come on and let's go introduce
usself.

Mizz Eagleton, I'm Mizz LaPorte and this is Mizz Bryce. Church sent
us out to welcome you. That all you got? Travel light, don't you?

I let her carry the overnight case while I hold onto the CD player, its
earphone stuck in my ear. Listening to Joan.

Mr. Nicholas is already at the house, says Mizz LaPorte, glancing
back at me. He say he your witness to the healings.

Yes.

What's that you listening to?

The gospel.

That's real nice to carry it around with you. Plenty of the young folks
does that, but it ain't no gospel they listens to. It's that rap. Ain't that
nice? Music, our preacher says, cures the soul. But I know some of that
music don't cure nobody soul. This modern world-stuff.

Ain't it the poet that say it music the greatest good we have below,
and all of heaven that mortals know. The greatest good we know, and all
of heaven we have below. Music or love.

Della gives me a conspiratory look, then says, We done advertised
you all around, you know, so we're expecting a real capacity crowd. But
I bet you always do draw a capacity crowd, don't you? You know you's

the first healing woman that I met. Do you think he'll follow you till you become human?

Say what?

Them that follows you say that you really heal and it ain't just rumor.

To tell you the truth, I'm not the sort of woman I'd imagined I'd become. . . . .

Preacher say that some people secretly prefer their flaws to their virtues, because they mistakenly think that it's virtues that make people the same, but flaws that distinguish them, that give them character. Preacher say that them is the sorta people that is enamored of they flaws, and them is the hardest peoples to free from they sins. 'Cause what they love best about theyselves is they flaws. They cultivates them. But if you is a true healing woman, he say you can heal some of them peoples. To one whom much is given, much is required.

When I arrive, he stands. They told me he would be Nicholas. Surely, they hadn't asked him his name. They'd heard about the man who was my witness, heard his name was Nicholas, and simply assumed this was him. Surely, they'd said Nicholas because everyone knew Nicholas was the one I'd always traveled with. A man named Nicholas. But the man standing here is the last man in the world I expected to find. Or maybe the first man I'd hoped for.

The author of *Corregidora* and *Eva's Man*, Gayl Jones is one of the most highly regarded African-American writers in the country. In the early 1980s, she spent several years in Europe, leaving a promising publishing career and a tenured professorship at the University of Michigan at Ann Arbor. While living in France, she published a novel in Germany. She returned to the United States, completed three more novels, and is currently finishing other new works of fiction and poetry. Beacon Press will publish her next novel, *Mosquito Woman*, in 1999.

Her awards include a *Mademoiselle* Award, a National Endowment for the Arts Grant, and a Schubert Foundation Grant for Playwriting. She has a reading knowledge of six languages and has been learning Japanese and Indonesian.